Penguin Education

Penguin Education Specials
General Editor: Willem van der Eyken

Resources for Learning
L. C. Taylor

Resources for Learning

L. C. Taylor

Penguin Books

Penguin Books Ltd, Harmondsworth,
Middlesex, England
Penguin Books Inc., 7110 Ambassador Road,
Baltimore, Md 21207, U.S.A.
Penguin Books Australia Ltd,
Ringwood, Victoria, Australia

First published 1971
Copyright © L. C. Taylor, 1971

Made and printed in Great Britain by
Hazell Watson & Viney Ltd,
Aylesbury, Bucks
Set in Intertype Plantin

Contents

Preface

This book is mainly about methods of learning in secondary schools. Of course, there is reference to what we learn as well as to how we might learn it, to education outside the classroom as well as in it, to primary and further education as well as secondary; but however large the periphery, the focus is on adolescents at their studies.

We can usefully fix our gaze upon this subject because, both in ordering each school's daily regimen and in organizing all schools into an educational system, we are awkwardly constrained by our assumptions, often scarcely conscious, about the way we should teach. But these may reflect past rather than present necessity, habit rather than convenience. Other less confining methods of learning may now be practicable.

As a nation we hope to provide a better quality of schooling for more children over a longer period than ever before; raising the school-leaving age and re-arranging the schools in a comprehensive pattern reflect this aspiration. But if we have fixed new ends we have failed not only to will the means but even to think them out adequately. 'Grammar school opportunities for all' is, alas, simply unworkable in terms of available resources. The credibility of comprehension has less to fear from Black Paper polemics than from White Papers on expenditure and the elevating of the comprehensive principle into a white hope so sacred that, like those Hindu gods, it is apparently expected to float along without ever touching common ground.

For if its opponents underestimate those social and political forces that make comprehension in the state schools the certain complement, I believe, of a mass democracy, its exponents enthusiastically gloss over the educational problems it raises. Thus over comprehension I find myself on middle ground – the surest place for getting attacked from both sides – accepting the necessity, and yet believing present intentions feckless. Both the shortage of money and the famine of well-qualified teachers in key subjects are chronic and not brief ailments, and the promise to provide for the many what was previously given only to the few, while presumably using the same teaching methods, amounts not to a policy but to wishful thinking. We must examine some alternatives to the hopeless cry for larger and larger buildings, and more and more teachers in ever smaller classes. A glance at the educational journals suggests a welter of possibilities – new methods and gadgets galore. It is not at all clear how, short of inconceivable expenditure, these could be mobilized to combat our perplexities; all the same I've felt it essential to contrive a coherent proposal for future action, for criticism alone is altogether too easy.

This perplexing exercise began with the prompting of the Nuffield Foundation. During my last two years of teaching I was able to work part-time with its 'Resources for Learning' Project – an opportunity reflected in this book. It is in no sense, however, an official report. The Foundation is not to be blamed for my idiosyncrasies, nor are my colleagues on the Project. Doubtless, in the manner of better scholars, I have sometimes copied their errors and have still found room to add my own; I can only hope similarly, from time to time, to have compounded their wisdom.

Without help from the Nuffield Foundation I could not have undertaken those travels abroad which are narrated in a section of this book. Foreign experience isolated from its full cultural context may, of course, be misleading; but total rejection on this score seems unduly severe. In particular we can profitably study those countries whose experience of comprehension is longer than our own and in which comprehension is more than the tripartite system under one roof. Such countries have been forced to try expedients we at present only contemplate; cash and conviction have permitted them to develop certain innovations for which we have scarcely yet felt the need. Even so, a reader may sometimes find some startling foreign novelty has been used in rudimentary form at his local school for the last forty years. So it may have been – there and in a number of other schools (and probably in the Middle Ages too). In education few things are really new; and in education, as in science, our passion for individual freedom makes us as fertile in 'original' local contrivances as we are relatively impotent in subsequent general application. Any attempt, therefore, to provide a conspectus of educational reform in British schools would turn this book into a *catalogue raisonné* of dimensions to which it cannot aspire. Further, when we contemplate innovations similar to our own but in foreign settings, we notice odd glosses which, by contrast, reveal our own hidden assumptions. So we travel to discover our own country, and, as the Chinese urge, wear other people's shoes to find out the shape of our own feet.

Among the many genuine limitations of this book there is one apparent limitation I must disclaim. Warden Spooner (of the spoonerisms) once preached at length to a sparse country congregation about Aristotle. Its bucolic members had never heard of the philosopher; even the tweedy gentry in the front pews, their memories dim, found the Warden's assertions a revelation – but then he was a very great scholar. The sermon done, the closing hymn begun, the Warden collected his scattered notes and cautiously negotiated the steps from the pulpit. At the foot he paused, then clambered up again. With hand upraised he stopped the cheerful song: 'Brethren,' he announced, 'wherever in my sermon I have said Aristotle, I meant to say St Paul....' Forewarned by that great man, I give notice, but in advance, that wherever in this book I say 'boy' I mean 'girl', and vice versa. To write 'boys and girls' every time is long winded, and there is no suitable disgendered term. Scholar, student, child, pupil – all have the wrong flavour. In desperation I've occasionally used all these terms, but the reader will often come across *boys* being taught by *schoolmasters* and he should make the necessary extension, accusing me of finicalness if he – or she – wills, but not of any callow anti-feminism.

My debt to others in preparing this book defies full record: educationalists at home and abroad; teachers in schools I've visited and those in schools that have worked in association with the Resources for Learning Project; members of the Project's Consultative Committee. In particular, though, I would thank Brian Young and Tony Becher of the Nuffield Foundation who initiated and have guided the Resources for Learning Project, and to whom therefore I principally owe the chance to toil at this book. Its argument reflects discussion with Tim McMullen,

John Vaizey, Michael Armstrong and John D'Arcy, my colleagues from the Project's early days. Those who joined the Project later have influenced details of the final draft in the course of
innumerable casual conversations. Yet other colleagues have
undertaken the thankless tasks of reading and transforming
messy scribbles into type. The Project's team is listed in the
Appendix (see page 243). Each of those so far mentioned by name
together with Willem van der Eyken, Brian Scragg and my wife
read the whole book in rough draft, and Dr Borge Holmberg read
the chapter on Sweden. They made many valuable suggestions
which I was glad to incorporate.

I am very grateful to these many friends and associates for
their help, but it is my family who have borne the brunt of this
book. A writer's necessary preoccupation, his absence in body or
in mind, makes added burdens for his wife and is made possible
only by her willingness to bear them. In this I have been singularly blessed. Unnoticed, roofs leak, drains clog, windows rattle,
week-ends and holidays come and go; meanwhile my family's
view of the man about the house has shrunk to a back bent over a
desk or, even less forgivably, a back disappearing to foreign parts.
I therefore dedicate this book to my wife, Suzanne, whose support sustains me, and to my children, Adam, Abigail and Jenni-
fer, whose support compels me.

Part One
Problems

Chapter One
Present Shortcomings

It is impossible to define exactly the purpose of secondary education. We can state the general purpose of most trades in a straightforward way: the aim of the manufacturer is to produce goods at a profit, of the doctor to maintain his patients' health, of the barrister to win his clients' cases. But how do we complete the sentence 'The aim of the schoolmaster is ...?' Sometimes a master will say to a reluctant boy, 'My job is to see you get through your maths exam', and for a moment a distinct purpose emerges. Few would wish to suggest publicly that exam passing is even a first approximation to what secondary education is about, yet it is hard to do much better without being abstrusely philosophical or vague. We want all children to have the opportunity to cultivate their talents, develop their individualities, live life to the full, become good men and women, care for their neighbours, have a sense of duty, learn how to use their leisure (and be trained to work), be quick to respond to change (and hold fast to eternal values in a fast-changing world) – and so on and on.

At the other end of the scale schools concern themselves ardently with the picayune. 'Lavinia', a headmistress gravely begins her report, 'is noisy in the passages'. Headmasters pronounce upon the permitted width of trousers or length of hair and wonder how, short of an equation, to describe the sharpest curve allowed at the point of a shoe. This amiable confusion of the sublime and the ridiculous achieves a heady splendour each year on speech-day platforms where the ritual boasting of minor triumphs is followed by the attempt of some brave soul to reveal the Meaning of It All. At a lower level, in masters' meetings, a prosaic discussion about the best way to handle lost property will somehow reach the point when a master asks, 'but what are we aiming at in this school?' In the stupefied silence the only possible answer is 'just about everything.' It is not very helpful. The connexion in schools between the ideal and the real seems as tenuous, if as enlivening, as the tip of the finger of God on the tip of the finger of Adam in Michelangelo's *Creation*.

Education then has little in common with limited and precise fields like business, medicine, the law. Its cares are as extensive as tohse of government and religion, and in consequence we try to squeeze into the school day a bit of everything. Whenever a new matter is recognized as a proper focus for general concern or public intervention, the demand grows for its inclusion in the curriculum. And how such matters multiply! Nothing is more important than personal relationships (what about marriage guidance from the fourth form upwards?) unless it be health (give them balanced meals, innoculations, a swimming pool). Our future as a nation depends on developing computers (add a bit more to the maths syllabus). Racial conflict will destroy us – unless the H-bomb, the motor car, drugs, environmental pollution, old age, get there first. So somehow there must be instruction in such matters. There is no end, it seems, to the things we ought to be doing.

Alas, the imperatives are now simply too many and too various, defying inclusion or coherence. Secondary education has become a bazaar for rival propositions: every adult from his memory, every parent from his heart, every taxpayer from his pocket, every employer from his need, reckons he has the right to speak his mind. Now boys themselves have suggestions to offer, and people will seek their opinions. The Schools Council recently conducted a survey among present and former schoolboys, and teachers and parents, on the importance of various aims of secondary education. The answers revealed a complete, a comic, disarray.[1]

In truth, people expect far too much. The beleaguered schoolmaster, marking a pile of books or admonishing a boy for larking about, may be surprised at the reminder 'a teacher affects eternity; he can never tell where his influence stops',[2] but the world at large has no doubt about it. The millenium, it seems, can only be ushered in through the schools. No wonder an American recently wrote an article on the teacher as 'victim of role inflation'.[3]

The perplexities that afflict education in general are felt with particular sharpness in the secondary school. To see why, we should compare the task of the secondary schoolmaster with that of the primary teacher on the one side and the university or further-education lecturer on the other.

In the primary school what has to be taught is, paradoxically, both more clear and less precise than in a secondary school. Less precise because, with the eleven-plus in disrepute, standards are less closely defined and examined;[4] more clear because the attitudes and skills are basic – not in the sense of being simple, but fundamental. If all pre-school and primary learning were blotted from our minds we should be hampered indeed; not so with secondary schooling. Primary education is more important, secondary education more intricate and recondite.

Because the primary school deals with universals, it can convey them in a great variety of contexts. A teacher can, if she wishes, keep the context artificial. She can sit children at desks and say: 'We'll read in turn round the room', or 'I want you to copy some sentences from the blackboard', or 'We'll do some sums'; equally, though, in the current mode, she can devise all sorts of situations in which children are led to practise speaking, reading, writing, number skills, the organization of knowledge and the arts of expression. They can do so, for example, in pretending to shop; or through projects like 'Our Postman' or 'Ships'; by visits to the zoo or to museums; and so on. The primary skills are needed everywhere. You do not need to label them and isolate them – periods for this, periods for that. You can have what is called an 'integrated day' – throughout it a teacher can look after certain children and help them to learn as their interests and needs dictate, much as a mother does. Not only can subject boundaries be eroded, so can those between in-school and out-of-school activities. What is learnt in school can be practised everywhere: it is reinforced by daily experience. Sometimes, of course (whether wisely or not), unnatural skills invade the primary day. A recent example is the attempt to teach French from the age of eight upward. Here the teacher has an ally in the willingness – the gullibility if you like – of the young. Prep-school Latin masters have known this for decades and exploited it, setting their charges elaborate exercises in formal grammar in a dead language, knowing that a remarkable number will consider it simply an eccentric game.

But for the poor secondary-school master daily life and lesson seldom coalesce. Everyday situations may be used to convey the fundamental concepts of quantity and relation underlying mathematics; harder by far to use them to teach quadratic equations. Similarly, in history, say, or geography, the subject matter strays far from the familiar – we are taught, many times removed, about the whole wide world in time and space. Science soon ranges beyond household happenings and natural history. The languages that occupy numerous periods are foreign indeed. All these artificial and complex matters a boy must learn – and more. Of course, no one person can teach them all. A boy cannot be left to work with a single master, so he moves from one to another – his day is well and truly disintegrated. Further, the relevance of what he is taught is not at all clear to him. Each master declares his particular subject vital for any boy who wants to understand the world, or himself; it is a prerequisite to this career or that; it is an essential preliminary to further studies of the most exciting kind.... Well, then, it's fun! No? Anyhow, it'll do him good. Unconvinced, the boy has often to be compelled: the artificial requirements of the secondary school demand not only more organization, but more discipline, control, order. So, too, does the greater size of the inmates. A little chaos of the kind that accompanies freedom is no great worry in a primary school;[5] it is altogether less amiable in a secondary school. For the teacher it is the difference between being run over by a bicycle and by a bus.

A rueful glance, then, suggests to the secondary-school master that his lot is more awkward than that of the primary-school teacher. How does it compare with a lecturer's in further or higher education – at a university, for example? The lecturer too has to convey sophisticated, unnatural skills and to insist on the mastery of information, but he does so under far happier conditions. The student has, after all, selected the subject he studies because he likes it or thinks it important to his future career. If he does not want to go to university he does not have to; if he does not care for university he is free to leave. How unlike the schoolboy. In general – unless and until he is a sixth former – he cannot specialize; he cannot refuse to do subjects because he dislikes them (for he might change his mind next year) or because he thinks them irrelevant to his future career (he might change his mind next month);[6] and, willy-nilly, he has to stay at school. Again, whereas the university selects its students, and can send them down if they do not work, the school must accept the boys it gets and cope with them. Moreover, the university is only marginally concerned about how well a student behaves. If he indulges in romp or riot, then the *student* will be blamed for his eccentricities and his waste of talent and opportunity, but the school is required to keep the boy off the streets, to insist on standards of behaviour well above those required by the law, to strive to make a boy use his talent and opportunities to the full. The school cannot, must not, shirk the blame for a boy's failure.

Thus the secondary school shares with the primary school the baby-sitting, baby-rearing function of education, but at an age when the babies are stronger, less amenable, and less easily entertained. It shares with the university the need to convey remote, complex information and skills, but at an age when its charges cannot be allowed a free choice and cannot understand the ultimate value of what they do. The school must look after boys as if they were children and teach them as though they were adults. These two conflicting requirements enclose it. In the secondary school alone both jaws of the educational trap meet and bite.

In all this the secondary school faithfully reflects the dilemma of the adolescents with which it deals. Primitive societies know only childhood, manhood, old age. We have added the long, confused, transitional stage of adolescence, awkward because it is artificial.[7] The adolescent is pampered yet caged, free from real labour but required to work, released from necessities and in consequence bewildered by possibilities, encouraged to taste but forbidden to eat. The confusion of adolescence is a measure of a society's sophistication; the length a measure of its affluence.

Once in Gambia, on a remote beach beside a listless sea, I came upon upon an old man leaning on his staff with a dozen boys sitting round him in a circle. They were twelve or thirteen years old, uniformly dressed in dingy white gowns. What were they, I asked my host, lepers? Of a kind, he said, temporary lepers: they were initiates. After a period of instruction, in a brief precise act of graduation, they would become men. In our terms they were at secondary school. They had to be taught certain special skills they could not learn within their own families, for which a wise man, a teacher, was needed. The skills and the knowledge a boy in Gambia may need in his adult life are few and slight, ours numerous and weighty. Their single teacher for a few days has grown with us into many teachers for five years or more.

Although the job of the secondary school, by definition, takes us beyond the primary, the basic, the universal, the degree of incoherence in the contemporary curriculum is quite recent. A hundred years ago those few who received any secondary education at all also had a sort of 'integrated day', in which classical civilizations were studied. For those destined to move in less happy circumstances, induction into elementary skills, together with some religious instruction, was enough. There were two nations: in one adolescence was long, in the other brief, and each had its own style of preparation.

But this simple and ordered pattern changed radically while Queen Victoria reigned. International trade and industrialization diversified the kind of learning that might lead to positions of power, giving modern languages and science a growing importance. New skills came to be required from the poorer sort too; hewers of wood and drawers of water were no longer enough. Worst confusion of all, the democratization of society made it less and less clear who would wield power and who would not; increasingly any skill and knowledge might prove useful to anybody.[8]

But the reverse was equally true. Anybody might find any subject useless. Those who modernized the curriculum in the nineteenth century argued that the new subjects they introduced were more useful than the classics. In some general computation of social needs, so they were. But so great was the diversity of possible careers that for any individual the most obviously useful subject might turn out to be most useless, and vice versa. Most of what was so laboriously learnt at school was entirely forgotten, or lingered uselessly like odd lines from a part in a play when the performance is done. . . . Old Boys in retrospect, young boys in anticipation, could each compile differing lists of subjects on which, year after weary year, precious hours were wasted. Utility providing such shaky justification, teachers of the new subjects increasingly deployed the arguments traditionally, and more cogently, used by the classicists they had displaced. Their subjects were not only useful to some but good for everyone. A modern language and its literature could also be studied like a dead one; science too could provide a disciplined routine of established exercises (so curiously described as 'experiments'). Squire Brown had roundly declared he didn't 'care a straw for Greek particles and the digamma[10], but what replaced them soon came to be scarcely more practical.

A blunt Englishman like Squire Brown might complain that classics had no 'real' use and he might well be blind to their 'true' use, their universal educational value, but he would doubtless understand their 'social' use well enough. They were the badge of a gentleman; they helped a man get on. In the same way the pure educational gold of the new subjects was transmuted by unphilosophical souls into the base metal of examination passes. Most of the curriculum might seem useless, but a collection of passes provided credentials required for profitable occupations. Not the thing itself but the symbol was useful. Already at school daily labour did not so much satisfy real needs as provide a coinage that did so.

As the medium of education the new subjects suffered, in comparison with the classics, a grave disadvantage: how could so many important subjects be dealt with adequately, in illuminating depth, with so little time available? Worse still, in the name of utility, the various disciplines yearly augmented their established store of 'essentials', hopefully pouring more and more quarts of information into the pint pots of time allocated to them – not just the established classics of English literature but contemporary work as well; not just reading and writing a language but speaking it too; not the history of Europe alone but of the whole world; and above all, more and more science. And then, as if the timetable were not already crowded enough, a number of new subjects – additional languages, social sciences – waved the invitation card marked 'Utility' and claimed admission. Erstwhile 'extras' and out-of-school activities – music, art, physical education – managed to squeeze in too, being useful for leisure and as education for the whole man. Next, the room being full to bursting, part of the corridor was loosely marked off as 'General Studies' and into it all the late-comers and gate-crashers were crammed. Finally there was nothing for it but to find a bigger space – a longer school day, more and more years at school.[10]

The growing fear that the learner might die of excess has been a major impetus behind recent curriculum reform. New courses have been devised which superannuate a lot of the time-consuming, traditional material, and rearrange the remainder in a more logical, economic order (though mysteriously what is finally included seems always to take up more time than ever). The touchstone of what to discard and what to retain or introduce is 'relevance', a much-used term in current curricular argument and one which, like the older notion of 'useful', conceals a radical divergence. Sometimes it means relevance *now* and sometimes relevance *forever*. In 'relevance now' the prime consideration is that the ideas should directly and immediately matter to the boy. It tends to be child-centred. With 'relevance forever' the prime consideration is that the ideas should be of permanent, underlying value, reflecting the mode of thinking used in the subject. It tends to be subject-centred. Ideally, both types of relevance should combine. When Jerome Bruner puts forward the hypothesis 'any subject can be taught effectively in some intellectually honest form to any child at any stage of development',[11] he has in mind both the structure of the subject and translating that structure into materials that appeal to the child at whatever age. The key ideas in the subject, recurring in increasing complexity as the child grows older, constitute a 'spiral curriculum'.

Such is the intention and the hope. In practice, discursive subjects taught in the vernacular tend to stress 'relevance now'; sequential subjects requiring the mastery of a 'language' tend to emphasize the structural 'relevance forever'. But usually, whatever the weighting, both sorts of relevance are claimed. Thus, the content of a new Nuffield science course is certainly more closely connected with contemporary experience than what it replaces; but more important is the opportunity it provides for learning by the experimental method – for thinking like a scientist. In English, literature and discussion about things which concern the adolescent replace *belles lettres*; but even more critically the subject is the arena for personal explorations in the widest of contexts, and their creative expression in words. Where a subject is useful, content matters in its own right; when it is relevant, it is process and involvement that count.

Now, we are concerned in this book with teaching method. Clearly the method we use will take account of practical consideration like the need for good order and economy, but it will also reflect our view of the purpose of teaching a subject. If a group of boys all have to know something in detail because it is vocational (for a particular trade or for survival in twentieth-century society), then putting them in a class and instructing them works well enough. If the subject is only potentially useful, class teaching becomes less suitable since all of the boys will have to submit to the full course of instruction which only some will directly use. When we shift our ground to relevance, class teaching becomes still less appropriate. To tell a boy that something may one day prove useful or creditable to him is incontrovertible if unconvincing. The proof lies in the future. With 'relevance now' the test is immediate. Unfortunately, what each person responds to as relevant to *him* is individual and elusive. In the fairy tale the King went out to search for happiness, heard a peasant singing cheerfully behind the plough, bought his shirt and hopefully put it on. Relevance too is the uncertain by-product of personal experience. How can it successfully be tailored by a teacher for all thirty boys in his class? Similarly some teachers argue that the essential, informing ideas in a subject, those of 'relevance forever', are not best conveyed by frontal teaching; they are better 'discovered' by the individual for himself so that they really mean something to him. Both relevance now and forever, then, point away from class teaching, the one towards a more personal selection, the other to a more individual progress. A classful of boys is just becoming involved in a poem or a discussion when the bell goes. Genuine discovery for the whole of Form III has to occur in the laboratory between 11.15 and 1.00 every Tuesday. When boys are taught in an uninvolved, passive way, a shift at regular intervals from master to master is sensible enough, but if the school is at all frequently to be the arena for personal exploration and significant experience, then its teaching and timetabling practices will need radical overhaul.

When we argue that a subject has relevance because it enshrines ideas and processes of general value, we pose a further problem. If certain ways of thinking are *generally* valuable, then they presumably occur in many different contexts. Thus, in 'new maths', thinking like a mathematician emerges as an exercise in symbolic logic that extends far beyond the traditional subject matter. We can think like historians in many contemporary human affairs, not just in past particulars. Is insight into the handling and structure of language best derived from a study of a single foreign tongue? Scientific method may be especially powerful in investigating physical matter, but its applicability extends much further. In asserting, then, that certain modes of thinking are universally important, we tend to detach them from any one context, from any one particular body of subject matter. For how many periods, over how many years, need a boy be made to practise a given mode of thinking in the context of a subject which, however apt, he finds repellent?[12] If the purpose of science be to convey possibly useful techniques and items of knowledge, there is no end to it; but how many 'real experiments' does a boy need to do before he understands the main elements in scientific method? Once he has grasped the basic process, might he not be scientific and experimental in areas of study that matter to him? After a relatively brief period of initiation into a mode of thinking in its most appropriate subject form, would it not be better to allow the boy more choice?

There are some who have generalized this detachment of the essentials of intellectual training from the content of particular subject disciplines. Their view appears in the rueful adage: 'Education is what you remember when all you were taught is forgotten.' It was admirably expressed by William Cory, an assistant master of Eton, in 1861:

You go to school at the age of twelve or thirteen; and for the next four or five years you are engaged not so much in acquiring knowledge as in making mental efforts under criticism. A certain amount of knowledge you can indeed with average faculties acquire so as to retain; nor need you regret the hours you spent on much that is forgotten, for the shadow of past knowledge at least protects you from many illusions. But you go to a great school not for knowledge so much as for arts and habits; for the habit of attention, for the art of expression, for the art of entering quickly into another person's thoughts, for the habit of submitting to censure and refutation, for the art of indicating assent and dissent in graduated terms, for the habit of regarding minute points of accuracy, for taste, for discrimination, for mental courage, and for mental soberness. Above all, you go to a great school for self-knowledge.[13]

Logically, the argument that it doesn't matter what you learn, only what you learn while learning it can be used to support either an enforced curriculum or the widest measure of choice. If it does not matter what boys learn, they may equally all do the same thing or different things. In practice, however, the down-grading of subject content undermines the arguments normally used to compel boys to take particular subjects, promoting the view that boys should acquire the important 'arts and habits' through suitable material of their own choosing.

Although current arguments about the curriculum point towards more choice and variety, a more independent style of learning, they quickly run into the barrier of class teaching, which was evolved to suit wholly different beliefs. With due guidance, thirty university students or thirty primary-school children working the 'integrated day' may, at any one time and in their own time, be learning thirty different things. Thirty schoolboys, while being taught in class, learn one thing – and someone has to prescribe *exactly* what that one thing shall be. We are accustomed in secondary schools to blame this inflexibility on the examiners. In so doing, we give scant credit to the varying modes of examining.[14] It is not that an exam forces us to adopt a single syllabus; rather that our teaching method forces us to adopt a single syllabus which may as well be one of those set by examiners. Worse, our method of class teaching requires that we fill out the syllabus outline with close detail, particularizing minutely, compulsory item upon compulsory item, period by period. It forces us to make a succession of prescriptive decisions and then to impose them upon boys, 'each for all and all for each'.

The importance of offering a greater choice of subjects and activities is often put forward as an argument for having large comprehensive schools. But the range of activities going on simultaneously in a primary school provides evidence that it is not small size alone but rather small size combined with class teaching that is the bar to flexibility. So long as we teach in classes, trying to extend choice puts us in an economic dilemma. If we have a small school and want to offer numerous options, all fully taught, then we shall be forced to subdivide our classes into groups of an uneconomic size. In a large school we may indeed be able to offer numerous options and still find each commands a class of economic size; but to cover the country in a network of schools of sufficient size, other considerations apart, will be a long and expensive business.

In sum, when we believe the content of a subject to be directly useful to everyone, it makes sense to collect classes of boys and to teach them. If we shift ground and encourage personal involvement and 'discovery', a more individual and fluid style of working becomes appropriate. Similarly, by emphasizing induction into modes of thinking, arts and habits, all of the widest value and significance – most aptly embodied in particular subjects but to be found and practised in many – we open the way to increased personal selection of subject matter. However, if boys are put into classes and taught, then we are bound to select among matters of indifference a single 'right' course for all to follow, to teach one set of particulars as though they were essentials. If boys are in classes and taught, then personal exploration and 'discovery' between bells, by subjects, is unrealistic. If boys are in classes and have to be taught, then we simply cannot afford to offer them much individual choice. Thus class teaching obstructs attempts to make sense of the curriculum. There is a strong case for examining any reasonable alternative.

The effect of our teaching method on the secondary-school curriculum is important but obscure; other constraints imposed by class teaching are more obvious and we can deal with them briefly.

First, class teaching tends to be passive. New courses may strive to make it less so but the weight of numbers undermines the best efforts. What size should a class be? For no particular reason we have picked thirty as the largest reasonable size in secondary schools. The Russians think forty perfectly all right. Sarah Fielding's Mrs Teachum had her number 'fixed to Nine, which she on no Account would be prevailed upon to increase'.[15]

For active scouting, Baden-Powell established patrols of eight. For sixth-form learning, where an easy exchange of views in discussion is important, sixteen is reckoned to be all that a man can handle. For discipleship, Jesus fixed on twelve, and one of those went astray. The size we select is a function both of what we can afford and of what sort of learning we intend. With the customary ratio of a teacher for thirty learners, we plainly have a sedentary, a passive process in mind.[16]

But beyond mere passiveness, classroom teaching requires actual docility. Mark Hopkins described education in his folksy way as 'a man and a boy on a log'. We have to translate that into a man and thirty boys in desks lined up, in Dickens's phrase, 'like figures in a sum'. If boys are to hear what the teacher says, then they must be quiet. Alas, the qualities that make a man an inspiring teacher may conflict with those he needs as a disciplinarian. Rules war with relationships. An aside in the back row of a classroom is as disturbing as an aside in the gallery of a theatre; a boy unwrapping an illicit toffee as distracting to his neighbours as a theatre-goer fumbling for his favourite chocolate among the crinkly papers. But the schoolmaster cannot simply rise above the intrusion; he has to ensure attention from every single boy, even at the risk of breaking the concentration of thirty others. A small child learning from a 'toy', a student from a book, work a bit, dream a bit, fidget, stand up and stretch – not so the schoolboy in class. We impose on adolescents in their most active years a relative stillness few of us as adults could sustain and we have to enforce it with an apparatus of entreaties and commands.

Because all thirty boys in the class are getting their information from a single source – the teacher – they must all, as we have seen, follow the same curriculum. Some meals are more pleasant than others, some presented more attractively than others; in general, though, we cannot expect boys to approach what is compulsorily set before them with the sort of zest they might display in choosing from a larder.

Again, a schoolmaster can teach only at one speed. To some boys in a class the message may be as clear as day, but they must stifle their yawns while the master sets out pound upon pound of tallow candles until even the blindest can see. A private tutor can vary the style, the depth, the speed of his instruction to suit the boy; the teacher has to set a pace he estimates to be right for a fictional average of the whole class. The same content, the same speed for all the thirty boys in it – the Americans call this the 'lock-step' of the class.

It matters greatly, of course, whom you are lock-stepped with and by. A single source of instruction is most effective when matched to a single known receiver. Since we cannot economically reduce all teaching to tutoring, we do our best to make our audience as homogeneous, as close to a single known average as we can. We 'stream' and 'set' boys, grouping them to their ability. A child in a bright, keen class is well away, but the reverse can be a disaster.

Classes made up of those who find academic work rewarding sometimes – and other classes often – develop a 'tail'. Some reluctant boys may just sit and dream in the back row, or play the fool with questions, sallies and antics that delight but disrupt the class; but the stronger ones may protect their self-esteem by a bullying assertion that work is sissy. They can all establish an unseen picket line between the master and those who would like to work hard. Whether in a form or in a factory a climate of ca'canny makes individual enthusiasm wilt.

Scarcely less important to a boy than his companions are the masters he draws in the lucky dip of the timetable. The Royal Society recently quizzed its members about the influences that led them to become scientists. Much the most important was a bright science master. Heads you win; but tails, alas, you lose. We do not know how many were deterred by a dim teacher. Indeed, the problem is more complex. The brilliant maths teacher may delight Smith but stupefy Jones; the new English master, however, may make Jones's spirits soar but completely puzzle Smith. Those who manage schools tend to shrug off these frustrating hours of incomprehension. It's life. You can't always work with people who suit you. But the stakes for a young boy can be unduly high. His tastes and skills are yet unformed. Further, he will, normally, have to stay with each teacher for a year. It may be a critical time in his academic development; it is certainly a long time to a child bewildered or stifled by a teacher he cannot understand. Moreover, schools tend to put their better teachers, however defined, into the classes made up of the more willing and capable boys.[17] Often, then, a boy shackled to bad company finds his difficulties compounded by having an incompetent overseer. Schools amply illustrate the sad paradox: 'Unto every one that hath shall be given, and he shall have abundance: but from him that hath not shall be taken away even that which he hath.' [18]

Lack of sympathy between a particular master and a particular boy is, of course, the leitmotive of masters' meetings. Sometimes it is explicit. 'I can't get Jones to understand logarithms', says the maths man. More often it is concealed within another theme: 'Jones is a fool and lazy too!' And the master who taught maths to Jones last year wonders if this can be the same boy he knew and found so willing. At home his parents worry about their son's unexpected lapse. Should they see the Head? And if they do, can he do more than console them with hopes for the best and a promise to speak to the master and boy concerned? For a boy can seldom be moved for one subject in isolation; he has to change classes, so that the change of one master means a change of many. Besides, the implications of grouping boys according to their preferences are extensive.[19] It would lead to a sort of popularity contest, and prove unpracticable. Some masters, like fashionable university dons, would need halls to contain their audiences; others would find themselves only slightly encumbered.

Because we have to group boys in classes of roughly equal size and assign masters to them, we are forced at present into constructing a timetable in which everyone changes classes at defined moments. The bell is king. It demands that we learn in episodes of rigid, equal length. It cuts short our brightest and our dimmest moments indifferently. The timetable becomes a sort of solemn Mad Hatter's tea-party. No matter what – how – where, when the bell goes we must all move round and face in any old order, one dish or another on the table before us. It may be necessary; it is certainly bizarre. Which of us would choose to study this way? For the constant disruptions make it painfully slow. A boy can, for example, learn the equivalent of all his school hours of French to O-level during a month's immersion in Paris; a buinessman gets further in a fortnight's intensive course in a language laboratory. Of course, motive is a key factor in the contrast. The boy in Paris wants to eat, shop, find his way around; the businessman wants to make sales and further his career. But lack of motive aside, learning in fixed instalments is calculated to nip in the bud the more delicate inducements to learning. It cuts across tentative understanding, cumulative absorption, growing excitement, half-formed invention and simple pleasure. Bell's gone – move on – and wake the Dormouse up.

No doubt this brief glance at class teaching gives an inadequate picture of the best practitioners of the art (as of the worst), but it may serve to display the method's main tendencies. Whatever its considerable defects, no other has yet proved acceptable over any length of time to more than a small minority of enthusiasts. Survival is a strong testimonial. Like other venerable institutions, class teaching no doubt evolved to meet particular social and economic pressures; it may persist, however, from habit and the difficulties involved in change. Do our present circumstances, our needs – which we now examine – suggest that some other method of learning may be more appropriate?

Chapter Two
Teacher Supply

We are accustomed to the awkwardness and inefficiency of class teaching. Boys and teachers survive it. A teacher, a parent, may at times feel particular concern for a boy whose needs are obviously not being met or one who cannot adjust his pace to the class; and we may at all times feel a general anguish, nodding a sad agreement to Henry Adams's remark, 'Throughout human history the waste of mind has been appalling.' Granted – but so inured are we to the inadequacies of class teaching that we seldom question the assumptions underlying the method or examine the familiar machinery supporting it.

Our present practices depend upon there being an adequate supply of teachers. Already when we collect thirty boys in a class and teach them as though they were one, various strains arise. It would be dismal indeed if the ratio, and consequently the teacher's ability to cope, were to worsen. To ensure, then, that we shall in the future at least be able to maintain the *status quo*, we must look at the statistics of demand and supply of teachers. We shall not look too far ahead – up to 1980 will probably tax our vision sufficiently – and we must first establish the broad outlines of our situation before trying to make out any of the more intricate details.[1]

It is estimated that by 1980 the school population will have risen from the present 8,337,600 to 10,534,100.[2] This prediction conflates the size of present age groups together with projections of those to come, the effect of raising the compulsory school-leaving age in 1972, and suppositions about the number of boys and girls likely to stay on at school voluntarily. Besides finding the extra teachers to look after these additional numbers, we have to remedy our present deficit. Currently many children in primary or secondary schools are taught in oversized classes. To meet all demands the Department of Education and Science calculates we shall need 113,000 extra teachers and that by 1980 they can be produced.[3]

This looks encouraging – at first sight. It is a little disconcerting to discover, however, that predictions made as recently as April 1965 were substantially revised in December 1968 by Report 51. Making projections is clearly a tricky business, and 'wastage' is a good example of the kind of unknown factor involved. Over 70 per cent of recent entrants to the training colleges have been women, for whom the training colleges often provide an alternative to universities with their bias in favour of men. Some women never teach at all. Others go into teaching and quickly marry out of it, or give up when they start to raise a family. Of course, many professional women in all walks of life are forced to confine their skills over long years within the home; but no other large profession – unless it be medicine – is so dependent upon women. The nurse, however, is part of hospital provision even while she trains. The teacher is not a permanent part of a school during the three, increasingly four, years she spends in a college of education. Over 40 per cent of those women so expensively trained are lost to the teaching profession within ten years.[4] In recent years some of the wastage has been ingeniously piped back into the schools by encouraging mothers with children of school age to teach part time, and mothers whose children have grown up full time. No doubt the years at teachers' colleges have value for those who become mothers, and the years of motherhood profit those who return to teaching. But in terms of estimating teacher supply, the going to and fro is a confusing factor indeed. As the DES Report 51 puts it: 'a slight change in the age at which women leave teaching in order to marry and have children can have a significant effect on the total number of teachers available'.

The effects of political decisions are only marginally less hazardous to teacher supply than marriage trends. The present estimate that we are 40,000 teachers short is based on the curious convention that when there are thirty in a secondary school class, the acceptable limit has been reached, but that forty is all right in a primary school. Government policy is to achieve an equality. An official spokesman declared 'our aim is to go on reducing the size of classes as rapidly as possible and to discriminate in favour of getting the size in primary schools down more rapidly than the size in secondary schools'. By *Circular 16/69* the Secretary of State repealed the invidious and restrictive regulation about class size, declaring a future intention to have a uniform pupil–teacher ratio, leaving it to the schools to deploy staff as they think best. However, if we use the old arithmetic of class size as a guide to an appropriate ratio, then to bring primary classes down to the thirty per class customary in secondary schools would add 70,000 to our bill for teachers.[5]

None would doubt the importance of ample staffing in a child's first years at school, but is this perhaps already unduly late? The researches of Basil Bernstein and others led the authors of the *Plowden Report* to emphasize that an educative environment in pre-school years is vital to a child's whole future. Proverbially, as the twig is bent so the tree grows, and Jesuits are credited with the axiom 'Give us a child before he is seven and he is ours for life.' Many educationalists now consider that nursery schooling may be the most important field of all in which to invest. Certainly we may expect an insistent demand for such schools as compensatory education in 'Plowden areas'. To run them we shall need more teachers.

But it is not in the nursery and primary schools alone that the present estimate of how many teachers we shall need seems conservative. The demand for education is an appetite that grows with the feeding. The more complex a nation's economy the greater the demand for a longer period of education or training; the more democratic a society the more anxious its citizens become to give their children a good start in the race. The prizes are open now to more people than before, the handicaps less arbitrary.

Ambition first showed in the grammar schools. The number of boys staying on into the sixth started to grow rapidly a dozen years ago in what became known as the 'Trend'. It took everyone by surprise. We seem likely now to be equally astonished by equivalent hopes among the less academic. At present the percentage of our fifteen to nineteen year olds receiving full-time education is 21·7 per cent in schools and 4 per cent in technical colleges – in all, some 26 per cent.[6] The equivalent total figure in America is 75 per cent. We may want to dismiss this figure because of American affluence; but we also lag behind almost all other European countries. Report 51 supposes that by 1972 everyone will stay at school until they are sixteen and that by 1980 we may expect 30 per cent of the sixteen to nineteen year olds to stay on voluntarily. If we add an equivalent or somewhat more generous increase in the technical colleges, then we may expect somewhere between 36 and 40 per cent of our sixteen to nineteen year olds to continue with full-time education. The Swedes adjusted their national plan to allow for 70 per cent; the French base theirs on 80 per cent.[7] It is difficult to estimate the effects a parallel increase would have in this country on the demand for teachers. Our present arrangements for the full-time education of sixteen to nineteen year olds are particularly confused and extravagant. An increase in numbers might well enforce concentration and so give economies of scale. All we can safely assert is that to provide tertiary education on a sale comparable to what now exists or is planned in other developed democracies would very substantially increase our need for teachers – and academically well-qualified teachers at that.

Unless all the demands we have examined – for smaller primary classes, nursery schools, more generous tertiary provision – are firmly blocked, we shall find the estimated need for 113,000 extra teachers by 1980 conservative indeed. Such major trends aside, teacher supply is also more subtly affected by changes within the schools. We have seen already that, in contrast to the primary school, a growing complexity, some would say infirmity, of purpose afflicts the secondary school. To take one example, lack of confidence in any established curriculum results in more and more optional subjects being offered up and down the school. Consequently there is proliferation of small groups of students with specialist masters teaching them. Report 51 sadly notes that 'though the proportion of oversize primary classes has diminished more rapidly than might have been expected, the reverse has been true of secondary classes. Secondary schools in deploying teachers seem to have pursued a number of aims of which classes over thirty was only one.' No matter how we try to fill the reservoir of teachers we find to our dismay that it remains obstinately empty; water is being drawn off to cultivate more and more fields. There is every indication that our educational expectations will rapidly increase. Even if by 1980 we could hope to meet present requirements we shall by then find our expectations so changed that the gap between supply and demand will seem as great as ever.

We have so far considered only global figures for teacher supply. The DES Report 51 understandably conflates primary- and secondary-school needs. There is, after all, a considerable overlap between the upper forms of a primary school and the lower forms of a secondary school. The qualities and qualifications that fit a person to teach in the one will fit him equally to teach in the other. Indeed with the present confusion over the age of transfer it is impossible to say where the primary school ends and the secondary school begins. All the same, constraints appear in the staffing of secondary schools which these global figures for teacher supply conceal. Thus, by convention, women or men, indifferently, teach children of both sexes in primary schools; but for the most part men teach boys and women teach girls in single-sex secondary schools. At present, as we have seen, 70 per cent of those at colleges of education are women, most of whom have gone into the primary schools where the latest population 'bulge' has been most acutely felt. As the bulge passes into the secondary schools and when the leaving age is raised, the ability of the teachers' colleges to attract suitable men will assume a new importance.

Further, in recruiting for primary schools we are scarcely limited at all by subject specialization. In a secondary school, on the contrary, it is not enough that a man should be a good teacher; he must also be a teacher specifically of maths, say, or science. In subjects like these, which bulk large on a timetable, the scarcity of teachers is grave already and likely to worsen. From sad experience training colleges expect to have few science candidates, and in 1968 only 520 of the 820 places available were filled.[8] Of the generation of teachers now emerging from the colleges, 63 per cent had in 1965 taken A-levels at school. Of these only 1800 had studied some science in the sixth form, whereas 10,000 had read arts subjects. Nor does the future hold out rosier hopes: while between 1962 and 1967 the annual number taking arts subjects to A-level doubled, the number of scientists not only fell proportionately but absolutely, from 32,700 to 31,700. Such considerations, quoted by Harry Judge in a speech to the Royal Society of Arts,[9] led him to forecast that, short of

some drastic action, science teaching will cease in most schools
within ten years. A succession of official reports – Appleton,
Dainton, Swann – while less precise in dating the apocalypse,
expressed similar disquiet, the most recent, the *Mott Report*,
positive alarm.[10]

Not only the subject but the level to which a candidate has
pursued it constrain a secondary school headmaster in choosing
his staff. For his sixth form at least he must find graduates.
Where college-trained teachers are in short supply, graduate
teachers are likely to be more scarce still. The Department of
Education and Science estimates that in maths and science we
have about a third of the graduates we need. The schools have
to compete for them not only with other parts of the educational
system but with industry. Between 1965 and 1968 the active
stock of scientists, technologists and engineers rose by some 4·6
per cent, but the employers needed an increase of 7·2 per cent.[11]
The situation in most other subjects is not critical, only bad,
and the schools' power to attract graduates disappointing. Because the expansion of universities had substantially increased
the number of graduates, it was officially and modestly forecast
in 1965 that the proportion of graduates in teaching should increase by 1 per cent; in the event the proportion declined in the
ensuing three years. Despite this, Report 51 says: 'after the early
1970s, the proportion of graduates to non-graduates in teaching
seems likely to increase'. This prediction is based on the belief
that more students at training colleges will take the four-year
Bachelor of Education courses. At present 5 per cent of the
annual intake of students do so; by 1974 the Report prophesies
25 per cent, of whom 40 per cent should be men. It sounds a
little optimistic. In any event, will such degree courses, tied
specifically to teaching from the start, tend to be a second-best
for those who cannot get into university? A recent poll among
older pupils at school did not suggest any impending movement
towards teaching by the more able, and least of all among those
with skills in short supply. Recruiting officers from other professions complain that they have too little chance to purvey their
wares to boys at school; teaching, perhaps, suffers from too close
and constant an exposure.

Estimates of meeting teacher needs by 1980 are less than reassuring therefore when we consider the secondary school in particular and not the schools in general, because in the secondary school we have to work within constraints of sex, subject and high academic qualification. We should notice, too, that questions of teacher supply are in the form: we shall need (at least) 113,000 more teachers by 1980 – shall we get somewhere near that figure? Our worry is whether we shall have enough bodies to man the classrooms at all, not whether we shall have any choice between bodies. The experience of headmasters already amply confirms this. Even in the grammar schools, so unfairly favoured, recruiting has become difficult. The shortage appeared first in maths and physics. A headmaster who used confidently to advertise for men with 'good honours degrees' will now search the mail anxiously for an answer, any answer, to his enticing offers. If there are, say, three candidates remotely fit to teach, he thinks himself fortunate; and these candidates are being pursued by many other headmasters besides himself. The lack of choice that once affected only maths and physics has now spread, at graduate level, to all the sciences and even, in less acute form, to modern languages and English.

Headmasters of secondary modern schools have far worse difficulties, but toughened by years of experience to every hardship, adept at extemporization, they have long since become inured to welcoming whomsoever they or the local authority can raise. Last year the younger boys had physics but the physicist has moved to another school and a retired chemist is the only possible replacement: for physics on the timetable read chemistry. A school develops strange specialities for brief periods. A teacher of French is ardent about Spanish as a second language; he starts a group of boys off on the subject but then leaves, and the subject withers with him. The wind bloweth where the available staff listeth.

These revelations of acute shortage may surprise parents and other laymen. They are commonplace to all but the most favoured secondary-school headmasters. Of course there are other occupations in which there are too few people with the right skills, but it matters specially in teaching. After all, these are the men and women who deal with our children, not those who entertain us, or produce cars for us, or serve us with our groceries.

And there are other reasons. In most other occupations if you have to make do because you cannot get the people you want, you can closely supervise, or group the weak with the strong, or mechanize. In teaching in Britain, to the contrary, there is no supervisor to overlook, no automatic check on results or mistakes. A nurse is instructed by a sister who is told what to do by a doctor who is regularly guided by a consultant. There is no similar interlocking hierarchy of experience and skills in a school. The degree to which a headmaster or head of department can actually control the performance of a new teacher is small indeed. Good or bad, each teacher copes as best he can. It is hard to think of any other trade in which such secure isolation persists. It is the condition of the teacher, unless he becomes reprobate or allows riot, for all his days. Getting reliable and capable people is therefore of overwhelming importance.

Most occupations are subject to constant change in equipment. General shortage of manpower, or a particular shortage of skilled men, is a particular incentive to mechanization. There are, or course, new devices to be found around the schools – projectors, tape-recorders, television and radio sets. The use made of them is, however, remarkably small. True, in language teaching the tape recorder makes a useful contribution in a number of schools; overwhelmingly, however, teaching still revolves around the long-familiar technology of blackboard and book. Even so, expenditure on books at present accounts for less than 1 per cent of the educational budget.[12] As for the much-publicized new audio-visual machinery, a measure of the actual value attached to it is to be found in a detailed survey of the surrounding region conducted by the University of Sussex: on all the 'software' needed to make the gadgets useful – programmes, tapes, slides, film-loops, film-rental – four-fifths of the schools spent less than ten pounds a year per school.[13] If a new Rip Van Winkle were, say, a doctor by training, he would find at his awakening that he could not function at all in a modern hospital; the equipment and the techniques would be mysteries to him. In a school he would have no parallel difficulties. Schools are like the very earliest factories: simple materials, walls, workers and overseers. The tools of the trade, the machinery and equipment, are rudimentary. I do not mean to imply that this is wrong; simply to emphasize that there is not much to counterbalance the skill, or lack of skill, of the individual teacher. Teaching is a job almost wholly dependent on manpower, and in the foreseeable future in the secondary schools the craftsmen we need are going to be in scant supply.

It might be supposed that such circumstances would deter us from any change likely to add further strains on attenuated resources. Not a bit of it: we have decided to reorganize all our secondary schools into a comprehensive pattern. However justi-fiable on other grounds, in terms of staff utilization it is a jump from the frying pan into the fire. Just why this is so we shall now examine.

Chapter Three
The Effects of Comprehension

I am going to assume that within the next twenty years almost all state secondary schools will become comprehensive.[1] At the present time opponents of comprehension have vigorously questioned the wisdom of the change, deploring that a momentous educational decision should have been made essentially on political grounds. Party manoeuvring on this issue is indeed unfortunate, but a clear separation of education and politics is both impractical and undesirable. For we use schools to transmit to the young what we think important for society as it is, as we conceive it will be, and as we wish it were. Any argument about the society we want will therefore have implications for the schools, and such argument is the very stuff of democratic politics. Communists may hope for the day when, all conflicts resolved, politics becomes merely 'the administration of things', but we who aspire to no such Byzantine immobility of opinion cannot remove education from politics without trivializing it.

Educational change might indeed proceed from purely educational considerations if our aims were clear and the way to achieve them known from incontrovertible research evidence. A measure of certainty, alas, lies only with the established order. The effects of any large change are so unpredictable that it will follow only from some glittering social or economic hope, ardently pursued. Such a hope quickly establishes the direction of 'worthwhile' research and make us give significance only to the findings we should like to believe. Thus, after the war, numerous research studies on the validity of intelligence tests provided ammunition for those who believed we should select children at eleven for differing styles of secondary schooling – grammar, technical and modern. Now, with equal conviction, all the 'important' research evidence points the other way. Reform starts with social or economic impulse; professional studies accelerate and sanctify the process.

Comprehension is now accepted in principle by all the political parties. Doubtless, nobler considerations apart, they have noticed that the idea of comprehension commands a wide sympathy. A recent poll showed 61 per cent in favour, 17 per cent against and 22 per cent undecided.[2] The parties now argue about how quickly and how completely the change should be made. The Conservatives, urging the principle of parental choice and the value of retaining schools of established merit, want to keep most direct-grant and many grammar schools, letting them co-exist with new comprehensives. Further, they insist, these comprehensives should be properly equipped for their role – an expensive and therefore a slow task in a time of financial stringency. Labour contends that under selection parental choice is a fiction, the overwhelming majority of children being in effect assigned willy-nilly to the secondary modern; and that retaining any selective state schools means that the comprehensives, bereft by neighbouring grammar schools of the most able children, are not comprehensive at all but secondary modern schools tarted up. Although in terms of enthusiasm there is a substantial difference between these political positions, there is agreement about replacing the tripartite system increasingly by comprehension. A new house is needed, but the Conservatives do not find the old one so intolerable that they are prepared, as Labour is, to burn it down, camping out in the ruins in an attempt to make the builders get a move on. Not only at Westminster, but at Town and County Hall, the argument centres generally around the tactics of introducing comprehension, seldom about the principle. Of 163 authorities 129 have comprehensive schemes approved for all or part of their areas[3] (although only some 26 per cent of children are yet being educated in comprehensive schools[4]). Twelve schemes are under consideration. Only twenty-two authorities have so far failed to submit plans.

The most extraordinary feature of current proposals is their variety. If the means available are few, the ways are all too many. For twenty years after the 1944 Education Act we rebuilt our schools so that primary education ended and secondary education began at eleven. It was a slow and difficult task, but at least the aim was clear. Not so with comprehension. A recent review listed eleven major variants in operation.[5] In differing parts of the country children transfer between schools at every age from

eight to sixteen. Our society has become more mobile: not
only may a boy from a grammar school in one area find himself
when he moves assigned to a comprehensive school in another,
but a boy from a sixth-form college may find himself back again
in a school, or a twelve-year-old from an all-through comprehensive find himself in a middle school where the range of subjects
and the style of schooling is very different. In certain boroughs
like Merton in London, placed near the boundaries of differing
authorities, children now leave the same primary school at many
varying ages according to which surrounding educational authority they belong to.[6] As if this were not confusion enough, the
Maud Report on local government, should it be implemented,
groups together existing authorities – say Nottingham City and
Nottinghamshire or Manchester and neighbouring bits of Lan-
cashire – in which, after protracted and often heated debate,
entirely different comprehensive patterns have been adopted.

The merit in this profusion of variants is obscure. Is it encouraged in the name of local autonomy? That surely is to lose
sight of the distinction between central decision and local administration. Is variety itself sacred? Indeed, seen from heaven
British education must seem as variegated as the British landscape, but for the mortals crawling upon the surface there is
rarely any alternative to their immediate environment. Is it
seriously supposed that a man will move from London in disgust with all-through comprehension solely to try the merits of
of the two-tier system in Leicestershire? To allow local decision on matters of general educational importance, such as the
age of transfer, is exactly like allowing local decision on matters
of general commercial importance, such as the system of weights
and measures. Children who move pay a toll in confusion. It falls
upon increasing numbers of them. The National Survey shows
that over 7 per cent of children move each year,[7] a rate which, if
continued, would add up, over the five years of secondary education, to one in three being affected. Despite this the government
has encouraged comprehension in a piecemeal, parochial form.
Was ever a change of comparable importance so chaotically
introduced – by an administrative Circular, number 10 of 1965,
and not a properly debated Act of Parliament?

This medieval confusion prohibits any accurate over-all assessment of the effect of comprehension on the deployment of teachers. One arrangement of schools – say, a two-tier system of middle and upper schools – will have certain effects; another – say, all-through eleven to eighteen comprehensives – will have others; a third – say, high schools to sixteen followed by sixth-form colleges – others again; and so on through the gamut of variations. At first sight, however, it may not seem clear why comprehension, in whatever single guise or in motley, should change staffing requirements at all. After all, the number of boys to be educated will not alter however we parcel them up. Why then should the staff needed to teach them not remain constant too? To show why not we shall examine one particular brand of comprehension – the eleven to eighteen variety, and one element in staffing – the use of graduate teachers. In case this choice seems arbitrary, we should recall that eleven to eighteen all-through comprehensives were preferred by the Labour Government and the NUT and the favourite of the majority of local authorities.[8] This was overwhelmingly the case in earlier sub-missions and remains true even of more recent reorganization schemes, where there has been time for second thoughts. Thus, in a group of forty-one schemes – the last large batch approved by the Department of Education and Science in the year ending August 1968 – twenty-five were of the all-through kind.[9] The reason why in considering staffing patterns we should focus on graduates will I hope become apparent. At this juncture we can simply assert that, so long as secondary education has a strong academic content, those with the best academic qualifications will constitute a particularly valuable minority.

This would seem a truism in any Continental country. In Sweden, for example, every child over the age of twelve is taught in all his academic subjects by university graduates who have had teacher training.[10] The need for such expertness is less axiomatic in England where by tradition schools have concerned themselves at least as much with character as with learning. Whatever our views, the grammar school practice of using graduates to teach in almost every form up and down the school is plainly a luxury we cannot hope to have on a comprehensive scale. Familiar saws will reassure us: 'It isn't what a man knows that matters but what he is', 'A teacher teaches children, not just his subject', and so on.

However, we here run into a problem as eccentrically English as cricket. The rest of the world keeps university education in the universities. The secondary school provides a general education; those who qualify then move elsewhere to pursue specialist studies. England (with some parts of its ex-Empire) has chosen to include two years or more of specialist studies at the top of the school, in the sixth form. This explains why most first degrees in England take only three years; the equivalent on the Continent or in America takes four or even five years. Now, we may argue about the relevance of graduate skills for teaching below O-level; it would be odd indeed to do so for the early university – that is, sixth form – years.

In studying how comprehension will affect the supply of graduate teachers we shall stand on incontrovertible ground, then, if we view only the requirements of those sixth formers aiming at A-levels. Most would urge the need for graduates much more widely than this: It is a measure of our plight that we shall find problems enough without enlarging our sights beyond such narrow bounds.

In an article published in November 1968, W. E. Egnar calculated how we should need to distribute our present stock of graduate teachers if a universal, equal pattern of all-through comprehensive schools were adopted.[11] Any such neat arrangement is, of course, an abstraction, far removed from complex reality, but his figures will serve to show in a rough and ready way the dimensions of our problem.

Mr Egnar tells us that the average size for all maintained secondary schools is 486 children; the average size for all-through comprehensive schools is 833. Supposing we could turn all our schools into comprehensives of 833, there would be 3382 of them. The average size for sixth forms in comprehensives is forty-four as against 107 in the grammar schools. Were the grammar schools abolished and their sixth formers evenly distributed, the average sixth form in our hypothetical 3382 comprehensives would number fifty-one. Since a few sixth formers will drop out and a few stay on for a third year, we arrive at an intake of between twenty and twenty-five into the sixth each year. A modest estimate of the number of subjects a viable sixth form should offer is ten, hence the size of some of the sixth form sets drawn from these twenty to twenty-five candidates will be wastefully small. In the grammar schools, with an average sixth form of 107 (twice that of our hypothetical comprehensives), the average sixth form set is only seven and a half. If, then, our present sixth-form habits are extravagant, any further dispersion of sixth formers at a time of a shortage of staff would seem to border on the lunatic. To complete our speculation, we should look at the equivalent distribution of 'good honours' graduates (those with first- or second-class honours), since grammar schools have customarily thought only these properly qualified for sixth-form teaching. In our universal all-through comprehensives the ration would be two modern linguists, one and a half historians, one and a half English teachers, two thirds of a mathematician, one third of a physicist and a quarter of a chemist. It looks unpromising.

We should now turn to some actual cases. In East Sussex there were, in 1965, nine schools in which a full sixth form operated. The LEA estimated that all-through comprehensive reorganization, if adopted, would require nineteen full sixth forms. In Somerset there were twenty-one and under all-through comprehensive reorganization there would be thirty-two.[12] Each sixth form needs, for example, a minimum of one (hopefully, good honours) graduate in maths, physics, chemistry, biology. Thus, in Somerset the minimum requirement of scientists under a bipartite system is eighty-four, under all-through comprehension it would become 128. In practice, of course, a teacher seldom wishes to be or can be timetabled to teach sixth formers only. The smaller the sixth form the higher the proportion of his time a graduate is likely to spend on lower school work. But even on the basis of actual present use, Somerset calculates that its stock of 221 maths and science graduates would have to increase to 354. As for good honours graduates, we may contemplate the plight of Renfrewshire, extreme in degree but not different in kind from that of other counties. Renfrewshire has eight good honours graduates in physics and maths and under all-through comprehension would have twenty-four secondary schools anxious to seize them.[13]

The case with arts subjects is equally awkward for other reasons. At present a half of all A-level entries is concentrated into four subjects: maths, physics, chemistry and English. Scientists traditionally concentrate on a very narrow range of 'basic' disciplines; not so those reading arts or social sciences. Other than in English, there are modest numbers of candidates in a wide and steadily growing range of subjects. As the number of subjects grows, so does the timetable problem of allowing as many different combinations between these subjects as possible, and increasingly of combining them with maths and the sciences. Schools with large sixth forms have managed to cope, but, in part at least because the subjects they want are not available, boys and girls from other schools have turned increasingly to technical colleges which now account for no less than 40 per cent of all A-level entries.[14] If, by dispersion, the sixth form became much smaller, then non-scientists are likely to have a very poor selection of subjects. Somerset could conceivably get an economist for each of its present sixth-form units. What hope would it have of doing so if sixth-form work were distributed, as all-through comprehension would require, in half as many places again?

This problem of sixth-form dispersion as a result of comprehension was neither unforeseeable nor unforeseen. In a letter to *The Times* on 3 June 1968 no less than twenty-five university vice-chancellors combined to draw attention to it. Nor, it should be said, were some of the earliest exponents of comprehension unaware. Robin Pedley as author of *The Comprehensive School* may seem rather euphoric,[15] but Robin Pedley as co-editor of *Forum* presided over a continuous and realistic debate on problems of comprehension in which the need to have sufficient concentrations of sixth formers frequently recurred. The Department of Education now recommends that an all-through comprehensive school should have at least a six-stream entry (though some smaller ones have been authorized in rural districts). Rhodes Boyson calculates that if the present proportion of 12 per cent of any age group take two or more A-levels, then in an all-through comprehensive a twelve-stream entry is needed.[16] Anything smaller will fail to yield a sixth form of the *minimum* size thought viable by the Inner London Education Authority. Such a school would number about 2000. If we assume, as Dr Boyson does, that the proportion of A-level candidates will soon rise to 20 per cent, then an eight-stream entry – a school of 1400 – will do. In human terms it is possible, from both American and Eng-

lish experience, to doubt the wisdom of such large congrega-
tions;[17] nor does a close acquaintance with large comprehensives
provide much reassurance that size leads to administrative ease
or efficiency. Just when, in government and industry, protests
against dehumanizing scale have led to an anxious search for
ways of devolution we have begun in education, where human
values matter most, to do exactly the reverse.

Whether one shares such misgivings about size or not, large
all through comprehensives imply costly building and, in rural
districts, a lot of travelling. One favoured way out of this problem, where distance does not prohibit, is to link two or more
schools together and to call them one. The inconvenience and
complications generated can be formidable. Such expedients are
often labelled 'temporary' but that word has as ominous a ring
in education as in taxation. Some education authorities have
avoided all-through comprehension entirely, preferring various
alternative two-tiered systems. In most of these children go to a
separate middle school until they are, say, thirteen or fourteen
and then to an upper school until they leave. In a handful of
places they stay in a high school until they are sixteen, and then
move either to a sixth-form college, usually attached to an existing grammar school, or to a junior college, designed (if differing
salary scales and other administrative puzzles can be resolved) to
unite sixth-form and technical colleges. The figures we have
looked at so far in this section illustrate the expense and awkwardness of all-through comprehension as a generalized arrangement; had we used any of the two-tier schemes as the basis of
calculation we should have arrived at far less eccentric results.

We do not need here to debate the merits of various rival styles
of comprehension. We should only notice, first, how chaotic is
the profusion of alternatives; second, that it is the need to concentrate enough graduate teachers and enough sixth formers in
one place that largely dominates the debate; third, that whether at
thirteen, fourteen or sixteen a tiered method (the common intention in all Continental comprehensive reorganizaion) seems the
obvious way to arrange this concentration; and, fourth, that all-
through comprehension is none the less most often chosen. It
seems a gamble based on the assumption that either great sums of
money for building large schools or new cadres of graduates to

lead the scattered platoons of sixth formers in smaller schools are miraculously about to appear.

London will furnish us with an example. An ILEA working party has recently produced a very able and thorough report, *Sixth Form Opportunities in Inner London*.[18] Its authors estimate that in order to offer a minimum of ten A-level subjects in reasonable combination, and assuming that sixth-form groups are not smaller than five, a sixth form should number not less than ninety (forty to forty-five in each annual intake). Many will find this arithmetic extremely conservative, wondering if ten subjects is enough, the combinations offered adequate, a minimum of five in a group a sufficiently heroic exercise in the use of scarce teaching resources. Some argue that the arrival of new A-level subjects, the anxiety to mix sciences and the arts, means that a good sixth-form unit needs to number at least 120.[19] It is devastating to find, therefore, that even the modest ILEA minimum of ninety is achieved by only a quarter of London schools with sixth forms, and that another quarter actually have sixth forms of less than thirty.

Of course, these inadequacies might be eased in the future by the expected increase in the number of those staying on at school. For how many, though, will A-level work prove suitable? And will the Q- and F-level proposals, now being debated, permit 'new' and 'old' sixth formers to compose unified groups and lead to a more economic use of graduate staff: or will they generate such a demand for further courses and combinations of courses that our predicament, especially in maths and the sciences, will become still worse?[20] The arrival of the new sixth formers may bring not added strength so much as added burdens. Certainly if the sixth formers in the direct grant and grammar schools of London were evenly distributed through all London's comprehensives, then each would make a braver showing in the sixths;[21] but this salvation seems remote indeed.

The remarkable fact remains, however, that, despite the obvious difficulties, London – and many other areas – has rejected the more easily instituted two-tier method of comprehension in favour of the all-through variety – chiefly because teachers demand it. This runs as the leitmotive through the ILEA report: 'It cannot be too strongly emphasized that we recognize the very powerful opposition of teachers generally to any arrangement other than the provision of a full sixth-form curriculum in all schools which are comprehensive or are already counted as developing on comprehensive lines' – which means in London all present maintained secondary schools bar one. This pursuit of all-through comprehension, even when it is visibly extravagant or unworkable,[22] echoes Tertullian's declaration of faith in Christianity: *Credo quia impossible* – 'I believe because it is impossible.'

How shall we account for this trend? In some degree, doubtless, it results from vested interest. In an intended two-tier system the top part may sometimes be an entirely new and separate institution (a sixth-form or junior college) in which case the grammar school resists the loss of its valued older boys. If, as is more often the case, the upper school is the old grammar school writ large, then the secondary moderns resist the loss of theirs. Many secondary moderns have persuaded their local authority, in anticipation of becoming comprehensive, to let them keep a few boys as a sixth form of sorts. It may mean the third forms being enlarged, or maths in the second forms being taught by the physical education specialist, but somehow the best teaching must be made available to the handful of sixth formers. Are these few, the harbingers of the many to follow, now to be annexed by the old grammar school? Comprehension was to give them a sixth form more abundantly, not to take it away.

Their objection to being robbed of the chance of a sixth form springs from reasons more noble than envy. For the sixth form is not, like the technical college (or the Swedish gymnasium, the American junior college) simply a place where a further stage of a boy's schooling occurs. The boy's changing relationships to other boys and to masters as he grows up through a school are regarded as the principal means of his *moral* education. In a fifth form, class teaching is a one-way process: in the sixth-form group there is the give and take of discussion. The older sixth former especially may learn a great deal from his junior partnership with masters in conducting house affairs, games, clubs and societies – all those curiously named out-of-school activities (in-school out-of-school as distinct from out-of-school out-of-school). The 'young master' (to whom at the end of the book Tom

Brown talks as an equal) recalls Harry East, now serving with his regiment in India:

'His year in the sixth will have taught him a good deal that will be useful to him now.' 'So it will,' says Tom Brown. 'Poor dear Harry, how well I remember the day we were put out of the Twenty! How he rose to the situation, and burnt his cigar-cases and gave away his pistols, and pondered on the constitutional authority of the sixth, and his new duties to the Doctor, and the fifth form, and the fags!'

The essential oddity of English schooling lies in the sixth form, in the belief that boys should not just be told how things are run but should, as seniors, learn from the actual experience of running them. So it is hoped – not without justification – that many of them will grow from children in institutions into co-operative adults in communities.

Now, we may argue that these ideals have suffered with the passage of time. Some observers, impressed by boys' earlier physical and social maturity, urge that fifteen year olds ought now to be prefects and sixth formers free as undergraduates. Others notice that many boys, having grown up in easy-going, 'democratic' families, find taking up positions of authority within a school unnerving and alien. Further, the sixth former's chance to experience responsibility is drastically curtailed by the translation from boarding to day schools (less jobs to be done) and by the explosion in numbers in the sixth (more boys to do them). The creation of larger schools reduces 'jobs for the boys' still further. A school of, say, 1500 does not usually generate three times as many teams, plays, magazines, as a school of 500. Put half-a-dozen Englishmen together, it is said, and they will form a club: so too schoolboys, and one of them is chairman, another secretary, another treasurer. A larger club or society may have higher standards but it will seldom generate more officials. In consequence a large majority of sixth formers now leave school without active experience of responsibility. The pressure of numbers has altered the quality of sixth-form teaching too, destroying the easy intellectual relationship possible within a small group of boys and between them and a sixth-form tutor.[23] There used to be a sharp break in the style of learning between regimented classes of boys in the fifth form, taught period after period, and the few individuals in the sixth, taught only a few periods in the week. Now the difference is small indeed, and most sixth formers too are constantly instructed.

Many boys may justly declare, therefore, that the fabled benefits of sixth-form education have not rubbed off on them: they remained at the passive, receiving end of teaching and had no chance to run things. But if such unfortunates denounce the value of the sixth as an empty myth, few schools would yet do so. Most masters, even in present less-favoured circumstances, enjoy teaching the subtleties of a subject to older boys who have chosen it. When a school goes searching for staff the existence of a sixth is often a tempting bait. Further, much of the most valuable learning in a school occurs between boy and boy in those out-of-school activities that transcend age division, so that in art, woodwork, music, drama, technical activities and the like, a creative contagion spreads down through the school from talented and technically competent sixth formers. The kind of discipline in a school, the burden that falls on a staff, the extent of the pastoral care they dare aim at, all vary according to the involvement of senior boys. It is no wonder, now the old restrictions of the tripartite system seem about to dissolve, that every school should want to keep its own boys in its own sixth, for the boys' own good and certainly for the school's.

It is easy, then, to understand why teachers, in consort with the parents they influence, have pressed for sixth forms everywhere. Contrary arguments about the proper size of sixth forms or the future supply of graduates are complex and uncertain. In their turn, local councillors naturally prove sensitive to their teachers' and their constituents' demands. Besides, who knows, if smoky Stoke cannot get graduates, sunny Seaford may. The national share-out is not the business of Sussex. The government might by Act of Parliament have instituted a chosen form of comprehension, or alternatively have gathered together all local plans before giving assent to any. Either way the implication in terms of teachers could have been assessed. Instead an astonishing variety of schemes – some dubiously comprehensive and labelled 'interim' – has been allowed, and local plans have been authorized successively as they appeared. Only now that the blanks in the map are being filled has it become clear that the multiplication of sixth forms presents a total bill for graduates or for buildings larger than we can hope to meet in the foreseeable future.

We should remind ourselves, however, that it is academic considerations alone – the need to offer sufficient subjects in varying combinations, and to have them taught by graduates – that require a large sixth form. The moral and social values of a sixth-form education may be experienced equally well, and by more boys and girls, in small sixths in small schools. It is worth investigating, therefore, whether there are any ways of meeting the academic needs of sixth formers, which would allow us to leave them without detriment in their local schools. Are we sure that sixth formers need the customary six to eight periods of teaching in every subject and always in small groups? Suppose, for instance, the Open University had been aimed principally not at adults determined enough to pursue a full degree course at home, but at the growing army of sixteen to nineteen year olds in full-time and part-time education whose academic and vocational needs so confuse our whole educational system.[24] Would the proposed combination of television lectures, related correspondence courses, regular sessions with local tutors and longer periods at conference centres, provide for sixth formers, in small or large part, in this subject or that, a reasonable alternative to so much teaching? Something similar is done in Japan. Perhaps it would not work here; perhaps there are other alternatives.

All we need register for the moment is that our concept of the sixth form makes going comprehensive uniquely awkward for this country. It is not that A-level candidates matter more than other boys, but that their needs affect the total size and structure of a school. If we accept a two-tier comprehensive system we shall meet resistance by teachers but relatively slight organizational problems; but if we want whole, all-through comprehensive schools – the most attractive arrangement in human terms and inevitable in thinly populated districts – then we are in trouble. Each school wants its own sixth, but a proliferation of local sixth forms, however desirable socially, is academic folly. There are not nearly enough graduates to go round. We are tempted, then, towards building big comprehensives. We must make a heap of boys such that 12 per cent of them (or more hopefully 20 per cent) going on to A-level will comprise a sixth form of sufficient size. And what is 'sufficient'? There must be enough sixth formers, even when distributed over a wide range of options, to provide in each subject a group large enough to justify frequent teaching by graduates.

Thus, in comprehensive reorganization, an army of perplexities follows behind sixth formers' needs, and these in turn are mounted upon our traditional assumptions about how they should be taught. *It is these basic assumptions about teaching method we might most profitably challenge.* In short, to defeat the serried ranks of problems we need to identify their commanding general, and to 'capture the general', as the proverb advises, 'first shoot his horse'.

Questions of teaching method posed by comprehension are not, however, confined to the sixth form.

Under the tripartite system the better qualified teachers instructed what were believed to be the more academically gifted boys. In grammar schools 80 per cent of the staff were graduate; in secondary moderns 18 per cent. Quite apart from whether this is right in principle (and such a division is not likely to persist in the egalitarian atmosphere of the comprehensive school) Douglas and others have tellingly demonstrated that selection of children to grammar school was, in practice, class-based: far more children from middle-class homes got places than the distribution of 'intelligence' through the whole population merited.[25] Comprehension was to put all this right. There would be a genuine equality of opportunity, an equal sharing of good teaching; all classes and differing talents were to mix together for the common good.

But the authorities in almost all comprehensive schools, in order to create manageable forms to teach, have also graded children by ability as the eleven-plus did. They have kept the best together, then the next best and so on down the line. This practice, familiar in all types of schools, is called 'streaming'. Sometimes a further division is employed and children are re-grouped, this time not by their general ability but by their specific bent for a particular subject. Such 'setting' most often applies in mathematics and languages. Some comprehensives, both in their streaming and their setting, do not discriminate class by class; instead they place children into broader 'bands' or 'blocks', each of which may consist, say, of three streams or sets, the subsequent divisions into classes being made usually by the alphabet. Whatever the variations, one wonders whether all the turmoil, all the protestation about comprehension, has simply resulted in the divisions previously embodied in separate schools continuing under one roof in the form of separate streams. The parallel emerges strongly in an admittedly slender study by Julienne Ford which shows that upper streams in the comprehensive schools she investigated are disproportionately filled by middle-class children and that friendships seldom occur across the streams or blocks.[26] A National Foundation for Educational Research study reinforces her local finding that, as an effect presumably of the expectations of teachers and the expectation of their companions, children seldom move from the streams or blocks they are first put into. These become almost as distinct and stable as schools were in the tripartite system, the theoretical possibility of transfer being little used in practice.[27]

Most comprehensive schools try to offset any social exclusiveness by a 'house' system in which children of differing ages and in differing streams necessarily meet; but the proportion of time spent in houses is generally small, and the interests pursued in this combination much less significant than those pursued in class. As the authors of *The Flexible School* point out: 'Children in the top streams mix mainly with other similar children, even in sports, and the houses are not much more than a place to hang your coat.'[28] We may, of course, count it an advance that in a comprehensive school children of various social backgrounds and abilities at least have the opportunity to mix in gym and music, art and games. This is true – so far as during school hours these activities can be timetabled across 'block' divisions, and in out-of-schools hours children from less encouraging homes can be induced to stay on. But it is odd to confine mixing to these peripheral activities. Surely the place where the less able and the less willing would profit most from good company is in the classroom, where, after all, most of the school day is spent. Hence the current preoccupation with 'unstreaming'.

This practice – putting into each class children of a wide ability range – is spreading fast. To some, unstreaming is obviously right not only socially but educationally. The TUC in submitting recommendations to the Secretary of State urged that the proposed new Education Act 'should at least prohibit streaming in primary schools and discourage it in secondary schools. ... There is evidence that streaming according to ability is damaging to the educational interests of less able children and irrelevant to the interests of the more able.' [29]

The TUC does not specify the evidence that leads it so confidently to dismiss streaming, but, as far as secondary schools are concerned, it presumably includes the celebrated Stockholm study by Nils-Eric Svennson.[30] Certainly there is no other work of comparable extent and thoroughness in the literature. Svennson was able to compare the academic performance, over five years, of equivalent groups of children in grammar schools in the north of Stockholm and in the new comprehensives in the south. These comprehensive schools were not merely unselective; they were unstreamed. Svennson's findings have been widely quoted by advocates of comprehensives in this country to show that, in what Swedes call 'undifferentiated' situations, the less able do better than if they are 'negatively selected' – i.e., put into secondary moderns or low streams. Further, what is more surprising, the more able do just as well as they would in 'positively selected' classes, that is in grammar schools or high streams.

Large-scale educational research is full of variables impossible to control, and, in his carefully documented study, Svennson's conclusions are modest and tentative. To follow the stages by which his own critical nuances have been cast off, and his work formed into positive 'evidence' to batter the sceptics, is a fascinating study in the generation of those myths which shape opinion. Thus Svennson found a definite pre-eminence in grammar school children, as against comprehensive school children, in grade 6 (thirteen year olds), but by grade 9 (sixteen year olds) this had vanished. Indeed his figures suggested that the trend had been reversed. Since, among other difficulties, his sample had shrunk from 2400 to 700 in that period, Svennson did not press the point and urged that further research was needed.

This has now followed. It points, alas, in exactly the contrary direction to Svennson's study. For the tests Svennson administered lacked what is known in statistical terms as a high enough ceiling. They were a fair enough reflection of what had been learned in common by both the streamed and unstreamed classes, but not of any extra learning done in either of them. Thus Urban Dahllöf found that the unstreamed classes took 73·2 lessons to cover the arithmetic syllabus on which the tests were based, whereas the grammar school stream took only 32·8 lessons, using the time saved for more advanced, unexamined topics. Dahllöf suggests that a teacher normally moves on from one topic to another when he believes a majority of the children in his class, say 75 per cent, have mastered it. When bright children are placed in unstreamed classes they may learn just as quickly as they would in a streamed class, but they then have to mark time tackling extra exercises – what is called 'over-learning' – while the rest catch up. Dahllöf, referring to his reappraisal of Svennson's Stockholm study and subsequent work done by Carlsson in Växjö and Borg in Utah, concludes:

There is a common trend in these three big studies. Although there are very often differences of small size, not even significant in the single tests, there seems to be a consistent trend, in the direction of the differences: pupils in positively selected classes tend to excel peers of equal initial ability level in comprehensive (i.e. unstreamed) classes, in these rather elementary tests, as long as the grouping difference lasts; while there seems to be no difference between the comprehensive classes and the negatively selected ones for pupils of comparable ability and social background.[31]

Now, we may well qualify this conclusion as based on mathematics and not relevant to other subjects; we may note the tendency to use tests of knowledge and simple skills – these being measurable – rather than 'insights' or 'attitudes', such qualities being more important but also more elusive. Since such controversies over research can recede to infinity, we may be more impressed by common experience and common sense. First, experience reminds us that for generations, whenever a school has been large enough to permit it, teachers have grouped children into streams or sets by ability. Plainly they discovered that their methods of instruction achieved the best results ('best' in relation to their educational aims in streamed classes. We may decide to use different methods of instruction, we may reject their aims what we cannot sensibly do is to retain both the traditional methods and the traditional aims and still expect equivalent results in a radically different – an unstreamed – situation. Second, common sense suggests that since one teacher can move at only one pace he will adapt that pace to include a majority – which Dahllöf quantifies at 75 per cent – of his class. A wider spread of ability will mean a slower pace; the quick, capable, keen worker in a class, as in a factory, may then be penalized. How do we avoid unstreaming becoming the unionization of learning? Presumably instruction given from a single source, the teacher, is likely to be most effective if matched to a single audience, an individual child, or failing that a group of children converging as narrowly as possible to a single standard. Such convergence was the purpose of streaming. The equal treatment of unequals, which is present in some degree in any class teaching will, by unstreaming, become very much more marked.

But the practice of streaming has also served a less obvious purpose than ease or aptness of instruction. We recognize two contrary imperatives in learning: first, that the individual should be free to learn at the pace that suits him; second, that he should contribute to, and learn from, a group. The streamed class (that is, a group moving at the average pace best suited to the individuals in it) provided a rough and ready reconciliation of these opposing requirements. Advocates of unstreaming unite in rejecting this workaday compromise, and in the process revert to the two distinct and conflicting poles. Some advance from the streamed class or set to individual work. But this amounts, in a very real sense, to a sharpening of streaming — an attempt to multiply the streams until there are as many streams as there are children. Freeing the individual to work at his own pace tends to be not less but more divisive than the class. This must be an unwelcome outcome of unstreaming to those who believe in greater equality. Some reformers therefore urge a different shift, namely from class work to group work, that is, from a class of approximately the same ability directed by the teacher, to smaller groups of varying ability often working autonomously. In turn this must strike those who want greater liberty as a sad outcome to unstreaming, for the pace and progress of any particular group may impose worse shackles on the individual than ever a class and teacher did.

Unstreaming, in whichever direction it tends, provides some

clear gains. Many children, we know, take on the colour of what is expected of them. Unstreaming makes it difficult for teachers to label groups of children; it may even deter children from labelling one another. So far so good. But unstreaming in itself does nothing to reconcile the familiar dichotomy of all democratic movements, the conflicting demands of liberty and equality. Individual work points one way, group work the other. Presumably – in varying degree according to the nature of the subject – we want both, now the one, now the other. Essentially, though, the streamed class was a balance achieved by sitting in the centre of the see-saw; in unstreaming we elect to balance instead by jumping from one side to the other.

We may believe this exercise to be necessary and beneficial. Certainly it is strenuous and unfamiliar. To suggest to a teacher that he should manage not a single class but on some occasions several small groups and on others thirty individuals working at different speeds and perhaps at different pursuits is to ask an actor to become a juggler. It requires new properties and new skills. Individualized work and group work are what the Swedes call 'tulip-roses' – things easy to say, hard indeed to devise.

To use inappropriate old methods of teaching in unstreamed classes is, then, to embrace frustration; to urge ill-defined new methods is to invite exhaustion or confusion. None the less, unstreaming inexorably spreads. The National Foundation for Educational Research in its survey of comprehensive schools noted in 1967: 'There was some evidence to suggest that unstreaming is becoming fashionable; many of the schools contemplated introducing non-streaming during the next two years.' It has now become quite commonplace. At present in England it is almost entirely confined to the lower forms:[32] but countries with a long experience of comprehension, like the United States and Russia, practise unstreaming, although with differing nuances, up to the end of compulsory schooling. More recently, Sweden has decided on a similar course. Unstreaming is a further extension of the same democratic impulse in some, the same social and economic calculation in others, that has already led to comprehension.

In sum, for reasons we have examined, comprehensive reorganization in its most popular 'all-through' shape requires a new army of graduates to man a multiplicity of smaller sixth forms, or a vast rebuilding programme; and unstreaming requires the wide-spread concoction by harassed teachers of programmes for individualized and group work. Given our present methods of teaching and our present resources neither of these developments makes sense. Both are being pursued. The situation is exactly that described by Professor Blackett who was involved with weapon and operational research during the war:

New weapons for old is apt to become a popular cry. There is a new form of escapism which runs somewhat like this, 'Our present equipment doesn't work very well: training is bad, supply is poor, spare parts non-existent. Let's have an entirely new gadget.' Then comes the vision of the new gadget, springing like Aphrodite from the Ministry of Aircraft Production, in full production, complete with spares and tended by a chorus of trained crews.[33]

Certainly some of the early enthusiasts for comprehension, from conviction or political necessity, purveyed a vision of comprehension as a miraculous new gadget. That is understandable. What is not understandable is that their illusions should have proved contagious, and that government approval should have been given to a hodge-podge of local schemes before thorough calculations were completed of the total national resources needed to implement the sum of those schemes. It is not the fault of those who were invited by *Circular 10/65* to choose from an array of possibilities: they were not to know that, added together, what they chose might turn out to be impracticable. Alas, what is best but illusory is the enemy of what is good and manageable. The proper objection is not to the principle of comprehension but to the chaotic way it has been implemented, not to the intention but to the drift.

In our present uneasy circumstances it may be profitable to look at what goes on in other countries where comprehensive schooling is more familiar. We should inquire particularly how they try to reconcile unstreaming with allowing boys to learn at their proper pace. How do they provide for those years, so awkward in their implication with us, between the end of compulsory schooling and the start of university? If they suffer, as we do, from a lack of well-qualified teachers in certain key subjects like maths and science, we should inquire whether they have found any way of compensating for the shortage. Discontented with our secondary school timetable – rigid, crowded, fragmented – we should seek out alternatives to our method of constantly moving boys about in groups from one teacher to another to learn this subject or that. We should especially welcome any arrangements that increase the choice and the activity allowed to a boy since such may contribute to his working more willingly. We shall need to assess whether any attractive and successful innovations we come across abroad are reasonably economic and whether they are workable in our circumstances. With some idea, then, of the sort of things to look for we can start upon our search, and where better than in the varied hunting grounds of America.

Part Two
Alternatives

Chapter Four
In America

The typical secondary school in America is a high school – that is a comprehensive school. Most are all-through high schools, grades 6 to 12, for boys and girls aged eleven plus to seventeen plus but without any equivalent of our sixth form. Two-tier arrangements are quite common – a junior high school for, say, grades 6 to 8 (eleven plus to fourteen plus) and a senior high school for grades 9 to 12 (fourteen plus to seventeen plus).

The range of subjects taught in high schools is far greater than in English schools. Such a range is most familiar to us perhaps at American university level, for writers like Linklater and Amis and Bradbury have had their fun with BAs in the art of the Mortician and college courses in Salesmanship, Sports Administration and Cosmetology. In parallel, the list of subjects in a high school seems to us catholic indeed. Thus, a new Californian high school offers, besides English, maths, science and French and so on, courses in leadership, band, school spirit (for cheer leaders), personal relationships, personal appearance, school magazine, driving. . . .

Such concerns are not unfamiliar in English schools. The difference is that whereas we put English, maths, science and French into the timetable, we keep leadership, school spirit, driving, school magazine, and so on, out of the timetable, relying on learning by osmosis or through voluntary clubs and societies; and we get in a muddle over art, music, workshop, drama, physical education, leaving them half 'in school' and half 'out of school' (say, fully in the timetable for juniors, chiefly in clubs for seniors). Such activities we treat as though, like divinity, they were either too important or too trivial for 'teaching'.

The ostensible gain in the American practice is that all talent is valued – skill in a band instrument along with skill in maths, skill in personal appearance along with skill in French. How far this equality is fact, how far folk-lore, is hard to judge – a bit of both presumably. The greater confidence and independence of the blue-collar worker in America, compared with his supposedly hang-dog equivalent here, is commonly attributed to a wider appreciation of manual skills; but consoling American middle-class notions of equality between white-collar and blue-collar do not bear serious examinations in terms of working conditions or pay or fringe benefits or range of opportunities or insulation against change.[1] In practice there is, of course, a hierarchy of skill-values in America, even if it is less obvious than in England; in anticipation, few high-school children would pretend that the 'college preparatory' courses have no higher status than parallel 'vocational' courses. Even so, in their post-Sputnik trauma, many Americans question the wisdom of high schools fostering, or appearing to condone, the customary democracy of skills.

Some have begun to wonder too about the effects, especially for brighter children, of the traditional organization of the high school. An American parent will speak of his child as a 'eight-grader', an English parent of his as a 'thirteen year old', for in America, with rare exceptions, children are kept in the grades appropriate to their age whereas in England they may stray beyond grade boundaries according to their progress, so that a boy may be taught with those older or younger than he is. Some high schools add to the egalitarianism of fixed grades the practice of unstreaming, but these are usually the smaller rural schools at the one extreme and the sophisticated experimental schools at the other. Most high schools have some streaming but generally of a less precise kind than our own and confined to broad 'banding'. Setting – that is, further fine division according to ability in a specific subject – is rare. But if grouping, whether by general or by particular ability, is less elaborate than with us, grouping by choice among optional subjects is far more extensive. This combination of rough banding and then of elaborate free choice within the band is clearly seen at the top of the high school. From the 10th to the 12th grade (fifteen to eighteen year olds) boys and girls are usually put into 'college preparatory' or 'vocational' bands. Colleges will usually lay down specific requirements for their candidates – for example, two semesters of physical sciences may be required – but a boy in the college preparatory band of his high school can choose from all sorts of science courses and bits of courses, perform at uncertain local standards, and still satisfy the requirement. As for a boy in the vocational band, the choice offered him in a big high school is bewildering indeed; he may graduate by electing courses in so higgledy-piggledy and unbalanced a fashion that we would need to go in for extensive redefinition to call what he gets an 'education' at all.[2]

This emphasis on the virtue of choice has important practical implication for the high schools. They tend to be very large – just as large as the neighbourhood allows. A number of city schools range between 2000 and 6000 and occasionally reach 8000. Only a really large school can produce enough volunteers to justify the provision of specialist teachers and specialist plant for every expected activity. We should note that, so long as we use our present methods of teaching, increased choice means increased size. Again, free choice makes American high-school timetables in some cases more wooden, in other cases much more complex than ours. In the smaller and simpler schools, in order to accommodate a choice of options, the few compulsory subjects tend to be given a regualr daily place, fixed points around which the confusion can revolve. In the larger schools, however, timetabling practices are more sophisticated by far. If you start by assuming that boys should be allowed to choose freely you end by trying to accommodate as many combinations of first choices as possible. In making up a timetable mere pencil and rubber gives way in succession to tag and hook, to punched-cards-in-bin, to the computer. For mechanical ease, high school courses are often numbered nowadays in the American college manner. Plainly, the range of combinations can be increased if, say 'French for beginners' (French 211) appears in as many time-table slots as possible: it may appear in periods 4, 8, 12, 16, in the week, thereby being available to boys doing certain chosen subjects, and again in periods 6, 10, 14, 18, for boys combining it with other subjects. One effect is, of course, that the size of the two French classes may vary greatly, depending on the popularity of other subjects in available combination; another is that any setting by ability – a quicker class, a slower class – is possible only if, despite the multiplicity of choices, there are so many French classes that you can still afford to run several in parallel. Further complexities may result from the attempt to enable a

boy to start French, say, in the 8th grade or the 9th grade or the
10th grade, because he chose combinations earlier in his school
career that excluded French. Of course, in a subject like French,
course 211 must precede 311; but you can do History 327 (history of modern Europe) without doing History 324 (ancient
civilizations) and Chemistry 302 without doing Chemistry 304.
In such non-sequential subjects free choice has curious side-
effects. A teacher cannot rely on a boy having done any history
before or doing any again. Consequently 'survey courses' proli-
ferate. Alternatively there is a tendency to make courses self-
contained. A master will try to make Chemistry 302 a coherent
'patch' – hence the bewilderment of English teachers faced with
American boys who often know quite a lot about an esoteric area
of science and have no 'fundamentals'. Further a chemistry
master cannot assume that a boy knows some related material
in his physics, nor the historian that a boy has done, say, any
French. Because of such wide choice, examining is perpetual and
it is local. The content, and the standard, of Chemistry 302 in
one school and its equivalent in another may vary greatly, so
that a boy's record at graduation indicates only the completion
of certain courses at certain grades as given by a certain school.
Of course, university requirements impinge on prospective candidates, but in so confused and localized a situation College
Board tests seek out potential ability and insight rather than
attainment and knowledge (though the distinction is not always easy), and universities, more than in England, reckon they
must start a longish way back to compensate for inequalities of
background knowledge.

This is, of course, a necessary simplification of the American
situation. There are after all some 27,000 autonomous school
districts in America. Certain 'essential' subjects – maths and
English – in part escape the implications of freedom of choice.
Some schools give firm guidance to boys choosing 'electives',
thereby restricting preference; a very few schools are European
in their insistence that a boy shall study certain subjects for a
certain number of years. Basically, though, the American way of
schooling is *a la carte*, the European *table d'hôte*. Judgement
about which is better is not intended here, only an emphasis on
the difference. For current American innovations are based on

the assumption that a very wide, largely undirected choice of subjects is educationally desirable. Such devices as computer scheduling, team teaching, programmed instruction, continuous progress, all fit in with this assumption. It is not, at present, our assumption. The question is not whether their clothes will fit us well or whether we can afford them: it may be that we do not need their sort of clothes at all.

We have developed certain educational habits which inhibit us from cheerfully offering a wider, freer choice among subjects to the children in our care. Suppose a boy in England is in form IVA. It may well be that he is taught all his subjects with the same group of boys; more probably he will be taught for about two-thirds of his timetable with that form and for the remaining one-third will be setted across the year by ability (say, in maths) or by choice (in a very limited range of options). The much greater selection between subjects allowed in America prevents, whether for good or ill, any similar form stability, and therefore any use of the form as an effective social unit. Further, even in a day school, we generally put a boy into a 'house' so that he has a continuing, if weaker, relationship with one man – his house-master or tutor – as well as a changing, if stronger, relationship with another – his formmaster. This concern with the pastoral function in education is an English oddity. With rare exception, it does not preoccupy American schools or even schools else-where in Europe. Doubtless the emphasis on pastoral care, on the teacher *in loco parentis*, derives from the boarding tradition; it may be less obviously justified and less effective in day schools. Parents may cavil at masters' interference and excess of authority, masters may object to being involved in burdensome worries about clothes and manners and hair and behaviour on buses, not to mention sex education, careers, X-rays, subsidized meals.... But the fact remains that the intention of English schooling is more inclusive than that of any other country. And so, in re-flection, is the role of the schoolmaster. In America, broadly, the teacher is a teacher; in England, in many day schools, he is teacher of his subject, helps a bit with games, runs a stamp club, is formmaster, house-tutor. Some teachers are more will-ing and better able to don these disguises than others, but the norm, the expectation, is protean.

In America teachers specialize in their own subject; specialist instructors deal with all games; there are separate specialist grade advisers; specialist guidance counsellors look after personal problems; specialist administrators cope with organization. Specialization is partly justified, partly necessitated by the size and the complexity of a school. At best it is a doubtful blessing. In one school I visited every sort of punishment lay aloft. If the teacher filled in a yellow card the boy in trouble took it to the guidance counsellor, if a red card to the principal or his deputy. When discipline involves being sent from Pilate to Herod and back again something is lost. Expertness in a particular function is matched by ignorance of any particular child and a spurious efficiency results which is bought at the price of remoteness and complexity. In the same way the specialist principal easily becomes removed not only from children but from his staff. A principal is not a headmaster. It would be odd indeed for a principal to teach; odder still that he should run an out-of-school activity. Principals, together with their deputies, are regarded as allies of the superintendents, men engaged on a career in administration, not in teaching. A few principals, specially if they are innovators, manage to become leaders of the team of teachers, but it is rare. Generally they are part of 'them' not 'us'. And, of course, all the centralizing of functions steadily undermines the position of the individual teacher. He is fit only to teach – from the textbooks authorized. There are, of course, ample signs of a parallel specialization through size in our own schools, but we still profit from an inherited belief that teaching and looking after the taught – the academic, the social, the physical, the spiritual care of children – are inextricably woven together. Put pejoratively, our way is Renaissance amateur, the American, twentieth-century professional. We need to register this difference clearly, for we may find there are bright new advances which improve the quality of instruction but which run counter to our inclusive, pastoral concept of schooling. Americans may hail such advances as true victories: we, at best, may find them pyrrhic.

The other major difference between American schools and our own is more obvious: cash. Not that the 'average' American school is more lavish; but the best, the ones that tend to experiement, the ones visitors go to see – these are grand indeed. The contrast between worst and best reflects the degree to which each high school serves its particular locality, one of urban or rural squalor, another of suburban splendour, the school being directly dependent on taxes voted annually in direct democracy by local taxpayers. A poor district may spend less than 300 dollars on each pupil, a suburb like Winnetka in Chicago over a thousand. Indeed, in any wealthy locality money is poured out for the local school with a religious prodigality. However, the faith is beginning to falter. In every school and junior college I visited there were stark tales of school bond issues refused and 'tax over-rides' rejected. Doubtless the mood will soon change. Nowadays property owners seem inclined to question whether they are getting their money's worth. Teenage crime, teenage excess, outspoken teenage criticism of adult society, goings-on at college, draft-dodging disloyalty ... is *this* the product of so lavish a provision of amenities, of so much freedom? As always, social criticism turns into educational criticism. The schools from which too much has been expected are now too much blamed.

The connexion between society and school is forced in conversation upon the visitor too. In present-day America it is hard to be politically neutral; and so too in education, where one man admires liberated young people, another growls at spoilt brats. The traveller to this scene, moreover, carries a case full of attitudes acquired before he begins his hurried journey. It is his own customs he needs to declare. What he writes, then, remains with the best technical will in the world, densely subjective.

In 1967, Gordon Cawelti, surveying American high schools, picked out twenty-seven major innovations.[3] Some of these were in the use of technical devices, some in the curriculum, some in methods of learning. Although it will provide an inadequate conspectus of American innovation, we must confine our attentions to novelties in the way high schools organize the transmission of skills and knowledge: that is, to methods of teaching and learning.

Prominent among these is 'team teaching'. The leading exponent of the practice is Lloyd C. Trump and a number of schools have now been built in America specifically to work to his principles. As basic timetable units, Trump replaces the self-contained class and individual subject teachers by a larger group of pupils and a team of teachers. Sometimes all the children in the designated group will be taught together, sometimes they will be divided into smaller seminar groups, sometimes they will work individually. Trump originally recommended (in recent writings he is less prescriptive) the following division of available teaching time: [4]

Large group instruction	(say 120 boys) 40 per cent
Small group seminars	(say fifteen boys) 20 per cent
Individual study	(one boy) 40 per cent

In this scheme the class unit of thirty disappears, though in practice it often survives in laboratory work.

Many advantages are claimed for team teaching. The large group assembly is an obvious effort-saver. If four classes are being taught about the American Revolution, why have four people lecturing in four separate classrooms? It is not only as easy to lecture to 120; the presence of a larger audience (often including one's colleagues), in a properly equipped lecture theatre, encourages careful preparation and presentation in place of casual chat from the master's dais. Further any one of the four teachers in the team need prepare only a quarter of the course, lecturing, by agreement, on the portion he enjoys. Similarly, he can specialize on his particular enthusiasm with each of the different seminar groups. Since there are only a dozen boys in the seminar, discussion and active participation is much easier than in the class. As for the merit of individual study, this is so obvious to all teachers that no dilation on the topic is needed.

There is a further benefit in team teaching. In almost all walks of life – in industry, business, medicine, the civil service, and so on – jobs interlock, the people who do them are interdependent and consequently subject to one another's appraisal. To the contary, the individual teacher in his classroom is wholly isolated. If he teaches badly, he has no friend in the classroom to give him advice. But in a team, how different it all is. Comment, scrutiny, discussion, help with this problem or that – these are readily to hand. They constitute for the less expert teacher a form of continuous in-service training.

Aside from these advantages there is one element in team teaching which has more significance for us than for its American originators. Problems of streaming and setting rightly preoccupy us in our new comprehensives. Team teaching, accidentally perhaps, seems to permit the necessary substance of grouping by ability without its objectionable shadow. Thus, although less able and less interested children are often excluded from both large-group instruction and individual study – comprising a 'class' to which more teaching of the orthodox kind is given – and although seminar groups are formed around boys' needs (which, being translated, often equate with boys' abilities), the timetable shows only the whole team of teachers and the whole group of children without invidious, public, fixed divisions.

So much in praise. Since in its present form team teaching is not very old, considered experience of its shortcomings in practice is less easily found. Certainly, the criticism of conventional class teaching implicit in team teaching has weight. The crucial question, however, may not be 'Is team teaching better than class teaching?' but 'Is team teaching the best available remedy?' Are there perhaps merits in class teaching which we underestimate through familiarity, and can these be reconciled and combined with the more important benefits team teaching promises?

Let us look again, then, at the elements of team teaching. First, the 40 per cent large-group instruction. Plainly, this need not exclude having boys in classes. It is a matter of timetabling, say, four parallel forms in the same timetable slot for one or two, or all, periods in a given subject each week. Such a practice is not unprecedented – the most common example is probably in sixth-form general studies. Whether such large-group instruction is the best way of exposition, whether the advantages of sharing and specializing between a team of expositors can only be achieved by this means – these are larger questions. It is sufficient here to note that a timetable constructed on a *class* pattern, as opposed to a *team* pattern, can very easily absorb large-group instruction.

At the other end of the scale is the 40 per cent individual study. This is neutral ground. It does not matter whether a boy boy doing individual study in a library is assigned for teaching purposes to a class and a particular teacher or to a group and a team of teachers. However, 40 per cent individual study can mean two separate things. It may mean that out of a total of forty periods a week sixteen are left untaught during which a boy gets through whatever work in whatever subject he chooses. On the other hand, it may mean something more precise: that out of, say, five French periods two periods on the timetable are designated for individual study specifically in French. The teacher in the French team has then to ensure that individual study is set to fit exactly into just those timetable slots. It means carefully designing the course; it cannot be done extempore. In this respect he is worse off than the class teacher who can decide in any period and any point in any period when boys are to work on their own. The attempt to get around this timetable constriction has led to the ultimate in team teaching flexibility, the 'daily demand computer schedule'. This permits the timetable to be modified every day to allow members of a subject team (within certain physical limits) to decide which boys or groups of boys will be in lectures, or seminars, or left to individual study. It is an enormous elaboration; in theory it might achieve something almost as flexible as the class.

For it is astonishing how the magic word 'flexibility' has been attached to team teaching, with implications of rigidity in class teaching. It depends, of course, on who is flexing whom. From the teachers' point of view (and, when the teacher is perceptive, even from the boys') the class can be remarkably flexible. A master may lecture, give a test, have reading round the class followed by questions, show a film strip or play a tape, set an exercise from a textbook, go through individual corrections, or have a discussion with his form as a whole or with half a form or a group or with individuals, tell boys they have been working well and can have a period off while he reads the racing form-sheet, and so on. It may be at times inefficient but it is certainly flexible. A team has to establish agreement; it often sprouts a 'leader'. A class teacher, on the contrary, is a committee of one. The allocation of who does what in a team is often very broad – one man, say, takes on poetry, another drama. Sometimes, however, a team aims at a more intricate fit between the pieces. In that event a teacher is constrained to make his bit of the jigsaw lock, in time, treatment and content, with the bits contributed by his colleagues; he cannot, like a class teacher, take the whole puzzle and cut it up at will. The claim that team teaching is more flexible than the class needs, therefore, careful examination. In effect it sacrifices spontaneous flexibility for variety of two sorts – first, in actually specifying variations in the size and composition of the learning unit and, second, in permitting a boy to be taught by several masters in the subject team, not just one.

This multiplicity of voices, which applies both in the large group assembly and in the seminar, spotlights the central difference between the two concepts of class and team teaching. In class teaching the responsibility for the progress of a group of boys in a subject is entirely and precisely placed upon a given master; in team teaching it is diffused. True, in a seminar a master has the advantage of teaching a smaller group of boys, but he is only doing a part of their teaching. He is never sure exactly what they were taught the day before or the week before by some other colleague – which asides, which red herrings, quite where they got to, what boy has not understood what. The class teacher may have thirty boys to cope with, but he has them for the whole year, he gets to know them, he does all their teaching in that subject, he knows exactly what they did the day before. Even discussion, therefore, may be easier in the class situation than in changing seminars. Certainly continuity of teaching is easier. Team teaching requires an almost daily collaboration between masters which, from personal difference or simple fatigue, can become burdensome. From the learners' point of view – in expertness, variety, uncertainty, relative freedom – team teaching is like having a clutch of mistresses, class teaching like having a wife.

It is easy to see why the Americans have (in educational terms) been attracted by promiscuity. As we have seen, in America boys can choose subjects so widely and combine them so freely that the compulsory, common core of work around which cohesive form structure is built scarcely exists. Team teaching, by splitting even within a single subject, is simply a further stage of atomization. The lack of a strong form structure is part of the low expectation of pastoral care in American secondary schools. Team teaching as an over-all pattern of school organization imposes, then, a smaller loss (whatever the gains) on Americans than it would on us.

In their pure form, Trump's team-teaching recommendations have not spread widely in American secondary schools: instead many useful, more modest variants have developed.[5] Indeed, it is hard to comment on team teaching because it has changed from a specific into a generic term, awkward to define. This slipperiness in terminology is, as we shall discover, endemic in education. Some teams consist merely of two teachers occasionally swapping over or sharing a lesson. In one 'flexibly scheduled' school I visited, the maths department had in practice opted out and preferred fixed groups with fixed teachers, but they declared they were team teaching because they consulted together. We should call this 'setting' with frequent departmental conferences. Usually teams are made up of people teaching the same subject. One school, however, has divided itself into units of 250 children and placed each unit in charge of eleven teachers of varying subjects. In effect, the school has become four much smaller schools which share certain specialist facilities. The 'team' now consists of each 'school's' entire staff; their conferences we would call staff meetings. Thus the term 'team teaching' lends authority to a very wide variety of changes.

Even in classic Trump team-teaching schools the standard components are often greatly modified. In certain subjects like maths, large-group instruction to boys of widely differing knowledge, ability and interest has proved so blunt an instrument that the large group has shrunk until it looks suspiciously like a mildly enlarged, setted class. Sometimes this is acknowledged and 'medium-sized groups' (once called 'classes') have been included in the canon. In the seminar – the arena for informed discussion, 'an essential education for citizenship in democracy' in Trump's view – 'teachers need to cast themselves in the role of listener, advisor and co-participant with the students' and 'students need to learn a variety of group roles – leader, recorder, observer'. Such roles are not altogether familiar and my experience of sitting in at seminars in various high schools was not often inspiring. Often the seminar dissolved into woolly chatter, or an uneven antiphony of long-winded obscurities from some participants and gnomic monosyllables from others. Some declare that in seminar discussions insights of particular value emerge which are accepted by the young because they are revealed by the young; others refer in exasperation to 'shared ignorance'. It is certainly an agonizingly slow process. Trump warns against impatience: because 'teachers worry that the group is not covering a predetermined body of subject matter [and] students are likely to have similar concerns, most teachers and students can easily miss the major purposes of the small group activities'. Indeed yes – and in consequence some seminars had, I found, been rendered down simply to the teaching of a smaller-than-a-class group. Similar deflation has occurred with individual study. The practice of using halls or libraries for supervised study during the day is far more common in American schools than our own. Individual study, when included as part of team teaching, has the appearance of an organized, carefully co-ordinated portion of the total learning process; in practice teachers generally work first at their teaching sessions and seminars and, for lack of time, leave individual study as mere homework done in 'free' periods at school.

When such erosions combine it is hard to know whether what remains should still be called team teaching (Lloyd Trump would not think it such) or class teaching modified by occasional shuffling of teachers and timetabled homework. To some teachers such a compromise, which leaves the responsibility for a form's progress squarely with a single teacher and yet offers some variety, is in any case the best of both worlds. When, infrequently, team teaching has rooted in secondary schools in Britain, it has generally taken this sensible, less radical form and has been given the more appropriate title of 'co-operative' teaching'.

It is, of course, the fate of many innovations to suffer radical change. Disciples notoriously distort their master's message and disappoint his hopes. But a doctrine may have an importance quite separate from the particular form its originator intends, the surviving church may usefully develop in directions quite contrary to the first embodiment of the gospel. Trump, in his original formulation of team teaching, conflated a general principle and a particular solution. The solution – large group, seminar, individual work – has proved awkward; but the principle has coloured with respectability a wide range of attempts to modify the established structure of the isolated teacher with his fixed class in a classroom box. Trump has offered one particular analysis of the total business of learning, attempting to separate what a boy learns best from a teacher, what from other boys, what on his own. By his example he has encouraged other attempts to dissolve the compound process of learning into its elements and to recombine them in new ways to suit present needs.

Team teaching is one way of altering the traditional arrangement of the teacher and his class. It institutionalizes variety in the way we group those who teach and those who learn. Ultimately, however, learning is an individual act. So, Trump declares, 'the school needs to see independent study as the culmination of its efforts ... the teacher's goal is to become increasingly dispensable'. Some innovators in America, going further, see independent study as the chief means of day-to-day learning in schools, not just, like Trump, as the 'ultimate educational objective'. For independent study, greatly expanded and 'individualized' to allow each boy to work at his own pace at tasks prescribed for him, promises to break the 'lock-step of the class', whereas team teaching may do no more than vary the company a boy marches in.

In some shape and measure self-tuition is of course familiar – 'Teach Yourself' textbooks, correspondence courses, assignment cards, and so on. Recent American developments in this field stem from psychologists like Pressey, Crowther and especially Skinner, whose work has been largely responsible for the sudden interest in programmed learning.

This, in the classic Skinnerian form, has the following requirements: the subject for instruction should be analysed into a succession of small units; each unit should be carefully arranged in the best sequence for learning; the material should be set out in a series of steps or 'frames' sufficiently small to ensure that the great majority of those taking the programmes can understand them; the learner should make frequent overt responses by, for example, writing in the answers in each frame; his correct behaviour should be reinforced (or wrong behaviour promptly checked) by his being given the correct answer immediately, normally in the next frame.

The programme itself should be preceded by a pre-test to ensure that those taking it have the essential skills or knowledge required to make sense of it. At the end there is usually a post-test to check that the programme as a whole has been mastered. Scores in these tests enable the writer of the programme to discover whether the declared, measurable objectives of the test are being met. By analysing the answers given to each frame, the writer can re-write those steps that defeat students, refining the programme until virtually everyone in the target population can get it right.

How unlike ordinary teaching this is, the devotees of the method point out. Schoolmasters have little beyond intuition to guide them in setting out material in the most effective sequence. Indeed, apparent intelligence at school may reflect less a boy's innate capacity to understand a topic than his instant skill at unscrambling the master's exposition, sorting out the relevant from the irrelevant and devising an ordered pattern.[6] Then, the schoolmaster has to assume that the boys' wits are working in step with his own, moving at the pace he sets. True, he can insert running checks into his exposition, but such questioning of particular boys may be intrusive and distracting to others in the class; and yet if he leaves the checking to a written test at the end of the lesson, by the time the corrections reach a boy, the subject is stone dead. In contrast, the programme allows each boy to learn at his own pace and keeps instruction, reaction, correction tied as closely together as in private tuition. But, most important of all, although the teacher may derive some general notion of whether his class has understood what he has said, he cannot retrospectively analyse his fugitive words in detail, cutting out this, adding that, to ensure he communicates effectively all along the line.

Skinner's assumption, based on animal experiments, is that you can by careful operant conditioning, small step by small step, teach most things to most people. A published programme generally specifies that, in a sample of those who qualified on the pre-test to take the programme, at least 80 per cent met the declared objectives of the programme in the post-test. A figure much lower than this would mean that the programme was not properly validated. The price for such a success rate is a programme that inches along. Skinner believes, however, that the danger of the learner getting bored is more than offset by the pleasure of mastery, the reward of being right. It is important not merely to correct error promptly, because it could mislead, but to prevent it arising, because it would discourage.

Pressey and Crowther take a different view of the place of error in learning. Suppose programmed material were presented in much larger chunks, at the end of which certain alternative answers are proposed, and the learner asked to make a choice; he may well make a mistake, but the kind of mistake he makes will in itself diagnose his particular needs. If he gives a wrong answer he can be directed to an appropriate supplementary bit of the programme that will put him right. In this way many varied ways of learning the material can be devised and each learner automatically directs himself, by his answers, down the route that suites him. Such branching programmes can either be put into a book or into a teaching machine. In the case of a book, the learner is told, according to his chosen answer, which page he should turn to next; in a machine, he registers his answer by pressing one of a choice of buttons and the machine then moves the programme on to the place that is right for him.

Such, very briefly, is the promise of programmed instruction and the principal difference between the linear Skinner approach and the branching Crowther development. There is ample evidence that both sorts of programme can teach effectively: but experience and research have modified many of the original dogmas of the method, especially those of the Skinnerian school. Thus G. O. M. Leith, a leading English authority in this field, declares:

It can now be seen that the most important principle of programming is not the set of characteristics suggested in the past, namely the analysis of teaching material into small steps, the requirement of frequent overt responding, the provision of immediate knowledge of results and so on, but the empirical tryout of teaching materials followed by revisions which ensure the specified objectives of the teaching are met.[7]

Such a retreat is tantamount to declaring that the really important feature of a much advertised new ice cream is the cornet.

Indeed, the initial promise of programmed instruction has proved disappointing. I asked in the Office of Education in Washington if I could visit a school in which programmed learning was extensively used. They knew of none. Manufacturers and publishers, I was told, had 'burnt their fingers badly over programmed learning'. In the secondary schools regarded as innovatory I found only two commercially produced programmes in use – *Temac* maths and *English 2600* – and then only as reserve, alternative material rather than the mainstay of instruction. Yet it was 'Education without teachers'[8] that had been the initial hope of the more extreme enthusiasts for programmed instruction.

The main difficulty with the use of programmes in schools has been motivation. Skinner's pigeons were rewarded by food; getting things right is, alas, seldom enough to make boys keen to move on to the next frame, and the scores of frames to follow. Pecking at small grains of information may be all right from time to time, but it is wearisome as the principal way of getting nourishment. Little tests can be inserted in a linear programme so that a boy who performs well enough can skip the subsequent explanatory frames, but for real flexibility branching programmes are needed. These tend to be bulky and costly. They require convincing wrong answers – which the better the programme are the less likely to be chosen – and then elaborate by-routes of re-instruction to bring the errant learner back on to the high road. Moreover, unless a full range of wrong alternatives is set out, many nuances of response remain uncatered for. It is all very complex and laborious. Because of cost, therefore, branching programmes, with all their advantages, tend to be confined in America, as in this country, to training in industry and in the services. The cheaper and simpler linear programmes (modified often with small 'skip-tests') have more immediate use for schools, especially when applied to the acquisition of the vocabulary of a subject, to hammering home basic concepts, key facts, important definitions, and other such irksome drills.[9] Programmes are not only efficient in such circumstances: they can avoid frustrating confrontations between those who teach and those who learn. For example, a set of programmed cards developed in America by J. N. Hook and W. H. Evans deals with common errors in the structure and use of written English.[10] A boy can be directed to a card for the particular piece of technical help he needs at the moment he needs it; and the teacher can avoid repetitive general explanations to a whole class, for most of whom the particular structure may have little relevance at that time.

Whether in short instructional drills, or in brief diagnostic and remedial sequences, linear programming is then a powerful and valuable addition to the armoury of a schoolmaster. But if it is used extensively as the principal means of learning variety becomes imperative. Such was the finding in a careful study by Doris Lee of programmed learning in some London schools.[11] The elaboration needed to supply sufficient variety leads to a complete programme *of* learning in which programmed learning of a recognizable, orthodox kind may occupy a very small place. Examples of this are to be seen in America in junior colleges or at first-year university level (equivalent to our sixth form) and, so far in less complete form, in schools.

Sam N. Postlethwait is Professor of Botany at Purdue University, Ohio. He grew weary of lecturing year after year to students newly arrived from high school on the elements of his subject. Nor did the process seem very efficient: despite his endeavours a substantial number failed their exams. He decided, therefore, to put his course into a more permanent form. This would enable him to validate his course, to discover which parts were not being properly understood and to improve them. He decided that his programme should retain much of the self-instructional quality of programmed learning, but that it should be far more varied. The result was the learning laboratory.[12] I saw it in use at the Golden West Junior College in California.

This learning laboratory consists of about forty 'carrels', that is, separate booths. The student sits at a table. Fixed vertically on a panel in front of him is a tape-player. The instructor, who may be a graduate assistant, can from a central point record material on to all forty tape-players. The side panels of the carrel are made of peg-board on which can be hung various specimens, pictures, or notes. Each carrel is equipped with a child's plastic 'microscope' for viewing photomicrographs and film-strips. In one corner of the room there is an eight-millimetre cassette-loop film viewer. In addition to this battery of available resources, each student has his textbook and a loose-leaf workbook for duplicated materials, self-tests, additional diagrams and notes, and a study guide.

At the beginning of each weekly or fortnightly session all taking first-year botany are called together by the lecturer for a compulsory introductory session. He describes the work to be done, points out its more important and more difficult features, shows where it fits into the over-all pattern of the course. At this session the duplicated study guides and tests are issued. Thereafter, at any time during the week, the student can work through the required section of the course in the laboratory. One student may take three hours, another ten hours. The laboratory opens early in the morning and remains open late at night, supervised relatively inexpensively by graduate assistants. 'Through-put' is at least 40 per cent above normal laboratory use. The student can work when he most feels like it. Examination results compare favourably with those of customary mass university instruction and scheduled laboratory sessions.

The study guide – and sometimes the tape – takes the student through the course in sequence: read such and such pages in the textbook; now listen to the tape; look at the specimen; answer the questions on sheet so and so in your workbook; look at slides x, y, z, on the microscope and at the related film-loop loaded in the corner projector; check what you have seen by filling in the diagram in your workbook; and so on and on. If the student gets stuck he can consult the instructor. As another touch of humanity, the tapes are not pre-recorded by the publishers; the local lecturer records the script, and can modify it at will. At the end of the assigned period of time there is another compulsory session with the lecturer, for comments and questions on the course. Any tests or other work required is then collected up for grading; and so to the next assignment.

At the present time the learning laboratory I have described at the Golden West Junior College is confined to botany. Plans are afoot to try it for certain basic maths courses. At Oakland

Community (Junior) College, purpose-built four years ago, self-tuition learning laboratory methods are commonly used in a wide range of subjects. The learning laboratory arrangements are similar to, but in my view less good than those at Golden West, and there are many signs of an attempt to do too much too quickly. There have been substantial modifications in the direction of more student–teacher contact. This had resulted both from student pressure and teacher pressure.

Student resistance to unmitigated self-learning, however regrettable, is familiar; teacher resistance less familiar. A senior man at the college, and a key figure in designing its methods, was a trained psychologist who had previously worked in the guidance and superintendent parts of a county school system. He described an attempt he once made to run a new school in which (following an analysis of student habits) the enlarged classrooms were, roughly, a combination of small library, cafeteria, club room and study. Casual contact between teacher and student – thought to be more important than formal association – was thereby maximized. It had not been a success. My interest was caught by my informant's description of a typical, unregenerate teacher's reaction. At first he would sit cheerfully watching boys at work. The boys were *learning*, and he wasn't *teaching*. Splendid. However, after a while, the teacher, it appears, would start wandering round, asking this boy or that how he was getting on. The usual result was a casual brush-off. Next, teachers took to asking boys specifically how they were coping with particular sections of work. This led to the master explaining whole sections of work, first to individuals, then to groups, and to the whole class. The Devil of teaching, in serpent disguise, had returned to spoil this Eden. My informant and his colleagues hoped that Oakland's learning laboratories would ensure self-tuition uncorrupted.

Oakland and Golden West are both junior colleges – in our terms, sixth-form colleges plus the equivalent levels in technical colleges. In such a context self-tuition avoids certain problems that it encounters in schools. The student is older than the schoolboy. There is the presumption that he has acquired some self-discipline. He expects mass lecturing and minimal pastoral care, whereas the schoolboy is accustomed to a closer relationship with adults. The student does not attend college if he does not want to: the schoolboy has no option (nor the school). The student selects his course: the schoolboy (in Europe more than America) has to learn what he is told is good for him. There is a particular puzzle for schools employing self-instruction in that it enables learners to finish their work at differing times. The student who finishes early can then leave, to enjoy his leisure. Not so the schoolboy. The burden on him (and on the school) is continuous profitable occupation, or a respectable semblance of it, and generally this is only feasible by keeping the boys in step in groups. Otherwise won't who's doing what, when, where become a hopeless muddle?

An approach to this problem in America is to be seen in the 'non-graded school'. A leading exponent of such schools is B. Frank Brown, once headmaster of Melbourne High School in Florida.[13] We have noted the normal American practice of the fixed grade by which all children of an age are kept together in all subjects. This clockwork egalitarianism has undoubtedly frustrated many able children, and may account for the zest for learning they often exhibit subsequently at university. J. B. Conant, President of Harvard, wrote in his survey of the American high school, 'I think one general criticism in order: the academically talented student, as a rule, is not being sufficiently challenged, and his program of studies is not of a sufficient range.' Following that crisis date in American education, 4 October 1957, when Sputnik pre-empted the skies, such criticism of grading has sharpened. Tests of general information administered by 'Project Talent' to grades 9 to 12 in high schools showed that 73 per cent of 9th graders made higher scores than the lowest 10 per cent of 12th graders.[14] The range of difference between individuals within each grade was between seven and eight times as great as the range or average scores over the four grades. When national standardized tests were applied to the 10th grade at Melbourne High School it was found that in maths, for example, only 15 per cent had, apparently, any business to be in the 10th grade at all. The rest should have been scattered between the 5th and the 15th grade (which is to say, the third year of college). Similar configurations appeared in all subjects – in English the range lying between grades 3 and 13. It is possible to have reservations about such tests, and the concept of linear progress underlying them, without doubting the general proposition that our present way (and even more the American system) of classifying children and then teaching to an average of that class is pretty clumsy. At Melbourne the grades were abolished. Instead five phases have been instituted in each academic subject, and boys and girls are placed in whichever is appropriate to their needs, subject by subject. Those who emerge beyond the fifth phase in a subject embark on a 'quest programme' in which they get scarcely any formal teaching.

It sounds great, though one's confidence is a little undermined by reference to the quest phase as 'designed to let curious students be creative with definite objectives' and to boys being given in time a quest quotient 'intended to identify all the components of the enquiring mind'. The determination to define the undefinable, to say what is better left unsaid, is part of the scientific-industrial-democratic process, especially advanced in America, of analysing, abstracting, improving, multiplying and, alas, sometimes ruining *en route*. Explicitness becomes a disease: 'We are condemned to words,' says William Burroughs. Thus, when we hear descriptions of non-graded school practices it is not that the ideas are unfamiliar; only that, like announcements over station megaphones, they are so precisely enunciated, so curiously distorted, that we can only with concentration and good will recognize them at all. 'Quest' in fact closely echoes the theory, if no longer the general practice, of sixth-form education; 'ungraded' has redolences of our custom of placing boys in forms by ability rather than age; and 'phases' within a subject are a reminder that boys in a high set may be doing work very different from their contemporaries in a low set. But the non-graded school aims to take our modifications of the basic class pattern a good deal further. For example, our modifications are made at the start of each school year and last, with rare exception, until the end of it. Melbourne aims at promotion from one phase to another whenever it is thought appropriate for the individual boy. The logic, then, of classification to suit each individual starts with the abolition of a chronologically determined grade by which a boy is fixed in all subjects in a class for a year, moves on to setting usually in sequential subjects but still within yearly limits, boldly extends to annual setting in all subjects, and finally arrives triumphantly at setting in everything without any limits of time at all – not setting indeed but a fluid continuum. The dissolution not merely of streams but even of sets hopelessly undermines the normal process of ordered teaching to a stable group for a defined period. It points to work being arranged so that each individual can go through it at his own speed. When the non-graded school is equipped with whole sequences of self instructional work it turns into the 'continuous progress school'.

A well-known exemplar of this kind of school is the laboratory school in Provo, Utah,[15] attached to the Brigham Young Mormon University. Set in a narrow strip between mountains and a lake, the place has the beauty and the remoteness of Shangri-la. To come here, as I did, from Los Angeles is to step back into another world. The university newspaper reports briefly the rioting of students in less happy places, and examines at length the prospects of the football team. The girls are required to wear skirts of a modest length; the boys look prime beef, milk-fed. Alcohol is forbidden (and the dissolute drugs of tea and coffee too). The buildings stand unvandalized and handsome. This is the naïve, vigorous, wholesome, confident America that Europeans used to mock and to envy. The University laboratory school is set in a quiet tree-lined street, with old buildings and uncrowded playgrounds. A quarter of the children in the school have parents on the university faculty, many of them Mormons. All are fee-payers. The University's Institute of Education works extensively in the school – a particularly good Institute because Mormons, like Quakers, have convictions that lead many of them into teaching. In sum, experiments in the laboratory school are done in a place, with children, with resources of expert knowledge and additional manpower, that are far from typical.

The physical arrangements for self-instruction in the school are unelaborate and effective. A big room holds about a hundred carrels – simple, home-made affairs. Sometimes boys and girls may work independently at a variety of subjects in the room; at other times they are scheduled for a particular subject. In the latter case a team of teachers is assigned to them. If a child gets stuck in a programme he can switch on an indicator light in his carrel. When one of the teachers is free he goes over to help. Of two smaller neighbouring rooms one is used for testing, one for instruction. When a boy has finished a programme he lets the instructor know. Subesequently a light in his carrel tells him that the test he should do is ready for him in the testing room. The lights can also summon to the tuition room a group of boys who have reached roughly the same place, or have run into the same difficulty with their programmes, so that they can be taught together.

The arrangements are well tried and on the whole satisfactory. A better way of keeping track of where each boy has reached in his programme, and a quicker means of making up *ad hoc* groups were being discussed at the time of my visit. A worse snag is finding suitable programmes. Indeed the shortage is such that the staff, helped by the university, has set about producing its own. I saw an algebra course in duplicated sections with a few accompanying cartoon film strips. Other maths materials were due to follow. The commercially produced *English 2600* is used and the staff have designed supplementary reading-and-essay courses on various themes: 'Life's great questions', 'Preserving individualism in a world of social pressures', 'Images of a hero', and so on. Frankly, the quality is not very impressive in comparison with the kind of new curriculum materials we have become accustomed to in recent years, but the energy, the faith in the method, is impressive indeed. In practice, continuous progress remains an aspiration. Complete self-instructional courses grade upon grade are not yet available. The children do not at present work more than a year ahead of their grade in any one subject (when they have worked themselves out of the top they can attend university classes). But the school is working by trial and error both at the contingency management problems arising out of self-tuition and at the problems of how best to construct courses. The design they had arrived at was similar in many respects to a new Swedish maths course we shall examine later.

For a school to produce its own self-instructional materials requires a rare and sustained heroism. Attempts are now being made to exchange experience and materials by setting up an association of interested schools. The government-financed

Regional Educational Laboratory for the Rocky Mountain area is backing work in self-instructional courses of the new, more complex kind. In Boston the Educational Development Corporation, drawing on government funds and on private foundations, has produced some social studies material, elaborately varied and orchestrated, still using the teacher as conductor but with the parts of the score written out in full so that children can be much more active than is normal. Schools in three states co-operate in PLAN, sharing self-instructional courses produced in a centre at Palo Alto in California.[16] The IPI Project based on Pittsburg aims to provide a mass of small separate units of work covering the entire elementary school curriculum.[17] These can be so combined that each child in an IPI school can, hopefully, be given a course prescribed to meet his specific needs. What the Americans call individualized instruction, a more varied and humane successor to bare programmed instruction, attracts increasing attention.

It would be sad if all this aroused exaggerated expectations. American skills in advertising invade education and generate a short-lived euphoria followed by a sharp reaction. And the failure of this trumpeted miracle or that breeds a general disbelief. In Provo the mountains seem to rise up immediately behind the university. I wanted to go scrambling among them, but my host laughed at the notion. Although apparently so close, they were in fact twenty miles away. The story goes that a New Yorker on holiday, similarly deluded and heedless of warnings, set off for a stroll in the hills. The next day a search party found him. He was standing on the other side of a little brook. They urged him to jump over and join them. 'No, sir,' he said, 'I'm staying right here. I know it *looks* small but I'm taking no chances.' A moral tale, I thought, for educational innovators.

Any survey of educational innovations in a country as large, as wealthy, as experimentally minded as America is bound to be arbitrary to the point of seeming haphazard. This remains true even if we confine ourselves to the relatively restricted field of methods of learning and deliberately omit – they are reserved for a later chapter – the more imposing technological innovations like television and the computer. A lot of American research has stemmed, as in this country, from the private foundations. In America they are legion. Their widespread activities have in recent years been added to by large corporations, generally made up of electronic firms and publishers, which combine philanthropy, research, promotion and sales in a volatile mixture. University education departments, which share in full the American passion for post-graduate research, contrive numberless experiments and have sometimes achieved a wide influence – witness John Dewey in his day and Jerome Bruner in our own. Further, in recent years university departments in specific subject disciplines have turned their attention to the schools, contriving new curricula which sometimes require a shift in methods of learning. The roll-call of such projects – Secondary Science at Princeton, Public Issues at Harvard, New Maths at Illinois and so on – is very long. Some of these new courses, produced by brilliant university scholars, have not been marked by realism, and our own practice of anchoring curriculum development in groups of capable teachers plainly has much to recommend it.

But the profusion of innovation in America has become especially daunting since the passing of the National Defense Education Act of 1965. The title is significant. By this Act central government funds became widely available for educational research and development. The importance of change has been enshrined in a network of government-sponsored regional educational laboratories, each required to promote and disseminate local novelties, to release teachers for curriculum development, to make supporting grants to schools. To report on their work is like trying to deal with dozens of somewhat smaller equivalents of Britain's single Schools Council, each less constrained by cautious terms of reference and less inclined to spread inadequate resources thinly in order to satisfy constituent sponsors. In addition to establishing regional educational laboratories, the government has disbursed large sums under various titles – notably for compensatory education for the under-privileged and for the use of technology in the schools.[18]

We might attribute the vast scale of American investment in educational research to their affluence, but there are other factors that explain it better. The Americans believe devoutly in their capacity to transform their physical environment (composed of unredeemed nature) and no less in their capacity to transform their social environment (composed of imperfect man). The instrument of physical improvement is science; of social excellence, education. It is this earnest, active belief in the malleability of men in the pursuit of perfection which gives education in general, and educational research in particular, a special importance in America.

Some of the Americans' worst educational problems arise from the grandeur of their hopes. They worry about their high school drop-outs: it slowly dawns on a European that by 'drop-out' they mean someone who chooses to leave school when compulsory full-time schooling ends. Because 70 per cent stay on in school voluntarily until they are eighteen, the 30 per cent who do not are drop-outs. By this token we in England have some 80 per cent of drop-outs. Similarly, the problems and deficiencies of American universities need to be seen in the context of twice as large a proportion of their population taking four-year degree courses as take A-levels in Britain. It is the massive effort to give ghetto children pre-school education – Operation Headstart – that has revealed inequalities of which we in this country are scarcely aware. Alas, in important ways, the very act of bringing a problem above the level of consciousness exacerbates it. To define is to accent. The poor have always been with us; the problem of poverty has not.

We can trace in American educational religiosity, then, a noble belief in an attainable celestial city and a heroic if hectic ambition to reach it *en masse*. Once it was hope that made Americans pursue innovation; now, often, it is alarm. Francis Keppel, as US Commissioner of Education, said, 'A few years ago, it was relatively unusual for anyone outside education to think of education as a burning national issue. But today when we legislate against poverty, we legislate against slum schools. When we legislate against unemployment, we legislate against weaknesses in vocational schools. . . .' That was in the halcyon summer days of 1964. His successor could now add racial conflict, an unparalleled crime rate (more murders in Washington alone than in all Britain), general aggression and violence, and an appalling drug problem to his list of ills for which 'the house of education is called to account'. Add to these social problems the clamorous demand from increasing numbers of ambitious citizens for more and more education and one sees why a few miraculous innovations are desperately needed.

Meanwhile adults agonize over the state of the nation, and the young riot and rampage. It is not the colleges alone which erupt: over half the high schools in California and a host in other states have now experienced strikes and boycotts. 'The bull,' says Norman Mailer, 'roars from its wounds.' But, for the most part, it is present deficiencies men object to, or more simply, their exclusion from the bonanza. In the din of protest it is hard to distinguish those who merely want a larger share of available riches from that ragged fringe who, from the twentieth-century equivalent of catacombs and caves, doubt the wisdom of the whole enterprise. 'All men desire peace,' said St Augustine, 'but few the things which make for peace.' There is little ground yet for suspecting a widespread loss of faith in the American Dream (as opposed to impatience about its realization), scarcely any sign of doubt about the approved method of realizing it – the unceasing, wholesale manipulation of men and of matter. The myth of the Fall unerringly picks out the desire for knowledge, which is the beginning of godlike power, as archetypically human: and in contemporary America how ardent the appetite, how exhilarating the greed! There, science seeks to map all the hidden places, mass media to expose them, business to exploit them – sometimes with creative, sometimes with destructive results. Of both sorts America provides numerous examples; of restraint or discrimination few indeed. Those who suspect they see in America today the future shape of other industrialized democracies must find the picture disturbing. The anxieties rather than the rewards of affluence and ambition impress; and one returns home like the country mouse, cured of all envy, thankful to live in what is still a relatively quiet and modest place.

Chapter Five
In Russia

An Englishman who visits schools in a Western European country or in America sees institutions which on the whole reflect
his own preconceptions. It is not so when he goes to Russia.[1]
Nowhere else does official control so exactly contrive that the
school should mirror society. The visitor needs therefore to take
account of unfamiliar conditioning factors if Russian education is not to seem merely bizarre. Fly to the United States or
to Sweden, say, and you can start straightaway looking at the
schools: much better to approach Russia by train, dawdling a
little to adjust to the alien air.

The express to Leningrad starts in Helsinki. Half the train is
Finnish, half Russian, and complicated shunting goes on at the
border. It trundles endlessly through stretches of landscape
where God at the creation plainly wasn't applying himself. A
vast, empty expanse, a no-man's-land – yet by comparison with
other areas in Russia heavily cultivated, well-settled, positively
cosy. The train's compartments are decked out in crimson plush,
polished mahogany, brass knobs and engraved mirrors, a reminder of Imperial days when the North European express made
its stately progress from Paris to St Petersburg.[2] I had visions
of vast Russo-Victorian meals in the dining-car: borsch, barons
of beef or rumps of reindeer; instead in the compartment there
was milkless tea, brewed over coals in a grate at the end of the
corridor, and papiermâché wafer biscuits – ghastly but free, a
first taste of the lack of choice in everyday things that Russians
put up with.

I survived the day by the generosity of my travelling com-
panion, an experienced German on his way to the annual fur
sales in Leningrad. Nibbles from packets and draughts from a
flask kept us going until the train stopped at last to allow supper
at a station restaurant. The German led me down the platform,
through the lofty booking hall, up the marble staircase. In a
country the size of Russia, the railway has great importance and

is housed appropriately. We weave our way through a dense crowd. Russian stations, I am told, are always packed with people, day and night. Such an astonishing variety of faces, as Soviet poets frequently tell us: 'At the Bratsk Station, brother of brothers, I see side by side Russians, Ukrainians, Tartars, Jews, Churashes, Bungats . . .' [3] and so on through the roll-call. Russia is not a country but a land-locked empire. When we reach the restaurant the fur-trader orders expertly for us both – an ample meal, if expensive. As for paying, well furnished with currency – nine different brands for use on his journeyings – he settles the bill for us both, and I set off for the State *bureau de change* to get roubles to repay him. In a bare room, decorated with faded notices, a patient crowd quietly gazes at a woman who sits at an enormous desk, slowly executing the complex rituals of her task. As a foreigner from the express, I am politely shown to the front. There is an abundance of forms, multiple rubber stamps, carbon copies, tear-off sections – a first glimpse of Russian bureaucracy. Out into the cold air and on to the platform again, I find the train gone. Panic and despair. Anxious questions reveal it has been moved elsewhere. I rush to where the finger points and there is the train actually moving. I leap on. It stops. Then reverses. Merely shunting – this time. I came to recognize that sense of being at the mercy of unpredictable events. Elaborate exactness over obscure detail can be relied on; but in matters of greater importance confused helplessness alternates with irrational, brusque decision – the twentieth-century State in surrealist extreme.

The train meanders on and in the warm compartment the fur-trader regales me with experiences from earlier visits. At last, the lights of Leningrad. The train slowly circles the city. We clank slowly into the station and stop far down a dark open platform. Enveloping greatcoats, wintry faces, men humping bulky cases, clouds of steam in the arctic air, dim lighting: it feels like wartime.

Russia was, by Western standards, a poor and backward country at the start of this century. There followed military defeat in 1905, war in 1914, two revolutions in 1917, three years of civil war (with invasion by four of its erstwhile allies), a famine in which more people died than in all combatant countries in the

First World War, Stalinist purges, the Second World War in which, as in the first, Russia suffered greater human loss and physical ruin than any other participant. In Leningrad alone, in a siege lasting 900 days, two million people died. The events of Russian history like the country itself are upon an epic scale. The ordinary individual shrinks in a land fit only for heroes, or the masses.

Of all this Leningrad is the apt symbol – both Peter the Great's city and the cradle of the Revolution. Here the Neva is as wide as a gulf – the bridges spindle across it; an army could camp in the square in front of the Winter Palace – crossing it on foot is an odyssey; the Nevsky Prospect is not so much a street as a practical demonstration of how lines in perspective meet at a distant point. It is a city imposed on a marsh by a madman determined to overawe and impress, a seventeenth-century Brazilia built to a motor-car scale long before there were motor cars. There are still remarkably few: a scatter of limousines, taxis on official or tourist business, and buses. There are not even any bicycles, so obviously suited to this great flat city. In the West a dozen enterprising capitalists could contrive to produce them, and doubtless live dissolutely on the proceeds. Western achievement grows in a soil that supports plants and weeds alike in profusion; corruption composts it richly and we are used to the whiffs. In Russia they have dug up the rich sweet loam of decay; the soil is more sterile, but it's thin, so that only what's officially cultivated can flourish.

Russian control and orthodoxy extend in full, of course, to the educational system and into the classroom itself. No semblance here of a Department of Education and Science anxious never to be seen to interfere; no possibility of any school existing independently of the State; no right of a headmaster to decide how his school will be run; no question of a teacher deciding what he will do. From time to time in pedagogic journals there appear criticisms, within the approved editorial limits, of current Soviet orthodoxies. At the time of my visit, for example, some of the problems of the unstreamed class were under scrutiny. Khrushchev indeed, in a memorandum in 1958, had floated a suggestion that there should be more special schools, so that talented children might be removed from the unstreamed comprehensives. Defenders of grammar schools in this country seized upon this apparent disenchantment with comprehensives. The arguments advanced in Russia certainly bore a superficial resemblance to those of our élitists. If, the argument runs, we have separate schools for those specially talented in ballet and music, surely we ought to have separate schools for those specially talented in academic work – grammar schools in fact.[4] When we want a good football team we put all the best footballers together: we do not have comprehensive football teams. The argument sounds convincing enough. But in practice the chief aim of an educational system may no longer be an academic first eleven but the best possible standard through the nation. As for ballet and music, we do not expect to have in society many professional ballet dancers or musicians – less than 1 per cent of 1 per cent of the whole will be so occupied. It is quite another matter to pick out not just a minute number of obvious highfliers, but, say, the 20 per cent destined for grammar schools, at which point on a normal distribution curve the candidates crowd thickly and choosing between them becomes uncertain. Further, whereas those talents likely to make for future success in music or ballet are relatively easy to distinguish in the young, academic talent is a much more confused and complex concept.[5] Hard cases based on special skills make bad general law.

Although Khrushchev used the argument from ballet and music schools he extended it only to other special talents, those of a scientific kind: 'It may be found expedient,' he said, 'to pick from among capable pupils at the existing schools particularly gifted children showing, for instance, an aptitude for physics, mathematics, biology, draughtsmanship, etc., and to collect them together at certain schools.' The context of his remarks is significant: his memorandum issued in 1958 is entitled 'Strengthening the ties of the school with life'.[6] The official commitment at the time was to extend the eight-year course into a ten-year course, up to the age of seventeen. Was the continuance of existing unstreamed comprehensive patterns over a further two years desirable? Khrushchev thought not. Already many children were staying on voluntarily for a ten-year course which was wholly academic. As with us, teaching designed to meet the needs of a minority going on to university was being applied to all those

whose hopes might stretch, however unrealistically, to such ambitions. Many in Russia were already unable to enter college.
Longer schooling would encourage still more to raise their sights
beyond everyday humdrum employment, and they would then
be frustrated. The trouble, thought Khrushchev, lay in the high
status of the professions, reflected in the curriculum of the
schools:

We still have a sharp distinction drawn between mental and manual
work.... This is fundamentally wrong and runs counter to our teaching and aspirations. As a rule, boys and girls who have finished
secondary school consider that the only acceptable path in life for
them is to continue their education at higher schools.... Some of
them even consider [manual work] beneath their dignity. This scorn-
ful and lordly attitude is to be found also in some families. If a boy
or a girl does not study well, the parents frighten them by saying
that if they fail to get into college they will have to work in a factory
as a common labourer. Physical work becomes a thing to frighten
children with. ... Such views are an insult to the working people of
socialist society. Such an incorrect situation ... can no longer be
tolerated.

Since it would not do for too many children to be taken
through an *academic* course to the tenth year, Khrushchev
favoured the retention of eight compulsory comprehensive years
followed by better opportunities for further education, full time
or part time, of a largely vocational kind. Any tendency for
those at school to feel superior about daily labour was to be offset
by making basic training in the use of a wide range of tools and
periods of work in a factory a compulsory part of everyone's
education. But the more such 'ties of the school with life', such
non-academic elements, intruded into the common curriculum,
the greater the need to provide excellent facilities for high fliers
when the years of communal schooling were over – hence
Khrushchev's proposals for special schools. Moreover, if such
intellectually gifted boys and girls stayed on longer at the common school, their reputation and their needs would tend always
to distort the character of the rest of the school. The tail, all too
vigorously, would wag the dog.

Khrushchev's reforms have now been largely undone.[7] Ten

years' compulsory comprehension has been restored as the official aim. A limited measure, two hours in all, of subject choice has been introduced in the 7th grade, increasing to three hours in the 8th and four hours in the 9th and 10th grades. The attempt to raise the quality, variety and status of further education of a vocational kind has been quietly dropped. The integration of factory work into the timetable proved awkward and unpopular. In some regions it lingers on, but it has vanished from the city schools of higher repute. The apparatus of examining which, it is feared, favours those from white-collar homes, the academic ladder up which an aspiring meritocrat can climb, has been restored in full.

Khrushchev, a peasant's son who did not go to university, showed in his reforms an acute awareness of the problem that plagues all secondary education: what should we teach? We neither traffic in what is self-evidently basic and important for everyone, nor can we choose confidently for each boy, nor allow each boy to make his own choice. In consequence the curriculum tends to be constructed around those academic studies which, by long tradition and by current practice, lead to the most respected careers. Yet, visibly, such academic studies at school really satisfy relatively few and society can afford fewer still to pursue them at universities or to make a profession of them. The 'German system', as the Russians call it – our eleven-plus and tripartite system – is one way of trying to ensure that the 'wrong' diet is not given to the 'wrong' people, nor that 'wrong' appetites grow with the feeding. Khrushchev tried another, compulsory polytechnic way of making the education of the many resemble more closely the sort of lives they would lead. The problem remains to plague the Russians – and us.

Of all Khrushchev's suggestions, the one about special schools for special talents has had most publicity abroad.[8] There are now four such schools, all directly affiliated to universities and emphasizing maths (which occupies a third of their timetables) and physics. The Moscow and Leningrad schools are largely day schools; those at Kiev and Novosibirsk, boarding. But these schools, unlike the ones maintained by the central Ministry of Culture for music and ballet, are strictly confined to *older* boys and girls – in our book, sixth-formers. They enter, usually by a mathematical Olympiad, at the age of fifteen and leave at eighteen for a special accelerated course at the supervising university. Similarly, although of 885 local authority schools in Leningrad forty are designated 'special' – twenty-eight for various foreign languages, seven for maths and physics, three for chemistry, two for literature – the specialism is grafted on to a common stock. Most of the children enter by right, not talent, because this is their local school. Subsequently, a limited additional quota is admitted. Experimentally, for languages, some arrive in the second grade; in other subjects in the ninth – that is, after the present eight-year common course is over. It is as though a group of our comprehensives had agreed to specialize in their sixth forms, emphasizing one or two subjects and allowing transfers from other schools at that stage.

In the first eight grades schools are almost identical. In Leningrad, School Number 320 mirrors School Number 1, although this is an 'English language' school in a rebuilt suburb. At this school, for me, the barrier of language was diminished, and I shall use it as my sample. Doubtless there are much worse schools that foreigners do not see – occasional references to them appear in pedagogic literature – but in their structure and practices all the schools, whether 'special' or not, vary little.

'I am on duty today. Today's October 24th,' announces a boy in English to his eleven-year-old classmates. 'Have you prepared anything today?' asks the teacher. 'Irregular verbs', they reply, and the boy at the front sets the class to reciting: 'Go', he says. 'Went', they reply. 'Come', 'came', and so on. He sits, and the whole class sings a song, known by heart, about Lenin.

The children sit at their desks, well-scrubbed, upright. All the boys wear high buttoned RAF-blue suits, a white shirt, a red scarf tied like a cravat; the girls, demure as mice, have a black and brown uniform enlivened by a white apron and the ubiquitous red scarf.

'Now to the text, "The Tiger and the Monkey",' says the teacher. The book is poorly printed, the paper hard and dingy, the illustrations few and dull. A girl comes to the front to read a section in Russian; the other children repeat part of the text to her; the girl translates, without the book, into English. Other

children take their turn at the front working through sections
of the story, until at last one is called to reproduce the fable in
her own words, the class correcting her errors. Whenever a child
is ready to answer a question or make a suggestion his hand goes
up, elbow anchored on the desk – no enthusiastic wavings, no
sound. When invited, he stands to speak and remains standing
until told to sit.

'Now we will act this fable.' A boy is chosen to take the tiger's
lines, a girl the monkey's; another girl fills in the narrator's part.
Acting consists of recitation. Others repeat the performance.

'Now,' says the teacher, 'we shall sing and dance.' A gentle gust
of embarrassed tittering greets this announcement. A gramo-
phone is started and the children join hands and skip awkwardly
in a circle chanting 'Round and round the village'. They move
the desks further back and try again. Then another song.

The lesson wore on, ending finally with exercises set for homework. The command of language was commendable; the techniques used allowed considerable activity. In this respect
language teaching, with its emphasis on speaking, differed
noticeably from other subjects. One class of thirteen year olds
had made coloured slides from their own paintings of a Kipling
story about Mowgli, and had recorded an accompanying narra-
tive on a tape. But whether a class was active or not the pervading
atmosphere was that of an excellent, old-fashioned nursery
school with the children grown large. Decorum was absolute,
control quiet and complete.

It was no different in a 10th grade class among seventeen
year olds. (In the corridor, on the way, a framed display of
'Famous modern writers of English' consists of photographs of
Shaw, Aldridge, O'Casey and Dreisler.) The 10th grade text was
Cronin's *The Citadel*, but in this period they had prepared
articles from the *Moscow News* – a government weekly which is
the only publication in English you can buy, for even the *Morning Star* is forbidden. The material was directly and densely
propagandist. Inevitably the literature in any school system reflects the dominant and accepted values of that society, but here
was a uniformity of view, a constant praise of the USSR that
boys of this age in England would find, if written about their
own culture, naïve and comic. Perhaps in private some Russian

boys become irreverent; here in class they read their pieces un-smiling. There were a few linguistic questions from the teacher. Discussion on matters of substance, still less argument, seemed wildly improbable.

To be subject to adult pressure is, of course, the inexorable lot of children the world over, but in Russia, the subjection achieves a rare completeness because the adults are themselves not free. Official opinion rules. The idea, for example, that one group of adults, the manufacturers, should use their utmost blandish-ments to persuade people to smoke, while another group of adults, the government, should use their propaganda to prevent people doing so would seem bizarre indeed in Russia. In such a context one sees their point. But the absence of any belief in the merit of dissent must bear hard upon children, or at least upon those who have somehow retained stirrings of independence. In the schools the general docility of the young before the old is further reinforced by two specific devices: the Pioneer organiza-tion and the parent associations.

In the halcyon days of Lenin, school uniform was forbidden. Now there is a uniform, not for this school or that, but for all children. The red scarf they wear is the sign that they belong to the Young Pioneers. Technically, joining is a voluntary act, but it would be an odd child, and a brave parent, who resisted the uni-versal expectation. I happened to be in the Museum of the Revolution when some children were receiving their scarves in a mass ceremonial. When they are fifteen they will join the Kom-somol – voluntary again. It is impossible to explain to one's polite hosts why an act so manifestly rightminded should dismay when it becomes universal. In each school there is a Pioneer room and a Pioneer leader – usually someone in his twenties who may later become a teacher. I spoke to four Komsomol members in the 10th grade. 'You may talk to them without any teacher being present,' said my host triumphantly. On that day, in place of the teachers, they supervised break and lunch. Those with red arm-bands were on classroom duty; those with blue on playgrounds and corridors. What else did they do? Well, the Pioneer organiza-tion was responsible for the compulsory practical work – each class worked in rotation on a nearby building site for about two hours every month. Further, each Komsomol was expected to collect a monthly quota of five kilograms of paper for pulping and recovery. The Pioneer leader arranged for Komsomols to help less successful students. They organized exhibitions, parades, ran holiday camps and extra-curricular activities. A Komsomol's helpful labours, carefully recorded, carry considerable weight in the competition for university places. It is rather as though in England everybody belonged to the Boy Scouts and each school had a resident Scoutmaster, who although controlled and financed independently of the school, would be responsible for part of its discipline, some of the supervisory chores, and most out-of-school activities. Each boy would know that his Scout record mattered greatly because the whole apparatus of State was run by Rover Scouts.

The school in its educative mission closely involves the children's parents. A teacher is expected to visit the homes of all the parents of children in her class. She holds a meeting at the start of the year to explain how the parents can help her. Their role is further explained in issues of the government magazine for parents, *Home and School*. The parents of each class elect three of their number to act as officers who are known as the Parents' Trinity. The Trinities from all the classes comprise the school's Parents' Committee, run by its elected Praesidium. Its chairman is a member, with the school's director and staff, of the Pedagogical Council which makes those decisions allowed to the school.

What sort of things are the parents, so amply represented, expected to do? Certain of their functions are familiar. They attend lectures. They help organize and supervise visits and excursions. They contribute to some of the 'circles' – our clubs and societies. They work a rota for the serving and supervision of school lunch – a very simple meal by our standards. At School Number 1 an architect among the parents had drawn up plans for modifying the rudimentary kitchen and eating place. When the school's director argued the need for this improvement with officials at the town hall she was accompanied by representatives of the parents. They might help too with part of the construction.

The parents have funds put at their disposal in the annual

educational budget. These can be used both to support their general activities and to meet individual needs. If a child comes to school ill-equipped – for Russian parents have to buy textbooks and exercise books and uniform – or he behaves badly at school, or his work falls off, or he plays truant, then a member of the class Trinity will visit his home. The member's report to the Committee may result in a contribution to alleviate any physical shortage or hardship. Where there is neglect, the parents will be lectured about its ill effect on their child. If reform does not follow, the parents may be summoned before the Parents' Committee. Should they still fail they will be reported to their factory Soviet. A notice then appears on the bulletin board pointing out that Sergei Ivanovitch is failing in his duty to support his son at school. The director assured me that this final recourse had seldom to be used.

It is possible to approve a more active role for parents in the life of the school than we are accustomed to without applauding these last extremes. They reflect a brand of thinking, not wholly unfamiliar now with us, that is communal. The claims of society are held to be supreme. There is no respect in Russia for the view that a man should be allowed to go to the devil in his own way – and certainly his child cannot.

We in the West also stress the claims of the community; we, too, look for circumstances to explain errant behaviour. Above all we do this with very young children. We moralize at them, and when our moralizing does not work we search out human causes. But in the secondary school new conventions become dominant. We no longer act as though a boy were the puppet of circumstance or the tool of God: we hold him responsible for his own individual action. The right to be held accountable is, for the schoolboy, the first and essential freedom. In Russia, the paraphernalia of parental involvement and of Pioneer support is marvellous, but it leaves a boy no independence, no elbow-room. He is not allowed the freedom of being ignored by his classmates. He cannot hope, by evasive answers and judicious silence, to kep his parents in useful ignorance, nor would they accept that such ignorance, or the pretence of it, was wise. How can you explain to a Russian that the consequent atmosphere of universal attention, hard work, obedience, seems stifling to a Westerner? Does virtue, if cloistered or constrained, become vice? The Russian determination is to re-establish Eden at the price of not allowing people to taste the apple. The objection is not that this is wrong or foolish but that it is demeaning.

But then, they would ask, are we in the West any more free, or rather do we allow less creditable people to control us, insisting only that their persuasions be tricked out in attractive disguises? What signs are there that Soviet children are abnormally constrained, forcibly compelled? Isn't there every sign of willingness? Indeed, the teacher's anger, the strident call for silence, the sharp order are rarer by far in the Soviet schools than our own. Disturbingly, a possessive motherly kindness seems more effective than any tyranny. In the fable the warm and benign sun removed the man's protective coat when the sharp wind could not.

The Russians have had compulsory, co-educational, comprehensive secondary education since the Revolution in 1917. Among Western powers America alone can match this experience. Further, until fifteen, when compulsory schooling ends, Russian children are taught in classes that are unstreamed and unsetted. American children in rural schools traditionally worked this way, but in the cities and suburbs egalitarianism has been eroded by allowing a very wide selection among many subjects, or among courses within a subject. Such fragmentation is not the Russian practice: all children, bar the remedials, are carried through the same curriculum at the same speed for eight years. In such circustances one would suppose class expectations to be fixed at a pretty low level. This is not so. The American comprehensive school impresses more by its plant than by its standards of work. J. B. Conant was perhaps a little harsh in saying 'school is the place where the band meets'; but in academic terms the American classroom, despite post-Sputnik efforts, still seems to be a democracy of comfort. The Russian classroom gives no such impression. Competent observers declare themselves surprised at the standards of work required even of the less academic.

How on earth do the Russians reconcile these standards with unstreamed classes? What do they do about children who cannot keep up – or, at the other extreme, those who find the pace too slow? 'Individualization,' I was told, 'is the function of the teacher.' In other words, the teacher is expected to help children who cannot cope. Such assistance may occur in an interval or at the end of the day. Further, one or two of the more able children may be designated helpers by a teacher in school, or the Komsomol organization may arrange for one of its members to tutor the laggard at home. I had been told that Russian children were often grouped in pairs – one able child, one less able – and learnt together in class that way. Also, I could find no sign of this attractive concept being part of the normal pedagogic canon: it is a rescue device only.

These helping-hand arrangements are, then, only of marginal importance. What keeps everyone going at a fair pace is the confidence and consistency of the teachers, the order and respectfulness of the children. The teachers know precisely what and how they are to teach. Textbooks are specified, the rate of progress laid down within narrow limits. The teachers have detailed guides setting out what methods they should use; extensive compulsory in-service training ensures they understand them;[9] regular inspection by the headmistress and by visiting inspectors ensures they observe them. There is no room here for the inconsistencies of our classrooms. With us, a child's progress is along a path traced in part by the predilections of individual teachers; in Russia you march steadily along, no matter who takes you or which school you are in. Move from Leningrad to Omsk and you scarcely change step. Such uniformity preserves the less able child from the confusions that would hinder and discourage him with us.

Recent research has established the influence of the home upon a child's schooling. We have seen how in Russia parental opinion is marshalled in support of the school. If a boy is struggling at the bottom of a class in England, he often misbehaves, whether from boredom, from despair, or from a need to assert his own self-esteem. How much of his academic difficulty is due to being a slow learner, how much to his misbehaviour, is hard to disentangle. In Russia the element of misbehaviour scarcely matters. The under-achiever will be criticized by his class companions at a Pioneer meeting – he is letting down his class, his school, his family, the Party. His parents will be visited by the teacher, by one of the Parents' Trinity, summoned by the Parents' Committee, and so on. When children are given marks in Russia, it is on a five-point scale. To get less than three is disturbing; but when it comes to marks for conduct, anything less than five out of five is regarded as a disgrace and a sign that the sky is about to fall about the child – and his parents.

Liberal adults in the West may deliberately restrict the liberty of a growing child, but adults in Russia who have known neither personal freedom nor the settled security in which it roots, themselves accustomed to extreme controls imposed for the highest ends, must find it not only justifiable but natural to control their children closely. The ill-discipline, the frustration, the time-filling langour of many children in our classrooms will not tempt us to dismiss the Russian achievement lightly. But schools are a product of the society they serve. Russian schools show that if the direction is clear, the route minutely planned, the NCOs well trained, if there is no freedom to wander or straggle, then a whole regiment can move at a surprising pace. It is not, however, just the schools but Russian society at large that is made, or is persuaded, or prefers (according to your political conviction) to see life as a communal march rather than a personal walk. To follow with conviction the Russian way in our schools would require in parallel an inconceivable revolution in our adult lives.

Russian attitudes in society, then, reflected in the schools, explain how the less able children in their unstreamed comprehensive classes manage to keep up with the brisk pace set. What about the more able children whose natural pace is faster yet? The attitudes and controls described can be of little help to them. Must they just put up with the fixed pace until the compulsory common course is ended? As far as classroom instruction is concerned this is broadly the case. Obviously, though, a teacher may encourage a capable individual to do extra exercises, or a studious boy may do his homework more thoroughly. Further, a small measure of options, starting in grade 7 with two hours a week, is now permitted, and the tendency for more able children to choose more difficult options may result in a form of rough streaming during the few optional periods.

Of greater significance, however, is what happens when school ends. The teaching day is shorter than ours – for fifteen year olds five hours suffice (but for six days a week). By 2 or 2.30 p.m. schooling is over. There follow various voluntary club and society activities called 'circles'. An unusual feature is the regular help given by adults outside the school staff. A Baedeker example is the circles in mathematics run by post-graduate students at Moscow University, their efforts reinforced by a correspondence course produced under professional supervision. Circles flourish particularly in the weekly boarding schools and in the even more popular 'prolonged day' schools, from which, homework done and the evening meal finished, children return home at about seven. In the ordinary schools a simple adding up of circle activities does not produce a total much more impressive than that of most English schools. But there is an alternative open to Russian children – the Pioneer Palace.

The significance of this institution seems little understood among Western educators – as though Pioneer Palaces were overgrown Scout huts or youth clubs. Of course, visitos are invariably shown the grandest examples, but the provision is widespread. The biggest of them in Leningrad, surpassed only by the Pioneer Republic in Moscow, is housed in 300 rooms of what was once a prince's residence on the Nevsky Prospect. The staff, mostly full-time, numbers 260. Children from nearby schools use the palace during the day and day-time courses are organized to help teachers run circles in their own schools. But essentially the palace functions from 3 until 9 each evening. Six hundred groups meet every week, each session lasting one and a half to two hours. Attendance registers are kept for each group. I examined three at random: they were up to date and absentees exceedingly few. The Pioneer Palace record joins the rest of the documentation of a child's career.

I wandered, with a schoolteacher guide and later with the director, from one group to another. The Cosmonaut's Circle was being instructed by a professor from Leningrad University in the mathematics of space flight. They met for one and a half hours three times a week, took frequent written tests, and as a *bonne-bouche* learnt how to jump with a parachute. There were many scientific circles, some dealing with those subjects like geology which figure scarcely at all in school syllabuses. Geography circles were popular and numerous, sub-divided for the study of different areas. Several groups, graded by their progress, met to learn English, and doubtless other languages. I saw a painting group (they met for two hours twice a week), groups for puppet-making, toy-making, acting. Chess players were taught in part by visiting Grand Masters. I watched classes in gymnastics, in high-jumping, in boxing. In the technical wing children started working with balsa wood and meccano, progressed through the handling of metals and other materials, and finally graduated to electronics and building large-scale working models – a three-foot tractor controlled by cable, a dumper truck with a pre-set programme of instructions, a radio-controlled crane. There was a ham-radio group, and another for radio and electronic construction, in which boys and girls repaired bits of equipment from local schools, made physics demonstration models, and were currently engaged in designing a small machine for a local factory under the guidance of a technician sent from it. The music wing, amply staffed, was enormous: there were rows of cubicles and a new concert hall was under construction.

The Pioneer Palaces offer serious courses, run by adults, in the widest range of subjects. Here a boy can study what he wants, sometimes working with a group, sometimes progressing on his own. In effect, when the short school day in the unstreamed comprehensive school ends another school takes over where volunteer learners stream themselves by choice and ability. There is no sign here of sensitive egalitarianism. Photographs accompanied by details of successful members of the Pioneer Palace hang in a permanent gallery of fame, and current stars are praised with a *brio* few head-teachers could manage on Speech Day. In the school a hardworking docility, here zest, impresses. Our emasculated youth club service provides coffee and table-tennis and dancing, a place for young people to meet off the streets, and seldom much more. The Pioneer Palace has an entirely different aim. It should be seen as a singularly impressive part of Russian secondary education.

There are no experimental methods of learning to be seen in use in Russian schools; rather a demonstration of what needs to be done to make the old methods work. It would be wrong to suppose, however, that there is no research in progress. In the universities, in institutes for psychology and pedagogy, fundamental research is organized on a large scale. Some of the experiments are surprisingly unorthodox.[10] Children scarcely out of nappies lisp numbers and play with higher mathematics, and so on.

But educational experiment is clearly distinguished from educational practice. In America, and increasingly in this country, the assumption is made that numerous schools, widely distributed geographically, should be involved with on-going experiments. Publicity is used to ensure the diffusion of interest. There is obvious merit in the practice, and some less obvious flaws. A school department about to make some modest improvement in its own syllabus may well feel inhibited by the promised miracles of some publicly-funded, officially sponsored project. The distant rumbling of band-waggons deters some schools; others seem enviably adept at leaping aboard. Sometimes a project, anxious to avoid exclusiveness, will take on large numbers of participants: one in this country (admittedly an extreme example), though still in an experimental stage, has 400 associated schools. To influence as many as possible as quickly as possible becomes the aim. The danger is that teachers, accustomed to transmitting laboriously acquired knowledge and skill, will lose confidence in the work they are doing long before anything clear or well made is devised to replace it, and, more important, before the resources are made available to them to adopt the proposed change. The Russians, on the contrary, keep experiment for the pedagogic institutes. Periodically official encouragement will be given to the discussion of some novel practice, some possible alteration; but in education, as in all other walks of life, when the discussion is over and the Party decision made it is binding on everybody. If their peril is that of turning any change into an insipid orthodoxy, ours increasingly is of creating a nervous orthodoxy of change.

It is easy to see why the Russians resort to central control. In the context of their geography, their violent history both remote and recent, Russian educational achievements are hardly credible. They may be the triumphs of uniformity, but talent in the young is not stifled. If unstreamed classes tend to make for equality, the Pioneer Palaces encourage excellence. If the syllabus up to grade 8 is common, thereafter specialist teachers and specialist facilities are increasingly concentrated. The ablest children are well catered for, boarding if necessary. But it is above all the supporting regiment of adults that makes the total educational enterprise so effective – parents, Pioneer and Komsomol organizers, the staff of Pioneer Palaces, the experts from all walks of life. A parallel to this adult reinforcement of the work of the school (if less organized), something like this community of values (if less complete) existed in the West not so long ago. In those times, authoritarian teaching of an established syllabus to docile ranks of children worked well enough with us too. It is tempting to sigh for such ordered days, but we are unable to return to them. The Russians demonstrate how the old ways can be made to work and can still produce results of a traditional kind of excellence in a comprehensive, unstreamed situation. The prerequisites are so unacceptable to us that it makes one doubly anxious to search out new ways. Alas, corrupted by ease, we should now find being part of a uniformly educative society oppressive.

The carpenters were putting up saluting stands in front of the Winter Palace when I left Leningrad. Ten days later the fiftieth anniversary of the Revolution was to be celebrated. I walked endlessly in the long evenings, well wrapped up, around a city which offered a double fascination: the curiosity of contemporary things and the evocation of past dramas. It was a marvellous experience. And yet when I heard from a hotel acquaintance that an earlier extra flight was being arranged for some of the fur-traders, their business done, I found myself agitating to get a spare seat on the plane with an anxiety I found perplexing. The impulse reflected a submerged sense of nightmare, of things marvellous yet horrifying – and somehow oddly familiar. It was not until we were bumping our way by bus over the tarmac to the aeroplane that I remembered. Trofimov in *The Cherry Orchard* cries, 'All Russia will be an orchard', but events have disappointed his hopes. Instead, all Russia has become a school. There is the uniformity, orderliness and lack of privacy, the public grandeur, the personal drabness; the same fervent official concern, the rectitude, the constant appeals for co-operation for noble communal ends; the same emphasis on fairness and equality – the sense that every casual impulse has remote implications, and in consequence a complexity of rules, regulations, conventions, expectations; the same helplessness before humour-

less, pervasive authority – the suggestion above, the threat
beneath. And in the midst, doubtless, laughter, friends and
simple pleasures no one can invade Young children seem able
not only to survive school but even to enjoy it, but those 'happiest
days' need an innocent eye. As Bulstrode found in *Vice Versa*, to
return as an adult is diminishing, stifling. Russian official practices seem almost always morally right, and in every way depressing. The last time I had felt that uneasy ambivalence of
respect and repulsion was when I had begun to grow out of
school.

The bus stopped beside the aeroplane. Armed police at the
gangway carefully examined our passports yet again. Landing in
Stockholm I felt all the exhilaration of an escape.

Chapter Six
In Sweden

Coming from Russia, perhaps I did not see Sweden plainly. Even in mid-winter, first impressions dazzle. People and things work well and look good. Somehow in this arctic air the unlikely marriage of efficiency and freedom has been consummated – the product, one supposes, of a long peace and the settled riches it brings, the absence of religious and ethnic strife on any serious scale, an industrial revolution so late that essential natural resources were from the start controlled by the State, and above all of manageable size. Sweden's population is less than that of London and it has an area twice the size of Great Britain to inhabit – a density of forty-nine bodies per square mile compared with our 612.

The sense of space can be chilling. My first wintry night in Stockholm I watched the children skating, floodlit in the park. The girls, their arms linked, circled the rink neatly in round, regular orbits like planets; the boys dashed after one another, all arms and legs, as explosive as stars. From somewhere far, far north, honed by a long journey across icy lakes, over bare rocks, between narrow trees, a sharp wind cut at them, and just beyond lay a black sea. Fair-haired and cheerful, dressed in their bright jackets, they made a brave show in the threatening void.

It is hard not to feel both pleasure and dismay in so clean, so well-lighted a place.[1] The absence of litter, of fly-posting, of graffiti, of things tatty, stained, unwashed and broken, is uncanny to the point of being alien. Whether over food and drink, or keeping open public places, or providing transport, or over shopping times, things seem arranged to suit the citizen as consumer rather than the citizen as producer. Envious of so many examples of pervasive good sense and good taste it is a relief of sorts to recall those surprising statistics about Swedish drunkenness, their worry over drugs, their alleged propensity for suicide.[2] It is hard, in fact, to find any public cause that justifies anger or effort. When a visiting Russian educationalist asked Torsten Husén what was Sweden's principal social problem, he was told, with pardonable exaggeration, 'where to park our cars'. Perhaps the human animal, adept at survival in difficulties, most ruthless and skilled of predators, cannot adapt to near perfection. As the naturalist Francis Galton put it, 'Well-washed and well-combed, domestic pets grow dull: they miss the stimulus of fleas.' So it seems do a minority of Swedes. For some restless human spirits it is apparently better to travel hopefully than ever to arrive.

In education Sweden has clearly been influenced strongly by America. Indeed conservative Swedes decry 'the American disease'. They mean by this the growing influence of the jazzy, the extreme, the meretricious, the sensational, the violent. Essentially, though, it is not an American affliction at all, but has happened to spread in America first. All Western European countries have willingly caught the disease, though its pathology may differ a little according to the patient's constitution. It is of interest, then, to watch another country that was once, like us, a liberal, middle-class democracy, adapting itself to the organized demands of the less well-off for a bigger share of the cake, which means in turn a demand that there should be more and more cake to share. As always, social and economic pressures have led to a re-examination of the educational system. In Sweden, as with us, it has meant a shift to comprehensive schooling.

There is a widespread belief that the Swedes decided to go comprehensive because of research findings. How unlike ourselves! As usual, we muddled our way into a major decision: only *now* has the National Foundation for Educational Research been asked by the government to consider comprehensive schooling, and then in terms which preclude direct comparisons with the tripartite system. It is indeed true that the Swedish decision 'was preceded by more than twenty years of study and thirteen years of experimentation',[3] but between 'preceded by' and any suggestion of 'because of' there is a vast gulf. We too have argued about comprehension for many years. It is amusing to find the Swedes referring in the early years of their debate to prior English experience, to the first comprehensives in London. The 1940 Swedish Schools Commission, under the chairmanship of the leader of the opposition Conservative Party and made up largely of teachers, reported *against* comprehension. Its secondary school members especially feared that insufficient provision would be made for the special needs of the less or the more able. The socialist government persisted with its inquiry and established a second Commission in 1946, this time predominantly Social Democrat and less densely pedagogic. The Commission found in favour of comprehension. When, however, the proposals were circulated to all secondary school faculties only three out of 234 were in favour. The next stage was the passing in 1950 of an Enabling Act so amiable and imprecise that it got through the Swedish parliament unanimously. This was the Swedish equivalent of our *Circular 10/65* except that it specifically labelled the new schools experimental and therefore did not try to compel local authorities to introduce them. Moreover, although variety in internal arrangement was encouraged, the basic age structure of the experimental schools was fixed after long debate in the Commissions – a nine-year continuum covering in each school the age range seven to sixteen. In 1957 yet another Schools Commission was set up. It sought the views of academics in pedagogic institutes and experts in related fields and got conflicting and uncertain answers. But by then the experimental schools had proved remarkably popular. A poll conducted by Swedish Radio in 1958 showed a sizeable over-all majority in their favour. Supporters noted the sharp rise in the number of boys and girls from experimental schools continuing into further education and precariously claimed the nature of the schools to be the essential cause. Husén demonstrated conclusively that early selection for grammar schools reflected not just a child's intelligence but his home background.[4] Svennson's massive Stockholm study, then largely unchallenged, served to stifle any fear that comprehension, even with unstreamed classes, would slow down the progress of the more academically able. When the 1957 Commission finally drew up its report in 1961 it firmly recommended the universal adoption of the nine-year co-educational comprehensive school. This the government translated into an Act in 1962. A year later, following the report of yet another Commission, another Act reorganized the education of sixteen to nineteen year olds. The agreed intention at present – though its implementation will take time – is to combine the gymnasium (sixth-form), and the continuation and vocational schools (roughly, the technical college) into a single institution.[5]

Much of the Swedish experience in going comprehensive is parallel to our own. For Husén's findings, even more convincingly displayed, read Douglas; for Svennson's cautious claims, stated more positively, read Pedley. There has been a similar shift in public opinion as revealed in the opinion polls. In both countries the purely educational argument seems in retrospect to have been the noisy skirmishing of guerillas in the hills. the real battle has been more fundamental, a conflict of views among statesmen about what makes for a better economy and a better society, and among politicians about what is acceptable to a mass electorate.

Whatever the similarities there are clear differences between Swedish proceedings and our won. The Commission of 1957, before making its recommendations, collected detailed plans from each municipality; a careful estimate of the total resources needed was compiled; a six-year programme for carrying out the change stage by stage was drawn up. It was even implemented. How shall we explain so sharp a contrast with our own ways of introducing comprehension? Continuity in government in Sweden has been an important factor. The party in power has not been tempted to rush changes through – on paper. The Social Democrats have ruled, except for a few months in 1936, over the last thirty-seven years, and in all that time there have been only three prime ministers. In addition, Sweden is wealthier than we are – though that might argue the need for even greater care on our part to match plans with resources. Sweden has a smaller population – but within an even smaller unit, a single county like Kent, we have managed to sprout many varieties of comprehensive schooling. The notion that our local authorities are free and the Swedish municipalities dominated by the central government is neither true nor would it explain the difference, for, as the 1944 Act clearly showed, in education as in other fields, parliamentary acts lay down the parameters within which local authorities move. Comprehension has been allowed to rest precariously on a ministerial circular which gave no guidance even on obviously national matters like the age of transfer: the Swedes preferred to investigate, debate and then decide critical issues. Explain

English education to them (or labour relations or social welfare) and you will be met with incredulity; they comment, according to temperament and perhaps candour, on the extent of our freedom or our anarchy. Plainly, we treasure difference; they treasure order. We choose to make a graft, occasionally steeling ourselves to prune a little; they tend to plough up and replant. Our decisions are almost always generous and enlightened: theirs realistic. Whether we shall be able to retain a profusion of local idiosyncrasies or whether in the long run we shall find it all unduly chaotic and expensive remains to be seen. In the foreseeable future we shall doubtless struggle to square every circle and somehow contrive to make the most irrational, unlikely compromises work – more or less.

Certain of our major preoccupations have no parallel in Sweden. For example, Swedish private schools, unlike ours, are few in number and insignificant in influence. And, in Sweden, the sixth form is simply a further grade in schooling: it is not confounded with concepts of moral growth through responsibility. Since in their secondary schools all academic subjects are taught exclusively by university graduates, the Swedes do not have to solve nearly so complex a problem in manning their new comprehensives as we do. But they have squarely confronted a central issue in comprehension that we, so far, have largely shunned: namely, if it is both socially and academically beneficial for children of varied ability to be mixed together in one school, is it good sense then to separate them by ability in the most important activity in the school, their studies? And if you do not group them into forms by ability how on earth do you teach them? How can you avoid boring the quicker ones and confusing the slower? In sum, is it better to stream or not to stream?

We have looked at the prevalent American way of dealing with this problem. It is to have a profusion of elective subjects. The more you can allow everyone to do what he chooses, the less question there is of anyone having been put into this form or that because of his ability. The drawbacks of this system have been noted: it runs counter to orderly progress over a period of years in a given subject; it results in very uneven class size; it leads to boys of widely differing ability and knowledge ending up in the same class; it is extremely complex to timetable and to run; it postulates large schools; it prevents a boy feeling he belongs to a settled form as a social unit.

Initially in their comprehensive reform the Swedes arrived at a compromise. Most subjects were to be compulsory and taken in settled forms, but these forms were not to be made up according to ability. It was urged, for example, that a group of children moving up from the primary to the secondary department of a school should be kept together. However, the two compulsory sequential subjects of maths and the first foreign language (English) were, in effect, setted since there were to be alternative general and theoretical courses. Further, there were five periods for elective subjects. At one extreme all the time could be spent on a second foreign language (German or French), at the other on handicraft; in between various standard combinations were permitted in which each of these subjects could be mixed in differing proportions with extra Swedish, extra maths and typing. Here was a workable middle road : the difficult subjects could still be taught in viable sets since only the more able boys would choose the theoretical courses or the second foreign language. The school would not undemocratically assign boys to graded sets; these would form according to the requirements of nature, not the dictates of man. And suppose a boy did not recognize his own natural propensities, who would then be the arbiter? The parents, it was decided, advised by the headmaster.

These hopes of a natural order have dimmed with time. At first there was a fear that headmasters would tell parents what they should choose. They were forbidden to do this. Thus a headmaster was not to say, 'In my opinion your son Erik should not take the harder maths and language option.' Various standard circumlocutions developed, the best known taking the form, 'If Erik were my son, I'd urge him to do the handicraft and typing.' In fact, whatever the advice and however it was put, parents proved remarkably tough in their ambitions for their children. Many unsuitable boys and girls turned up in the advanced theoretical maths and English classes. As a result, for their elective periods, far fewer boys and girls than had been expected chose the easier options, and the harder option sets, notably those in the second foreign language, tended least suitably to be the largest. The pundits had estimated that less than two-fifths would choose the tougher academic route: in Stockholm more than four-fifths did so. To the complaints of those teaching form subjects to mixed ability groups were now added the objections of those who dealt with more esoteric subjects, in which the case for separation into ability groups seemed especially strong.

One way out of such a dilemma is the English one of apparently allowing choice but vesting the final decision in the headmaster or some other authority. Thus, the appearance in the 1944 Act of parental choice over what school a child should attend turned out to be a sham; and happily each year the 'right' proportion of children (though a different proportion in various authorities) prove 'suited to' grammar or technical or modern schooling to fill the available places. In this way political promises are translated into local fact. But the Swedes in their educational reform unequivocally located the ultimate choice with the parents, and there has been no going back on that. So now, since voluntary setting has proved unworkable, it has been decided to reduce setting whether by ability or by choice almost to vanishing point. The National Board of Education has recommended that from 1971, mathematics should be taught in unstreamed classes. English is expected to follow suit some five years later.[6] The total amount of time for elective subjects is being trimmed to three periods in the 7th grade and four in the 8th grade, out of a total of thirty-five periods in the week. But the sharpest cut is planned for the 9th, the final year. At present there are nine branches for a boy to choose among – five designated theoretical and four practical. The same phenomenon of youthful – or parental – ambition has resulted in so few taking the practical alternatives that they have shrivelled. Even the 9th graders are therefore to have a unified curriculum in unstreamed classes with only a few optional periods – five in their case – in simple continuation of what happens in the lower grades.

In all of this the Swedes have firmly rejected the American practice of a multiplicity of options, preferring the European habit of a common curriculum, with only slight variations by choice, throughout the years of compulsory schooling. This has been insisted upon, now even more stringently than at first, in the exceptional circumstance of unstreamed classes. They have arrived at a positively Russian solution, but without on the one hand being able to count on the docility of the young or on the other have the compensatory, extra-curricular Pioneer Palaces. How then do the Swedes hope to have everyone doing more or less everything together, undifferentiated by choice or ability, and yet to avoid crushing both the exceptionally slow and the exceptionally quick beneath a juggernaut of uniformity? How do they aim to reconcile organized equality with individual quality?

The uncertain answer is 'individualization'. If the quick and slow are to be together in one place, no one man can hope to instruct them at a pace that suits them all. Instruction to the whole class will have to be reduced substantially; some sort of learning that caters for individual differences in ability, speed and interest will have to be devised. In Sweden, because the commitment to unstreamed comprehensive schooling is absolute and the standards of the grammar school a recent experience, the demand for new materials to meet the new conditions of teaching is clearer than it is yet either in England, where streaming and setting continues, or in America, where organized academic rigour in state schools is a folk memory. The transition to full comprehension in Sweden would have been less anxious and awkward for teachers and parents if specially designed teaching materials had been provided in advance; but until demand becomes loud, treasury departments in a democracy always prove hard of hearing. Now, belatedly, the Swedish National Board of Education has set to in earnest upon the task of providing the materials the teachers need.

In Sweden research and development in education is financed almost entirely by the state. The results have been impressive.[7] We should not dismiss them as the product of Swedish wealth since, unlikely as it sounds, for research purposes the Swedes are comparatively poor. In financing research it is absolute wealth, and not *per capita* income, that counts. The Swedish treasury, by law, can authorize up to 2 per cent of the educational budget for research; much less than 2 per cent of our total educational expenditure would produce a far larger yield. Nor can the Swedes turn to accumulated wealth in foundations of the sort that have been so active in England and even more in America. The limited central funds available in Sweden are channelled, through the two people who manage Bureau L4 of the National Board of Education, into universities, pedagogic institutes, teachers' colleges. A substantial portion at present is devoted to designing individualized courses for use in schools, in the gymnasium and in vocational training.

In trying to devise such materials for classroom use the Swedes have drawn on two sources of experience outside the schools: on industry and on correspondence colleges. Swedish arrangements for training workers do not permit the variations to be found in apprenticeship arrangements here. In recent years self-instruction has been used increasingly. In the training courses for motor engineering, for example, the 'stations' system allows the trainee to move from one area to another, working at his own speed from printed materials, tapes and models, doing written and practical exercises under the control, at each station, of a specialist instructor. By these means a course that once took three years has been reduced to two years and the proportion who pass has greatly increased. In parallel, in Britain, many of the best items of programmed instruction have been written for use in industrial training and for technical training in the Services. In both cases the educational programme has advantages the schools lack: the purpose of the training is clear; its success is measurable; if he doesn't choose to work the trainee can quit or be fired; variety is built into practical training in a way that is not paralleled in most academic subjects; the economic value of technical training is direct and the argument for adequate financing therefore cogent. All the same, what is found to work well in technical training may be illuminating for schools. The Swedish 'stations' method, for example, has arrived by trial and error at an arrangement closely similar, as we shall see, to the Dalton Plan which many schools used in the 1920s.

If, in designing self-instruction in schools, the Swedes have found industrial experience useful by analogy, their experience of correspondence colleges has proved useful by simple transfer. We have in England many correspondence colleges, all but one run for profit. In Sweden there are only two and one of those, Hermods, has been a widely respected, non-profit foundation for many years. It is said the only thing all Swedes have in common is that they have at some time begun a Hermods course. In Britain correspondence courses provide a valuable alternative, sometimes a supplement, to what is provided in educational institutions. In Sweden a good deal of Hermods's work is specifically designed for use *within* educational institutions. We have not let correspondence courses into our schools except to fill some temporary or bizarre need – a master's long absence, for example, or to occupy a pupil who at the end of his schooldays determines to learn, say, modern Greek. In Sweden they have had a few secondary schools in which for years boys and girls have done most of their normal work by correspondence courses.

Sweden has been forced to this by geography. Certain regions are scarcely inhabited at all. In the northern wastes, as in the forests in the south-east, when you have collected every child of secondary school age, you scarcely have a class of each age, and if you then separate out the grammar-school children, as Sweden used to do, you are reduced to so thin a scatter of children that you are forced to make up an all-age class. In such areas, schools employed one or two teachers who could instruct only a few children at a time and in a limited range of subjects. It was decided to supplement the teaching force with materials, supplied by Hermods, intended for independent study by the children. The results achieved in the graduation exams were, according to an official Board of Education inquiry, entirely in line with those of children taught conventionally – neither significantly better nor significantly worse.[8]

Now Sweden has gone comprehensive, such grammar schools no longer exist. I did, however, see a gymnasium (for sixteen to nineteen year olds) still run in this way in Torsås. *En route* a small plane releases solitary passengers at a succession of airstrips as quiet as British Rail halts. Then a drive through crowded forests. Ships' masts used to be exported from Torsås to England, then pit props and timber for houses. At one time more people in these parts could understand English than the strange language affected by the northerners around Stockholm; even now, the English ports are more familiar to some of them than anywhere in

Sweden. There used to be a small school in Torsås which provided for the years of compulsory schooling; very few children aspired to anything beyond it and these used to be sent away to board. In 1958 the *korrespondens gymnasium* was begun. The lower school is now a comprehensive *grundskolan* and a number of its teachers help in the gymnasium although this is a separate institution. The number staying on for further studies has grown steadily and has now topped a hundred. In some remote northern *korrespondens gymnasia*, however, the total may still be as small as thirty, spread over the three years of the course.

In the gymnasium the timetable distinguishes between the hours during which boys must be together (for example, to take physical education) and a block of time for correspondence studies. Usually there is more than one teacher in the school and they divide their time between class teaching and supervision. During supervision boys can get help with whatever correspondence courses coincide with a teacher's specialisms. Usually a boy spends about two-thirds of his time (class time and homework) on the correspondence courses and a third being taught, the proportion varying a bit between subjects. At Torsås boys often come into school only for three days in the week, working otherwise at home, but some schools have built special study rooms and require daily attendance.

Swedish 'sixth formers' do not specialize to any significant degree. They have at present a choice between five main theoretical lines each with a number of minor variants, but every line includes nine subjects to be taken in the *Studentexamen* – roughly our A-level, the passport to university and also to many quite ordinary jobs. In the first year of the *korrespondens gymnasium* the students concentrate upon the three or four subjects of least ultimate specialist importance to them. They follow the courses supplied by Hermods, sending exercises and tests to Malmö for correction, finally taking oral and written exams which mark certain defined stages of their studies and count cumulatively towards their final certificate. Halfway through the second year the students board for a month at the Hermods hostel in Malmö, getting intensive tuition, using well-equipped laboratories, preparing for further exams. In the third and final year the stay at Malmö increases to about two months, culminating in a final examination of the four subjects which the student has chosen to follow most deeply. It is a nice blend of correspondence work and direct instruction, local support and central guidance, home and away. While most seem to find the method stimulating, I was told that 'a certain maturity' was needed. In general it has proved for these older boys and girls an economic and effective way of learning.

When teachers in the comprehensive schools found they urgently needed individualized work for their unstreamed classes, they turned to the correspondence courses already in use in small country schools. These did not work properly in the wholly different circumstances of the new comprehensives. The materials were too difficult, too bookish, especially for those less good at or less inclined toward academic studies. There was then a flurry of interest in orthodox linear programmed learning. At one time ten publishers produced such programmes. Only in scattered topics in maths and languages do these survive. The Board of Education has instead sponsored more sophisticated styles of individualized work for schools. One of these, the IMU maths course (which we shall examine more closely later) has been designed at Hermods by people skilled in teaching by correspondence; but it makes the usual correspondence course seem naïve indeed. Nothing of a comparable sophistication or so well-tested has yet appeared in any other country. Attempts in Sweden to devise similar self-instructional materials for school use in other subjects – such as German and English, civics and religious education – are less advanced and have revealed awkward problems, but the approach is thorough, determined and on the whole imaginative.[9]

The Swedes then pin their hopes on individualized courses as a means of reconciling a common curriculum with unstreamed classes. Such courses are expensive to produce. But the American alternative of a wide selection of options is expensive on other counts. Because they deliberately limit choice, Swedish schools, although comprehensive and covering a nine-year age span from seven to sixteen, remain generally quite small – with rare exception they contain between five and eight hundred children. The uncomfortable dilemma of fewer options or larger schools affects our comprehensive planning particularly acutely where extensive choice becomes unavoidable – in the sixth form. At the moment the Swedes too have a similar if less acute problem, for pending the time when all further education for sixteen to nineteen year olds can be concentrated on a single campus, the gymnasium for the more academic is usually tacked on to the top of the comprehensive. Many of the 'lines', especially in remoter schools, are taken by very few boys. Torsten Husén believes that the next bout of reform will involve cutting down the number of periods of teaching gymnasium students receive, from the present thirty or so a week to about fifteen, and the provision of individualized courses in compensation. The first example – the SAG history course – has already appeared.

However much we may learn from the Swedes' present intentions we have still more to learn from their past mistakes. The move to total comprehension was marvellously planned – except where it mattered most, in the classroom. Teachers adept in formal instruction were suddenly told to deal with children of widely differing abilities, interests and intentions, mixed in un-streamed classes. Some simply continued in the old way; others obeyed the official exhortation and, on top of their daily exertions, tried to evolve varied work to match varied capacity. It was an unrealistic expectation. I saw some of the results: the children were more or less occupied at individual exercises but the work seemed dreary and the atmosphere lacklustre. The government preached to the teachers about their new responsibilities, insisted on their attending vacation courses, urged them to design effective individual assignments. The teachers finally, in 1966, went on strike.[10] After a long and bitter struggle they got a large pay rise, five days of paid in-service training a year,[11] the expansion of research into teaching problems and the development of suitable courses. Will we learn from their hard-won experience that wholesale reform in the character of schools depends for its quality and success less on new buildings than on change in the classroom, which means the proper support and training of teachers: and will we act on that knowledge in advance?

Chapter Seven
Past Attempts

In education few things are new. The problems change little, but now this one seems most urgent, now that. In our hunt for different ways of learning, we can usefully match our journeys in space with journeys in time, learning as much from browsing in the Reading Room of the British Museum as from any more distant travels. Some old notions ripen with time until they are ready for us and we for them, and we may hope to find in the recorded experience of teachers in past times practical devices whose virtue we can now rediscover. During the war a research worker examining the British Museum's great Linnean Collection of plants came across a nettle two hundred years old. It stung him.

There is, of course, no end of past experiences we might examine, so we had better remind ourselves of the sort of questions we want to answer. For example, what alternatives to instruction from the teacher have been used not as an occasional variant but as the normal means of teaching in secondary schools? Has anything been found to support a teacher who may have to cope with an excessive number of children or with work at a level beyond him – for we know in certain subjects we can no longer count on the supply of well-qualified teachers meeting an exploding demand? Did our predescessors come across ways whereby learning could be made more active and more individual in content, style and pace than class teaching allows? Nothing so far tried can have worked really well or been suitable for general application; if it had we should not still be asking such questions. But even partial successes could profit us, since we may have means to remedy whatever defects foiled those early experiments. Leonardo da Vinci, we are assured, invented a workable aeroplane; only now can it be built to fly.

The most obvious alternative to a system of education based on teaching is one designed around the absence of all teachers. There are those who believe in Nature as a nurse. In the extreme, this view has been enshrined over the ages in wistful fables, from Romulus and Remus among the wolves to Tarzan among the apes. Alas, such hopes of a higher moral order in the animal kingdom reflect our petulance and disgust with man rather than our careful observations of nature. The celebrated Wolf-boy of Avergnon remained disturbingly animal:[1] he became no Mowgli.

However, most writers who despair of the artificiality of a human upbringing do not insist on such total isolation among the animals. They exclude books and similar artificial aids, but admit the active presence of a tutor to explain the curiosities of Nature. Thus Emile, his library confined to one book, *Robinson Crusoe* ('the best treatise on an education according to Nature'), is amply instructed by Rousseau, the Swiss Family Robinson untiringly attend to the observations of their father, and the courtiers submit to Duke senior's 'books in the running brooks, sermons in stones' in the forest of Arden. Indeed those who see nature as a nurse use her chiefly as the source of innumerable texts, sermonizing the fall of each sparrow. It's a depressing habit.

We can conceive, however, of an alternative way for nature to teach. We might selectively contrive the experiences available and remove the interpreter, allowing the learner to draw his own conclusions 'naturally'. Indeed, since natural environments are hard to find (and dangerous and uncomfortable), our real choice lies in any case between varying artificialities. Topsy was naïve in supposing she 'just growed', though we perceive she was not educated. The devising of educative environments in which a child can wander freely has marked the nursery school movement, whether Froebel or Montessori.

Alas, at the secondary level the process is more complex. As far as moral education is concerned we may still be able, more or less, to fence in a carefully cultivated area in which boys can be safely left to learn naturally – that is imperceptibly – what we think they ought to learn. Such an enclosure the Victorian public school aimed to provide. Nor need teleological contrivance be confined to morals. We can arrange things so that boys discover for themselves important elements in their academic work. This heuristic method dominates current curriculum reform. It is a powerful method; but the more genuine the 'discovery', the slower and less certain learning by it becomes. Will all the boys get the point? How long will they take getting it? When there is a lot to be mastered, mere exposition quickly intrudes. Thus, the ascending hierarchy of artificiality in learning extends from random experience uninterpreted, through random experience followed by explanation, to contrived experience with little explanation, and finally to explanation before experience and as a substitute for it.

'I hate books,' wrote Rousseau, 'they only teach us to talk about things we know nothing about.' True. But since we cannot contrive an adequate variety of experience in a manner sufficiently orderly, succinct and safe to meet our complex future needs, we find ourselves forced to plant the 'natural' environment with books. Some rare spirits have in effect educated themselves by browsing in a library. A Charles James Fox, a John Stuart Mill, a Margery Kemp, an Augustus Hare, may well derive most of their intellectual nourishment this way; and doubtless many men have, like the young Cobden, pieced letters painfully together to become, through character and wit, scholars and men of affairs. Such exertions do not suit less heroic mortals; but, suitably selected and mediated, books have often been a supplement to and sometimes even a substitute for a teacher.

When, however, we consider the education of the many and not just the few, can we envisage a book-based system of learning, as distinct from one that is teacher-based, being a practical expedient? Here we must move uneasily among nuances. A book-based system is not one in which teachers are forbidden, any more than a teacher-based system is one in which books are banned. At present, although books are hopefully distributed, the day-to-day business of learning is dominated by the schoolmaster. If he is late for the period he'll blame the boys for their chatter: they know perfectly well, he says, that they should get out their books and study them. If one day he found that they'd taken him at his word, he'd fear that they'd taken leave of their senses. For although a particular structure in a foreign language or a particular topic in maths is set out with detailed care by the author of a textbook, the boy waits to be taught it by the master. The textbook, except occasionally in literary subjects, acts chiefly as a compendium of exercises for homework. So it is hard to know at whom the textbook is aimed.

The normal sequence of instruction is that the book helps to guide the teacher who then teaches the child. Curiously, this is exactly how Comenius in the early days of printing saw books being used:

We might adapt the term 'typography' and call the new method of teaching 'didactography'. Instead of paper, we have pupils whose minds have to be impressed with the symbols of knowledge. Instead of type, we have the books and the rest of the apparatus. The ink is replaced by the voice of the master, since it is this that conveys information from the books to the minds of the listener, while the press is school discipline, which keeps the pupils up to their work and compels them to learn. . . .[2]

Of course, Comenius' notions were based upon the prohibitive cost of books in his time, but in our secondary schools the multiplication of copies does not seem to have made much difference. One wonders whether, as Marshall McLuhan suggests, we have exhausted the possibilities of 'the Gutenberg technology' or have yet to explore them seriously. At least until a boy gets into the sixth form (and often even then) books are not a prime device for learning but a weak supplement.

Our schools, then, provide no ready answer to whether a system of learning might be devised which is based on books (teachers being present) in the same way as our present system is based on teachers (books being present). Either system might use *things* extensively – objects for observation, experiment and manipulation. We use a book-based system extensively in our universities; doubtless many attempts have been made by individual teachers to make it work in schools. But perhaps the earliest systematic effort to adjust the balance in education – to make the book weightier and in consequence to move the teacher further from the centre – was that of Charlotte Mason, the founder of the Parents' National Education Union.

Charlotte Mason started to teach in 1861. Parish schools were then run in a parsimonious way and most middle-class children in their earlier years were brought up at home. At the secondary stage, some boys were sent to private academies as various in quality as those run by Mr Squeers and Dr Strong,[3] others made shift with the local public grammar schools or, increasingly as this century wore on, travelled to those which Arnold and his disciples had shown could be redeemed and made fit for the sons of gentlemen. For middle-class girls, however, there was scant provision indeed. Most had to stay at home. Despite her earlier intention to teach poor children, Charlotte Mason found her life-work in devising means to improve 'home education', and which was the title of her most influential book.[4] But the significance of her work is not confined to little girls in pinafores set to their labours by harassed mothers or inexperienced governesses. Schools, even secondary schools, came to use her methods. However, whether in a school or a schoolroom, Charlotte Mason did not assume that the child had access to a qualified teacher. On balance she thought this lack an advantage, for it made more room for books.

Too much faith is commonly placed in oral lessons and lectures; 'To be poured into like a bucket,' as says Carlyle, 'is not exhilarating to any soul'; neither is it exhilarating to have every difficulty explained to weariness, or to have the explanation teased out of one by questions. 'I will not be put to the question. Don't you consider, sir, that these are not the manners of a gentleman? I will not be baited with what and why: what is this? What is that? Why is a cow's tail long? Why is a fox's tail bushy?' said Dr Johnson. This is what children think, though they say nothing. Oral lessons have their occasional use, and when they are fitly given it is the children who ask the questions. Perhaps it is not wholesome or quite honest for a teacher to pose as the source of all knowledge and give 'lovely' lessons. Such lessons are titillating for the moment, but they give children the minimum of mental labour, and the result is much the same as that left on older persons by the reading of a magazine. We find on the other hand that in working through a considerable book the interest of boys and girls is well sustained to the end; they develop an intelligent curiosity as to the causes and consequences, and are in fact educating themselves. . . .

But surely, says someone, a child will get what he wants better from the lips of a teacher who knows how to explain and to approach him on his own level, than from the pages of a book written for his elders! Here is one of the fallacies that we as a 'school' exists to combat. For his intellectual diet the child wants more meat, stronger meat, meat more various in quality than any teacher can afford, and he is unfairly dealt with if he is not from the first brought into touch with great minds through their own written words.

Having found the right book, let the master give the book the lead and be content himself with a second place. The lecture must be subordinated to the book. The business of the teacher is to put his class in the right attitude towards their book by a word or two of his own interest in the matter contained, and of his own delight in the manner of the author. But boys get knowledge as they dig for it. Labour prepares the way of assimilation, that mental process which converts information into knowledge; and the effort of taking in the sequence of thought of his author is worth to the boy a great deal of oral teaching.

Do teachers always realize the paralysing and stupefying effect that a flood of talk has upon the mind? The inspired talk of an author no doubt wakens a response and is listened to with tense attention; but few of us claim to be inspired, and we are sometimes aware of the difficulty of holding the attention of a class. We blame ourselves, whereas the blame lies in the instrument we employ – the more or less diluted oral lesson or lecture, in place of the living and arresting book. We cannot do without the oral lesson – to introduce, to illustrate, to amplify, to sum up. My stipulation is that oral lessons should be few and far between, and that the child who has to walk through life – and has to find his intellectual life in books or go without – shall not first be taught upon crutches.

If the teacher's instructional function was to shrink into a few words 'to introduce, to illustrate, to amplify, to sum up', how should his (more commonly, her) time be occupied? As a start the teacher had to select the books that were to be used. This was a subtle task in which the children's docility could be misleading.

They are kittle cattle, and though they will plod on obediently over any of the hundreds of dry-as-dust volumes issued by the publishers under the heading of 'School Books' or of 'Education', they will keep all such books in the outer court, and allow them no access to their minds. A book may be long or short, old or new, easy or hard, written by a great man or a lesser man, and yet be the living book which finds its way to the mind of a young reader.

The teacher needed to be able to distinguish between 'twaddle and simplicity', and to be prepared to 'experiment or test the experiments of others, being assured of one thing – that a book serves the ends of education only as it is vital'.

The teacher was directly concerned, too, with ensuring that 'education is a discipline'. The day had therefore to be suitably arranged, and certain habits of work inculcated:

It is desultory, unorganized work which fatigues both body and brain, while the rhythmic regularity of prescribed effort is wonderfully ⬛⬛⬛ ⬛⬛ ⬛ ⬛⬛⬛⬛⬛ ⬛⬛ ⬛⬛⬛⬛ ⬛ ⬛⬛⬛⬛⬛⬛ ⬛⬛ ⬛⬛⬛⬛⬛⬛⬛ ⬛⬛⬛ ⬛ ⬛⬛⬛⬛⬛⬛ of subjects make for relief and refreshment and not for fatigue; the things that tire a child are too long lessons and too long school hours. It is a constant effort to pull together 'wits that are woolgathering' that fatigues child and man, and not rapid work done with full interest and attention. . . .

As knowledge is not assimilated until it is reproduced, children should 'tell back' after a single reading or hearing, or should write on some part of what they have read. A single reading is insisted on, because children have naturally great power of attention; but this force is dissipated by the re-reading of passages, and also by questioning, summarizing and the like.[5]

The aim of such reading was to substitute knowledge for mere fact or information (no Gradgrind here), to let each child feed on the ideas he found relevant to his own needs, in the books he read:

Education is a life. That life is sustained on ideas. Ideas are of spiritual origin, and God has made us so that we get them chiefly as we convey them to one another, whether by word of mouth, written page, scripture word, musical symphony; but we must sustain a child's inner life with ideas as we sustain his body with food. Probably he will reject nine-tenths of the ideas we offer, as he makes use of only a small proportion of his bodily food, rejecting the rest. He is an eclectic; he may choose this or that; our business is to supply him with due abundance and variety and his to take what he needs. Urgency on our part annoys him. He resists forcible feeding and loathes pre-digested food. What suits him best is pabulum presented in the indirect literary form which our Lord adopts in those wonderful parables whose quality is that they cannot be forgotten, though while every detail of the story is remembered, its application may pass and leave no trace. We too must take this risk. We may offer children as their sustenance the Lysander of Plutarch, an object lesson, we think, showing what a statesman or a citizen should avoid; but who knows, the child may take to Lysander and think his 'cute' ways estimable! Again, we take the risk, as did our Lord in that puzzling parable of the unjust steward. One other caution; it seems to be necessary to present ideas with a great deal of padding, as they reach us in a novel or poem or history book written with literary power. A child cannot in mind or body live upon tabloids however scientifically prepared; out of a whole big book he may not get more than half a dozen of those ideas upon which his spirit thrives; and they come in unexpected places and unrecognized forms, so that no grown person is capable of making such extracts from Scott or Dickens or Milton as will certainly give him nourishment. It is a case of 'In the morning sow thy seed and in the evening withhold not thine hand, for thou knowest not whether shall prosper, either this or that.'

This acceptance of the individual mystery of learning lies close to the centre of Charlotte Mason's thinking. She would quote Matthew Arnold: 'Knowledge is information touched with emotion.' What information a child would invest with an active response and so transmute into knowledge was a personal matter. 'We grow by our affinities'; each child has his own and they occur at varying moments. A child should therefore have a 'generous curriculum' full of 'books and things' (for nature study, paintings and music were prominently included in her curriculum) with which to build his own relations. Her objection to the normal process of teaching was that the teacher too narrowly intruded *his* ideas, *his* affinities, *his* relations upon children. How much more would she object to the current stress by experts in programmed learning on 'target populations' whose measurable 'behavioural changes' reveal whether the precisely defined objectives of a set of learning materials have been met. Such men would trim materials until all inefficient redundancies are removed. Where cold fact or mere technique holds sway, perhaps; but as a habit in education, never! Their vision is of cultivated land, watered neatly by sluice, dyke and lock: Charlotte Mason's is of the teeming sea. Children, being young, need direction to those waters which experience has shown to be profitable and some instruction in the use of a net; thereafter let them cast and draw in freely.

I merely set the work for the given term and the children occupy themselves with it. I believe that the fact of working on a given curriculum produces a sort of intellectual and moral aloofness on the part of the teacher, which is wholesome for the children as tending to give room for the development of personality, and it is necessary to be a person, before one can become a moral person.

Education is an Atmosphere, a Discipline, a Life. By this we mean that parents and teachers should make sensible use of a child's living (discipline) and should nourish his mind with ideas, the food of the intellectual life. These three we believe to be the only instruments of which we may make lawful use in bringing up children. An easier way may be found by trading on their sensibilities, emotions, desires, passions; but of this the result must be disastrous. The reason of this is that habits, ideas and circumstances are external and we may help each other to get the best that is to be had of them; we may not, however, meddle directly with the personality of child or man, we may not work upon his vanity, his fears, his love, his emulation or anything that goes to make up his essential personality.

Charlotte Mason did not merely preach this personal reticence. One of the student teachers at the training college[6] Charlotte Mason established remarked:

She avoided expressions of personal opinion lest they should act like 'suggestion' on those who loved her. She distrusted personal influence as limiting and belittling the person influenced and she steadily set her face against any form of personal influence over any with whom she came in contact. She laid down principles and waited for others to think along her lines of thought and find the right solution. She would not deliver those she loved from the growing pains of thinking for themselves, and sometimes those who did not understand took her silence for consent when they suggested things she did not wish. They little knew that she was only waiting for them to think clearly for themselves.

Such firm principle and firm habit, with great freedom within the bounds they set, make Charlotte Mason seem attractive and, alas, alien, for we cannot discover certainties in whose power we have such trust that we are content to restrain our continual manipulations. In our stereotype of the Victorian middle class we perceive the prescribed order, the hard-and-fast rules; we have little appreciation of the liberty those rules made possible. They chose to live, as it were, in a stiff collar; it left the neck untouched for ordinary movement and was felt sharply only when there was any excess.

Charlotte Mason's work survives almost invisibly, for the PNEU 'school' is no monumental pile of old stone, gothic brick, or stylish glass and concrete. It is not dashingly *avant-garde*, except in the sense that a clock that stops sometimes seems ahead rather than behind the times. Its members are scattered all over the globe, where business has temporarily taken their parents: children of a UNESCO expert in India perhaps, of someone working an oil rig in Indonesia, of an officer seconded to train Arabian levies. Wherever they are, in desert and jungle, children who belong to PNEU may solemnly sport the school cap and tie, read the school magazine and exemplify the motto 'I am. I can. I ought. I will.' Usually a child's mother is his teacher. She's armed with the recommended books, the syllabuses based on them, and with suggestions for supplementary activities. Charlotte Mason's cardinal principles guide her: she must listen while her children 'tell back' after a single reading or hearing; she 'mustn't get between the book and the child'; 'what a child digs for is his own possession – what is poured into his ears floats out as lightly as it came in and is rarely assimilated'. She is kept in touch by a magazine, the *Parents' Review*; she can write for help; twice a year she can send her children's exam papers to London for comment (never marking). Since Charlotte Mason's time many thousands of children have learnt this way. When in later years PNEU children go to ordinary schools, they generally impress teachers as being uncommonly well-grounded. They give point to Charlotte Mason's assertion that 'The great educational failure we have still to deal with is in the matter of books.'

Aside from these children in remote places, there are a number who gather in privately run PNEU schools in this country – at primary level generally, though a handful aim at the secondary years. Once, though, a far wider influence seemed likely. PNEU began to make inroads into the state schools and seemed set to fulfil Charlotte Mason's hopes of 'a liberal education for all'. A Miss Ambler had tried PNEU with a normal, large class of forty-five in the elementary school at Drighlington and her results encouraged other schools in Yorkshire to follow suit. Then, in

1917, H. W. Household, the County Secretary for Education in Gloucestershire encouraged five schools to try the method; a year later, at a little ceremony, a seedling oak was planted symbolically in the grounds of the PNEU training college at Scale How to celebrate the fiftieth. By 1936, when Mr Household retired, all but thirty schools in the county had adopted PNEU methods.

The movement waxed and it waned. Just after the Second World War an acquaintance of mine, fresh from training college, went to teach in a school in Gloucestershire. He came upon a cupboard crammed with books – strange books he thought for children. There in bewitched piles slept copies of North's translation of Plutarch's *Lives*, the *Life of the Ichneumon Fly*, *Twelfth Night* and the rest of those 'living books' of PNEU, preserved by the reverence of schoolmasters for the printed word and the solicitude of civil servants for public property. Once, to buy them, schools sold produce from the school garden, or got permission to keep pigs; parents combined in fund raising with an ardour they now attach (the ample supply of books being the province of the State) to swimming pools. Perhaps the achievement of so many copies was itself a disaster: when the precious books were bought in rationed quantities the teachers arranged the children into small groups to work through them in differing order. In such PNEU periods no class teaching was possible. But those piles of books my friend had come across were in full class sets – teachers raised and trained in an older tradition had turned them into classroom readers.

And perhaps Mr Household was right in doubting whether less able teachers should be let loose suddenly on PNEU and whether Charlotte Mason was unduly sanguine about the almost automatic virtue of the method. Whereas it is commonplace now to believe that children, lightly guided, can get their learning in an independent fashion from 'books and things', in those days the 'masterly inactivity' Charlotte Mason recommended required faith of a high order. The primary school now leads safely to a secondary school and even, most safely of all, to a comprehensive school, but the all-age elementary school of her day from which some children left for grammar school at thirteen and others at fourteen to hunt for jobs, was doubly involved in competitive anxieties. It suffered the same sort of pressures that still afflict the secondary school. Must these lead inexorably to boys moving together and step by step, through a set syllabus, taught, in safe dependence, by a master?

In that same troubled summer of 1914 in which Miss Ambler tried first to apply PNEU in a State school, Norman McMunn, a master at the Stratford-on-Avon grammar school, thought he had hit upon quite another alternative.

Norman MacMunn's analysis of the shortcomings of the traditional way of teaching in *The Child's Path to Freedom*[7] includes many of those criticisms which Charlotte Mason made. For example, a master in his teaching cannot allow sufficiently for natural variations in pace: 'clever boys are tied with stupid boys in a sort of three-legged race'. A boy 'loves difficulties as he loves light and air, but he does not love to be seized by the hand and rushed across broken country, hardly setting foot to earth, by some wiseacre who knows everything but the nature of his victim'. How and when each individual learns best is an unpredictable business.

The extent to which children differ in their method of work is almost incredible. Some boys tend to work almost incessantly with their prep: others write only when reminded by their partner, and seek nearly all their knowledge through conversation. Under the didactic system no allowance is made for this difference (depending mostly on whether the boy is stronger in visual or in auditory memory). ... Each must seek his own information, absorb it and reproduce it in his own way. There is no royal road to the mastery of any one subject, and a fact that would have a profound effect on one boy at a given moment leaves another quite indifferent until his moment of responsiveness arises.

Above all, the traditional way of teaching is wrong because it is too passive.

Knowledge sought is good, knowledge unsought is not true knowledge. ... No boy full of sap and vigour would reduce himself to the rank of a servile listener for five hours a day without some stimulus. ... To ask a child to concentrate its mind on lessons learned under conditions of silence and inertia is to ask more from it than it is, in general, in its power to give. That is why punish-

ments and rewards play so large a role in the administration of a
school conducted on traditional lines.

These ills are readily diagnosed, but to prescribe a cure is less
easy. Charlotte Mason's sovereign remedy lay in books and things.
MacMunn agreed that a boy should work 'with free activity'
among 'endless material to which he can be almost incessantly
responsive'. As a grammar-school teacher, however, he had to
ensure that boys covered set syllabuses, a task he could not fulfil
by encouraging quiet, personal infection from literary master-
pieces. Could dull but required labour be got through effectively
only by a resort to class teaching? Beyond books and things and
schoolmasters, what other resources were there?

To whom, then, must we turn? The traditionalist can only answer
'to nobody'. To the open-minded man of logic there is an alternative
answer, but an answer that will probably condemn itself, at the first
blush, as unconscionably absurd. It will come, in any case, tenta-
tively, timidly, interrogatively. To the boys? What an absurdity!
Boys teach one another! There would be a bear-garden in half an
hour, if not in ten minutes! What inaccuracy! What neglect of vital
principles! What subterfuges of pretended activity! What a chance
for ragging and for escape from all the restraints of healthy discipline! ... Is it not so? ... No, disappointing as it may be, para-
doxical as it may be to those who have never seen the boy beneath
the schoolboy, *it is not so*! It is precisely the contrary.

In a sense, of course, boys teaching one another was nothing
new. It is called, in most schools, cheating. If you can't (or
prefer not to) cope with your homework alone, you can work
through it with one or two friends in the same situation, or you
can work through it with someone rather more expert. Such
casual devices sometimes become quite stable: homework syndi-
cates form among equals, or a boy expert in one subject will be
induced to perform in it regularly for the benefit of others.
Similar arrangements sometimes creep out into the sunlight
of official approval. Such was the system of Amiculi in Jesuit
schools. George Moberly, as a boy and later as headmaster at
Winchester, thought well of an arrangement in college by which
an older boy was responsible for helping up to half a dozen
younger ones with their studies.[8]

To MacMunn such partnership was too random; moreover it would lead to the more able boy always 'leading his partner by the hand'. He advocated what he called 'differential partnership'. The notion had first come to him when he still taught his class as a unit.

I was standing before my class one day, wondering what verb I should give the boys to learn, when it came into my mind to ask myself why I gave one verb to a whole class, and whether there was any well-founded reason why masters gave twenty boys one particular thing to learn at one particular moment. I found it very difficult to give myself any valid reason for this proceeding, and I at once decided to try the effect of giving as many verbs as there were boys. The result was remarkable. The bottom boys in the form, spurred to effort by the mere fact that for the first time they knew things of which their class superiors were ignorant, at once showed an interest in their work such as they had never displayed before. After that, and so long as I taught collectively, I set my work on this principle of letting one boy teach another through being in possession of different information; and when I reached the partnership stage of my experiments I saw no reason to depart from this plan.

MacMunn therefore devised materials in such a way that boys could be mutually useful in their questioning. For example, in a French class pairs of boys worked from reciprocating booklets. From the red booklet one boy asked '*Comment vous appelez-vous?*' and (armed with the correct answer '*Je m'appelle —*') waited for the other to hazard a reply. Then in his turn the boy with the blue booklet would ask '*Quel âge avez-vous?*' awaiting an answer in the form his booklet showed: '*J'ai — ans.*'[9]

Similarly, a boy would set his watch to 9 o'clock and then to 11.30, asking '*Quelle heure est-il?*' His partner would do his best to answer, checked by the questioner who held the correct version: '*Il est neuf heures*', '*Il est onze heures et demie*', and so on. There were sentences in which a boy's partner had to supply the missing word. One boy would pick up a book: '*Qu'est-ce que j'ai fait?*' His partner tried to arrive at the required answer: '*Vous avez — un livre*'. Hide and seek offered possibilities: where was the pencil hidden? '*Le crayon est sous le panier.*' Toy models – a car, a cow – could replace classroom objects in the game and so provide an extention of vocabulary, opportunity for repetition, and nonsense situations that boys enjoyed – the cow in the car is under the desk. Boys played table tennis games in French and made up dialogues for glove puppets. They contributed to an illustrated card dictionary – not just individual words, of course, but sentences, direct speech in 'balloons' with the parallel indirect speech beside it, and so on. The card dictionary was the origin of MacMunn's picture encyclopedia in English that ran ultimately to fifty thousand cross-indexed cards, many of them contributed by boys, and used extensively by them.

But differential partnership was less easily translated into other subjects. MacMunn's little manuals turn history and geography and English into quiz-games, and maths, of which he confessed complete ignorance, into mental arithmetic. He admitted therefore the need for other methods of learning.

I think we may take it for granted that partnerships may well become the chief means of giving scope to the boys' spontaneous effort. But to say this is not to imply that we need be too bigoted in our heresy and exclude, for example, the purely individual work that boys might be encouraged to carry out in their school library, or to deny the value of an occasional lecture by a master. . . .

My method of using printed books is to cut them up into sections and rebind them in paper covers. . . . I have frequently the opening sections of half a dozen different books in use at one time. . . . Once the number of sectional books has become really large, it is easy to set every pupil in a school to do work exactly suited to his particular development. Hence those who follow the partnership plan of teaching will not content themselves with the meagre resources of the old school of teachers. And the fact that even beautiful editions of books can be cut into sections at a fairly small cost per head and lent to boys will help to enlarge the range of material brought into play.

MacMunn reckoned this more active method of working suited almost everyone:

I find that 6 per cent is the maximum number of boys who find a difficulty in applying themselves even to the most active kinds of work. . . . Eventually, I am convinced, no boy would slack except through ill health. . . . All this comes almost at once if he is no more than twelve or thirteen – uncorrupted by much past imprisonment. With a boy of sixteen it may take from six to eight weeks to reawaken his sleeping power of initiative. The worst are the 'cage-birds', as I call them – the dutiful little slaves of the system of repression.

MacMunn, like most educational pioneers, did not consider his 'discovery' simply more efficient technically: it promised great moral gains. No longer would boys act like prisoners released momentarily from the cells. 'Every inhibition of school hours tends to suggest a corresponding licence in the playground or in the home. Correct speech in the classroom suggests outside an orgy of slang, silence suggests noise, the preaching of beauty the almost wilful cult of ugliness – and so on *ad infinitum.*' Through differential partnership boys would become co-operative and self-governing, learning both respect for the needs of others and self-respect.

In March 1914 'some hundreds of guests', including some leading educationalists, came to watch MacMunn's boys at work in a demonstration at the Stratford Public Library. It was all very impressive. But MacMunn found a grammar school confining. His methods and those of his colleagues were in stark contrast. Exam strictures were severe. He moved, during the second half of the war (from which ill-health precluded his active service), to a prep school with a sympathetic headmaster. Beside working his 'partnerships' in class, MacMunn instituted at this school a number of clubs and societies of an academic sort, entirely run by boys. By now MacMunn felt he could organize a school entirely on the active principles he espoused. The effects of partial freedom were, he had always said, not to be compared with complete freedom. When the war ended he leased Tiptree Hall in Essex and brought up some war orphans at his own cost. Alas, two years later bankruptcy threatened and he was forced to take in fee-payers. He feared, and found, that their parents had conventional expectations: they thought his methods appropriate only to their more wayward or delicate sons, and would not accept his insistence that boys should learn in so eccentric a style from nursery to university. His passionate refusal to compromise meant that numbers were small and times hard. By 1924 his health was hopelessly undermined. He took his faithful few to a house in Rapallo and then to San Remo. There, a year later, he died.

Education so firmly based on a belief in the goodness and the wisdom of each child is, alas, hard to envisage on any large scale. It is said that if over a period we trust two year olds in a cafeteria they choose a balanced diet: the snag is precisely that in academic matters our artificial society demands an *unbalanced* diet. Without, then, following MacMunn to his single-minded, generous and brave extremes, we may still speculate usefully on whether a system of learning might be devised in which the schoolmaster is less central, his boys much more so. Can boys indeed be used to help one another to their mutual benefit? Can the lineaments of Chaucer's ideal student be seen in a boy: 'Gladly wolde he lerne, and gladly teche'?

MacMunn had no doubt in the matter. Moreover, when a master allowed boys to act as nature intended, he turned from being a drudge and taskmaster into a friend and an inspiration.

He [the new sort of teacher] will set to work with infinite respect, with enthralled attention, to help on this new and marvellous being along the path to the realization of a higher human type... he will rejoice unceasingly that it is his lot to be among the first to be at the work of beginning to recreate the world through the laws on which the world is founded.

Ah, how fair the asphodel, how green the grass, in those Elysian fields to which the weary souls of teachers, turned lecturer, researcher, inspector and writer, so readily ascend!

Charlotte Mason and Norman MacMunn wanted children to get instruction without it being pre-digested by the teacher. Helen Parkhurst shared their distaste for the conventional classroom method.[10] She too found it unnaturally passive, preferring 'learning by doing'; she too lamented the inability of any one teacher to take proper account of the variations of temperament, interest, ability and pace in any group of children. None of these innovators expected to do without the teacher – only without so much of the teacher teaching.

Charlotte Mason wanted the child to learn as far as possible directly from worthwhile books and profitable things; Norman MacMunn did not dissent, but (his experience being in a secondary school) he thought more structured, direct learning unavoidable and invoked the boys themselves as the means of providing it. Helen Parkhurst urged a more narrowly prescribed route through books and other resources than did Charlotte Mason, and a more casual community of learners than Norman MacMunn. Her devices were the 'assignment' and the 'subject laboratory'.

Although her direct concern was with school and not home education, Helen Parkhurst's starting point had much in common with Charlotte Mason's. A Victorian mother or a governess might well find herself trying to educate simultaneously half a dozen children or more spaced in age over a considerable span of years. In parallel, Helen Parkhurst when she was just sixteen was appointed to teach in a village in rural Wisconsin where forty children, ranging in age from seven to fourteen and officially spread through eight grades or classes, got their schooling from a single teacher.

I had thus to provide occupation for seven classes while I gave oral instruction to one class. To get every pupil busy on something until I could overlook his work occurred to me as the best solution to this difficulty. To make this plan a success I had to get the older children to help the little ones. They, and especially the big boys, responded to my appeal. With their assistance I transformed a store-room into a schoolroom with each corner marked off for each different subject. ... Even in that stolid backwoods community no one objected to these unconventional experiments because they were a success. The attendance rose rapidly; the children were orderly and obedient and they worked with a will.

Of course, in setting work to occupy some children while she looked after others, Helen Parkhurst was doing what teachers had been forced to do in rural schools the world over since schooling began; nor was the use of older pupils to help younger ones new. But the organization of such methods into a system that could be applied to a large secondary school was quite another matter. A handful of American schools, notably at Winnetka (Illinois) and Lincoln (Nebraska), had made the attempt with considerable success, but it was Helen Parkhurst's variant that proved the most infectious. She had tried her method in 1919 in a school for crippled children. In the next year the 'Laboratory Plan' was applied in the high school of Dalton, Massachussetts, and with astonishing speed the Dalton Plan spread around the world.

The Dalton Plan did not involve a change in subject content, or curriculum – it was simply a method of working. Helen Parkhurst made the distinction clearly:

Just as we need proper food to nourish and sustain our bodies, so do we need proper food for our intellect, which the school curriculum is supposed to supply. But a constant supply can only be secured by an efficient method of transportation. Many of our essential physical products are grown far from the consuming center. Transportation is therefore the key, and in the Dalton Laboratory Plan I had tried to provide, through the reorganization of school procedure, a vehicle which will transport quickly and safely a new and better curriculum to starving intellects. ...

In the Dalton Plan the child was to do more:

The curriculum is dead without the live motive power of the child; it must work by boy and girl power.... The basic principle of the Dalton Plan is that the pupil is made responsible for his own work and progress; he is made to feel that it is his own concern rather than the teacher's, that it is his own job, the success of which depends on his skill, initiative and industry. Having made him responsible for the job he must be allowed freedom to organize his work, his materials and his time (in short, his school life) and to secure whatever help from his teachers, his books, etc., he finds necessary for the successful completion of his task.

The first stage for a school moving over to the Dalton Plan was for the staff in a subject to break up the curriculum into portions 'say, as many as there are months in a school year'. These units of work were then to be set out in the form of detailed assignments. The boy's first assignment each month would declare the purpose of his work, the problems he would learn to solve, the skills he would acquire. The assignments, typed on to cards, would then tell him, step by step, what he should do. A good assignment conveyed some information, references to reading, helpful suggestions, 'interest pockets', questions to be pursued, and written or learning work to be completed.

So constructed an assignment can almost be made to serve as an assistant teacher. It is also well to indicate periods where consultation with the instructor is advisable, as, for instance, by adding to a mathe-matical assignment the words 'After you have finished the required problems come to me and I will explain the next rule before you go on.'

In cases where experience has revealed a marked disparity of in-telligence between the pupils of the same age and form, it is some-times well to modify the assignment in order to bring it within the reach of, say, three different categories. The minimum assignment will merely require the essentials for a firm foundation, and its execution should not put too great a strain upon the least gifted pupils in the class. The medium assignment would be given to the next group of moderately intelligent children, while the maximum assignment would be reserved for the star pupils.

When assignments were scaled by difficulty in this way the teacher could suggest to each child which was most suitable, or simply let each child choose. In the latter event, however, 'some-times the weakest have to be advised not to attempt too much'. The problem was not reluctance but ambition. Sometimes assign-ments could be written specially for an individual boy. A boy who had been absent might, for example, need a specially abbre-viated version; one who had finished what was set might be given, or be helped to design, an assignment that took him down an interesting by-way in his favourite subject – or be allowed to browse at will. The indefatigable Mr Spriggs, who taught maths in a Daltonized school in England, insisted that individual assignments evolved by the boys themselves should be the rule, not the exception; but normally the making of assignments was done in a secondary school by the whole department of masters teaching a particular subject. Helen Parkhurst urged a further stage of collaboration: 'intended assignments should be posted in a master's commonroom, so that connexions might grow between subjects, and that sometimes a common topic might be chosen upon which all the customary disciplines might for a while agree to concentrate'.

To match this different way of learning, Helen Parkhurst urged a different distribution of rooms.

Do away with classrooms in the formal sense, and substitute work-shops or laboratories where the pupil can browse intelligently. ... At home a child moves about as an individual from room to room with-out confusion. Usually he moves in order to get something he wants.

Similarly a boy was to go to whichever subject laboratory he chose, in order to find the resources to complete an assignment – books, apparatus and equipment of various kinds. There were human resources too – the teacher, of course, and in addition boys in the same age group doing similar assignments, or older boys working at that time in the same subject laboratory.

These laboratories are not supervised study-rooms, but workshops where the pupils collaborate with each other or with the teacher. ... She does not attempt to throw information into their minds as one shovels coal into a furnace, but rather studies their needs to discover what she can do and what she should know in order to help their research. ...

How on earth was the school to keep tabs on all these children beavering around, and how were children to be guided through the complexities that their new freedom implied? Each assignment of work carried a time-weighting. Such and such was to be read and a summary made – that counted as two Dalton 'days'' work in that subject; a map was to be filled in – one 'day' for that. Every boy had an assignment card, divided into subjects, and each subject into day units. When he finished an assignment he checked his work with the subject-teacher in the laboratory and filled in his own card. This might show that on the first calendar day of the month he had done, say, four Dalton days' work in maths; on the second calendar day, two days of geography, one day of history and two days of French; on the third, five days of English. Each morning first thing, for about fifteen minutes, a boy went with his class to the class-teacher, who examined their assignment cards and advised them accordingly. All this budgeting of time Helen Parkhurst thought essential:

Because children are prone to waste the time of others, but never their own, we make time theirs from the start. ... Under this method even the antipathy which most pupils feel towards certain subjects disappears, for it is seen as a weakness which can be remedied by a proper distribution of time. Children feel and frequently bear witness to this development of their capacity to take an interest in and to understand studies which they formerly found repugnant and incomprehensible.

Dalton assignment work did not have to be an exclusive diet. A common pattern was to have 'laboratories' in the morning and games, art, music and the like in the afternoon. Even in the subjects that were Daltonized regular time might be set aside for a class to meet formally with a teacher – a process we would call 'teaching' but which was rechristened 'conference time'. Further, when each boy finished an assignment he marked up his 'days' done, and the subject-teacher conveyed this information on to a chart; since this showed the point reached by every member of the class, the teacher could make a 'special appointment' with a particular group of pupils engaged on a common task.

Sometimes a whole grade is summoned to meet the teacher at a certain hour; sometimes only a few pupils are called together. Thus the subject specialist collects those who have, in spite of their different mental speed rates, arrived at the same point in their work and are ready to receive the same materials. In the event of a whole grade being called, the teacher posts the announcement 'this laboratory is closed until such and such a time' on the door of her laboratory.

Presumably this was pretty irksome. Might there not be other times when boys were frustrated because the laboratory they wanted to work in was full?

Preference is given to those who are less advanced in the subject, and to those who have only that subject to finish in order to complete the month's work. The teacher tells the children that he wants six, eight or ten as the case may be to volunteer to go to another room for the present and a sufficient number goes immediately without demur. It is a good training in self-denial.

Even such awkwardnesses, it seemed, happily worked for good.

For the Dalton Plan (like PNEU and Differential Partnership) was not simply more efficient academically, but morally and socially better. From such an experience of independence and responsibility children would acquire a proper confidence and self-respect. In addition, the Daltonized school was a co-operative community. Masters were no longer taskmasters and inquisitors but people to whom a boy could turn for help. At any one time in the laboratories boys of varying ages would be at work, free to assist one another.

When the pupil's working time is spent in company with others above and below him in age and position in a school, where he is constantly liable to be called upon to give help or equally at liberty to ask it, his attitude to the community is, of necessity, totally different to that which he assumes when playing from his own hand.

Helen Parkhurst displays in full, then, the combination of head in the clouds and feet on the ground of most educational innovators. Are the earnest souls she describes the children we know?

It would be folly to deny that all children enjoy a truly fine mental meal more than a poor one.... Children are prone to waste the time of others but never their own ... the mere fact of a common job and a common table is certain to breed keen discussion among children. ... When groups of individuals meet in their travels through the laboratories as they are bound to do, they settle down to work together.

Few of us, alas, will share such uniformly hopeful views. But Helen Parkhurst's belief in her Plan and in its central principle of 'learning by doing' suffered no crippling doubts:

There is, in fact, no limit to the application of this principle which will, I confidently believe, transcend in course of time, the frontiers of school life and bring about in the world of men and women a regeneration of human society that will be the triumph of the future – possibly of the far future.[11]

For all this heavenly nonsense her Plan was thoroughly practical. The first school in England to use it, the Rosa Bassett High School for Girls in Streatham, remains faithful to it; the curriculum at Bryanston was based upon the Plan at the school's foundation and is still; it strongly influenced Gordonstoun; the school her admirers built in New York for her still flourishes. But there was once a sub-Dalton plan for five and half year olds; a certain Commander Coote adapted it to gymnastics; in India the Bureau of Education planned its widespread introduction; there was a Dalton Plan in the Army, and considerable interest in its possibilities for industrial training, and so on. Helen Parkhurst's book was translated into seventeen languages. By 1926 she could write,

we have reports from hundreds of schools using the Plan in Great Britain, Germany, Austria, Norway, Sweden, Holland, Russia, China and Japan. In each of the last three countries there are now over a thousand schools which have put the Dalton Plan into operation, and in Great Britain a much larger number.

What happened to them all?

It is arguable that the Dalton Plan (and other variants of independent learning) never really died, that the notion of 'learning by doing', like a stream in full flood with Helen Parkhurst, went underground, now to emerge as springs in unexpected and apparently unconnected places.[12] There are points of similarity between the 'stations' system in Swedish industrial training and the Dalton Plan. Where – infrequently – the individual study element has been properly organized, then Dalton-style arrangements now re-appear as one element in team-teaching. But, above all, there is a close likeness to the Dalton Plan in the latest fashion in primary education, the 'integrated day'.

Leonard Sealey, a former Leicestershire Schools' Inspector, has said:

An Integrated Day is one in which there are no class lessons as such. Instead, each child makes a unique synthesis of his learning experience. The classroom is subdivided into specially-equipped working areas. Normally, one area is associated with science and mathematics, another with reading and the language arts, a third with work in the visual arts; and a fourth serves as a general purpose area. Occasionally, teachers may work in pairs, accepting dual responsibility for two classes. This arrangement allows teachers to give some specialist attention to work relating to their own interests or particular abilities. There are many possible variations on this theme.[13]

A visiting American teacher, Edward Yeomans, greatly impressed by the integrated day writes of it:

To anyone familiar with the adjustment problems among her twenty to twenty-five students which the teacher copes with every day in the primary grades of our [American] schools, often with an assistant or a student teacher to take one of the reading groups or to supervise recess, it is something of a revelation to see forty to forty-five children going about their work with little need of direction or restraint from the teacher. In rooms which have a span of two or three years of age, younger children ask older ones to help with a difficult word in the reading or with a dull saw in carpentry, but the degree of inter-relationship is no less in a room that has children of the same age only.

Yeomans quotes a Leicestershire head teacher:

Contrary to popular belief, the Integrated Day does not mean 'we can do anything we like all day'. It involves a choice of subject and not necessarily a complete choice of subject content, so I have found it essential to have work planned to prevent time-wasting questions such as 'I finished that. What do I do now?'

The head teacher then describes the advantage of this freer choice among assignments:

The flow of work is no longer interrupted by the division of the day as on a fixed timetable ... the mood of the class is livelier ... personal attention is easier ... the amount of work produced on any one assignment on any one day is not limited – other than by the child's own capacity ... the children help one another ... few children are 'lost' in this type of situation, though some prefer to be directed. ...

In all of this there is an exact continuity, often indeed an echo, of the Dalton Plan. The fact remains that those responsible for the integrated day and for other attempts at a more independent style of learning seem unaware of any connexion, little less any debt. Why has the once triumphant Plan been so obliterated?

Plainly, the Dalton Plan required a major change in the role of the teacher who was now expected to move from the centre of the stage. The same self-denial is a feature of many recent courses put out by curriculum reformers. When teachers make the change but then relapse into their old ways, disappointed reformers suspect the cause is vanity, but this is too easy an explanation. It is affection and anxiety which make adults – parents as well as teachers – resort to continual explanation and exhortation, not the love of hearing their own voice. We may accept that a boy's long-term growth is best served if we let him learn securely for himself, but whereas a primary-school teacher can exhibit appropriate patience, in the secondary school it is the boy's short-term interest that worries us,[14] for the day of reckoning is at hand. So we push, desperate to do all we can to help, now. Under the Dalton Plan, when boys worked too slowly through assignments, made mistakes, got absorbed in unexaminable detail, indulged in 'profitless' speculations, not to take over must then have felt to many of the most conscientious teachers like culpable neglect.

It could be argued that under the Dalton Plan many children did more and better work than ever they did when shoved along in the classroom, but what about those who did not, or those who found the new freedom required an unwelcome sobriety? Some Dalton Plan schools developed an admirable flexibility, but many of them must have suffered from a problem that affects all innovation – the energy, the passion, needed to change familiar ways tends to exclude compromises, nuances, tolerance. In the Dalton Plan the innovator's ardour for conversion was reinforced by strictly practical considerations: *all* the classrooms had to be rearranged as 'laboratories'; in *all* subjects assignments had to be written and the related books and equipment provided, and so on. Such wholesale transformations, physical and psychological, must have taxed the initial good-will of many amiable but uncommitted teachers and children. The sort of event recounted in *The Diary of a Communist Schoolboy*[15] was doubtless repeated elsewhere if in less extreme and dramatic form:

September 27th
The Dalton Plan is being introduced at our school. It's a system under which the skworkers [teachers] do nothing and the pupils have to find out everything for themselves. At least, that's what it looks like to me. There will be no more classes, and the pupils will merely be given 'tasks'. These will be handed out a month in advance, and may be prepared either at home or in school, and when your 'task' is finished you get examined at the lab....

October 1st
The Dalton Plan has begun. All the desks have been crammed into one room, which will be the lecture hall. Instead of desks we'll have long benches and tables. Vanka Petukov and I loafed all day about these labs, and I felt silly. Even the skworkers don't seem very clear how to go about this Dalton business. As usual, Nikopetozh turned

out to be the most sensible among them. He simply walked in and gave the usual class, except that we had benches instead of desks.

October 3rd
The Dalton thing is a wash-out. No one can understand a thing, not even the skworkers. The skworkers discuss it every evening amongst themselves. The only novelty so far is that we have to sit on benches and have no place to put our books. ... The boys say that this plan was invented by some Lord Dalton, of bourgeois stock. Now I wonder what the devil we need this bourgeois plan for?

The Dalton Plan failed to develop any central supporting agency. The Dalton Association in England, for example, gave advice to its many members and provided a forum for discussion, but it did not produce materials for use in the schools. Some few assignments were indeed published in the early days by way of a sample, but the Dalton gospel rested essentially on local inspiration. Helen Parkhurst saw assignments carrying a far larger weight in the process of instruction than Charlotte Mason ascribed to her reading lists and related guides; but whereas these were supplied from PNEU headquarters, the Dalton Plan envisaged teachers in each school composing their own assignments. A busy mother, acting as PNEU teacher to her child in a remote corner of the world, recently complained that what she really needed was the educational equivalent of frozen peas, whereas what PNEU provided were some peas to plant and six books on horticulture.[16] The Dalton Plan actually believed in frozen peas but thought teachers should plant, grow, cultivate and refrigerate their own. Alas, although such ardours may appeal to a first generation of enthusiasts they prove unattractive to those who follow in more humdrum days. Inevitably, Dalton assignments tended to be sketchy and to be based on the books the teacher happened to know or the school to possess. Frequently the teacher would set boys to read unaided long sections of the very textbooks which, in class, he would go to great lengths to interpret. The burden on the less literate boy therefore was especially heavy. Weighty, too, the assignment must have seemed to a boy whose interest or motivation was slight. Of course, such a boy might learn remarkably little in an ordinary class, but at least he was quiet and tidy at his desk. During the long timetabled hours everyone could indulge the fiction that he was working; alas, contrary fact emerged with clarity in the light of Dalton day.[17] Worse, when masters found they could actually see the product of each boy's ruminations they felt compelled to check and to improve what they saw, for the Dalton Plan came to England at a time when education was closely tied to external exams and, in reflection, progress at school was measured in marks given for written work. Under the Dalton Plan children no longer sat listening by the hour; the time available for writing grew. The convention that written work was always to be corrected resulted in masters disappearing in a blizzard of paper.

These worries about keeping a check on what each boy was up to, about marking, about exams, about formal discipline, pressed least heavily on the progressive schools. The original Dalton concept of a teacher designing assignments to be done by all individuals easily stretched into designing assignments to be done by each individual, and then into encouraging each individual to design his own assignments. Consequently, although there was general agreement among orthodox Dalton and progressive Dalton schools that a boy should be allowed to work more actively and individually, there was the widest divergence about what limits should be imposed on what was done.

The introduction of fashionable Montessori principles into progressive secondary schools had come to mean that it was best to let each boy learn as he willed at what he willed. Justification was by choice alone. It was an educational Reformation. A quiet progress through accepted syllabuses in well-established subject disciplines was no longer enough: a positive, willing, individual understanding was to replace it. There had been for many generations scattered protests against the comfortable corruption of learning into a mindless routine. In the 1920s, however, the reformers achieved a new self-consciousness and common elements appeared in their programmes.[18] Of course, they fell out violently over details: progressive sects multiplied and argued immoderately. But the world at large ignored their differences, and noted merely that there were new dogmas abroad which amounted to a separate protesting church.

At its best the freedom to choose did indeed result in a lively and a deep personal involvement in a project or some chosen piece of study; at its worst it led to the choice of easy options by the idle, a haphazard confusion among the flighty, a narrow utilitarianism among the dour. Further, the old educational rituals, dimly comprehended, were accepted by boys as being, however mysteriously, good for their souls. Time had invested them with authority. But the new gospel of individual choice, however far extended, still fell short of the genuine wishes of some, the passing whims of others, and the settled conviction of a few that the best choice for them was to keep clear of schools altogether. The progressive schools consequently exhibited an uneasy compromise in which freedom alternated with a sharp, erratic discipline, the more painful to the high-minded teacher and the querulous boy because its sanction was 'reason', which is personal and encourages argument, not 'tradition', which is given and does not.

Progressivism in an extreme form was embodied in England only in a handful of new schools, all of them independent and most of them remote and boarding. Elsewhere it managed to fuse imperceptibly with the ancient orthodoxies into an established, respectable, middle-of-the-road Anglicanism. In America, on the contrary, the progressives, invoking the sacred name of Dewey (who in later years, alarmed by excess, became a leading anti-Deweyite),[19] dominated many of the fashionable suburban state schools and seemed set to invade the stolid rural areas. The Second World War, however, raised fears for national security; an emphasis on the disciplined learning of essential skills led to a retreat from progressivism which Sputnik turned into a rout.[20] Since then, in a counter-reformation, the traditional subjects have been reinforced by new syllabuses, and a new canon of approved doctrine established. And now, once more, in the familiar see-saw of education, the objections to formalism, however enlightened, the insistence on a child-centred approach, are in the ascendant again.

Meanwhile the Dalton Plan disappeared with 'life adjustment' and the other brands of progressivism it had facilitated. It stood in people's minds for individual study. This can mean anything from a narrowly controlled progress through traditional subject matter to an untrammelled exposure to a variety of experiences, but such nuances were lost in the general consensus that an alternative to class teaching had been tried and a lot of hanky-panky had resulted. In the public mind, and within the educational establishment, when the progressives embraced the Dalton Plan they gave it the kiss of death.

And yet in speculating about the practical difficulties which may have undermined the Dalton Plan, and about the guilt by association which afflicted it in its American home, we may be missing a more general cause of decline. In education, where nothing is new and where aims conflict, appreciable change seems chiefly to occur through exaggerated emphasis now this way, now the other. We flourish by excess and by contraries. Each year in Egypt the Nile floods; twice yearly in Cambodia the Mekong at its delta reverses its flow. In the process the rivers transgress their familiar banks and deposit riches on lands gone stale from use and time.

Chapter Eight
Help from Outside

In PNEU, Differential Partnership and the Dalton Plan, as in our travels abroad, we have examined attempts to improve the quality of schooling by making learning (even within secondary-school contraints) less uniform in pace, content and style, less subject to rigid timetabling, less passive, less exclusively dependent on a constant instruction by the isolated teacher to his class – the teacher who, in certain subjects and at the higher levels, is already in dangerously short supply. There may, however, be devices we do not at present connect primarily with schooling which could help towards a solution of our problems. We shall examine three of these briefly: the correspondence college, broadcasting and the computer.

The correspondence college in this country provides 'an unnoticed and unofficial safety net' for adults whose educational needs have not been met by the normal apparatus of schools and further education. This second chance and alternative role has now been embodied in the Open University. Not by books and correspondence alone will the zealot pursue a degree: periodic lectures by radio and television and residential courses with tutors will sweeten his solitary labours. The Open University is the lineal descendant of the Dawn University and other experiments by the National Extension College, the BBC, ITV and various universities, to combine correspondence courses with broadcasts and tutorial conferences. The once austere image of learning by correspondence will never be the same again.

In some countries, however, correspondence courses are still intently pursued under forbidding circumstances and by youths we would regard as still of school age. In Africa at present, less than 5 per cent of the population can get any secondary schooling. Were the Nigerian Government, for example, to build a new school every week till the end of the century, still, the Ashby

Commission reported, there would not be enough. In such circumstances, the more determined boys build on whatever rudimentary start they may have received by working on their own.
In a suburb of Lagos the British Council maintains a modest and
useful Centre. A high boundary wall marks out from the surrounding undergrowth a quiet space in which the library building stands. Against the inside of the wall a continuous run of
corrugated iron sheeting and frail timbers forms a long open
lean-to, furnished with rows of trestle-tables and benches, and
lit by occasional dangling bulbs. On the suffocating night I was
there, these huts were crammed with teenage boys, labouring at
obscure tasks set by men in London and Oxford in preparation
for exams set by others in Cambridge. In contrast, the Japanese,
with their capacity for organizing everything to extremes, have a
huge network of sixty-five high-school correspondence colleges
aimed at the 33 per cent of boys and girls who do not go on to
the three-year upper-secondary school. A quarter of these now
manage to graduate through correspondence and the proportion
is expected to grow rapidly by the supplementary use of television and of peripatetic tutors in factories.

In both the Nigerian and Japanese cases, however, we are dealing with boys and girls over the local compulsory school attendance age, with the volunteer learner. The children who
came under the control of the headmaster of the Department of
Education Correspondence School in New Zealand have no such
option, nor do those in the outback of Australia, taught by correspondence and radio.[1] Still, like PNEU children, they stay at
home, so that problems of management and discipline are dealt
with by their mothers. There is little experience of children of
compulsory school age being gathered together into institutions
and then of their learning directly from materials supplied from
'outside', as formerly in some remote grammar schools in Sweden
and in a handful of PNEU secondary schools in this country.
Normally when children and teachers gather together it is
assumed that children should be formally taught and that the
school should rely on its own teaching resources.

The Dalton Plan challenged the dominance of teaching by
letting children learn from assignments, but it did not question
the entire self-reliance of teachers in each school. They were

expected to design their own assignments, which often turned out to be little more than prescriptions for reading, with ancillary questions, in certain familiar textbooks. Some correspondence courses, too, are adjuncts to specified texts, but they have to do much more than simply set out material to be learnt, because they cannot count on the teacher being present. A textbook is generally written at a level of generalization well beyond the experience of those who read it. Its words may, in Pindar's phrase, 'be vocal to the wise. but for the crowd they need interpreters'. If the textbook is read around the classroom then a master will keep prompting his boys with 'What do you think that means?' He will try to connect the text with the boys' own lives, providing comparisons; he will tell them what to pay most attention to, refer to related material previously encountered, suggest further reading in the library. In sum, he will try generally to make the topic interesting, and check that the boys have noticed what is most important. Class textbooks can be relatively brief and cheap because a teacher is expected to enlarge and explain them. They are indeed books of texts, concise subjects for elaborate sermons. But a correspondence course can count on no interpreter. It should, therefore, provide more examples and fuller explanations, clearer directions, more frequent recapitulations, more diagrams and illustrations.[2] Because the print alone must teach, the designers of correspondence courses have a burden placed upon them (which many neglect) to produce something more attractive, more lucid, more lively, more emphatic, than any textbook. Part of the blame for the apparent inability or reluctance of the schoolboy to learn directly from the textbook may lie with the style of the book itself. The problem of how to use language, line and layout to create the equivalent in print of the emphasis and variety of speech has already exercised the better correspondence colleges. It is no accident that the Swedish Government, in urgent need of materials for independent learning in their unstreamed comprehensive schools, turned to a correspondence college to provide it.

In this country, neither poverty nor isolation has driven us to use correspondence courses systematically for children of school age. None the less, the National Extension College could cite in 1965 seventy-five secondary schools that had used its

courses in the previous two years.[3] That correspondence was regarded only as a recourse to meet some unusual individual need
was reflected in the small number of children involved – some
275 – and their enrolment for a large spread of courses – thirty-
four in all. The heads of the schools gave the following reasons
for invoking correspondence courses: compensating for a shortage of specialist staff (the most popular course was O-level physics, ingeniously based on a box of inexpensive apparatus);
easing the conversion to some unfamiliar syllabus, such as new
mathematics; widening the choice of subjects, or of topics within
a subject, or of combinations among subjects, especially in the
sixth form; helping the boys who were out of step – those forced
to repeat exams, those who had been absent, those transferring
from schools where the necessary earlier stages of a subject had
not been taught, those who had made an early choice excluding
a particular subject which they subsequently needed. But although the use of correspondence courses had been occasioned
by such special needs, some teachers noted more general advantages. For example, boys a bit lost in a subject, although regularly
taught, found the systematic way things were set out in a correspondence course a valuable reinforcement; individual work at
a course provided a useful introduction to the more independent
style of learning in the sixth form and university; and some boys
and girls simply preferred working on their own to working in
a class. Dr Borje Holmberg, Director of the Hermods Foundation in Sweden, puts 'at least 50 per cent' of those who enrol for
a Hermods course in this category.[4] They like to be free of classroom strains – competition, censure, exposure – and appreciate
the chance to arrive at their own conclusions (not always those
officially approved or demanded) without their personal search
being cut short by premature disclosure from a quicker com-
panion or an impatient teacher.

Correspondence courses, then, have generally been used by
volunteer learners, adults and older pupils, or by children in their
own homes. In Sweden and elsewhere, correspondence courses
have sometimes been used by children still at school, but only
those of the more academic cast of mind living in remote places.
In this country, correspondence courses appear in schools only
to meet exceptional circumstances. So narrow a base will not

bear large and confident extrapolation. All the same, suppose the skills required in the writer and designer of a correspondence course were applied to stretches of the ordinary curriculum, might we not find independent work a more realistic proposition in secondary schools than it now seems? We should then have correspondence learning without the usual isolation and, teachers being present, without the awkwardness of corresponding – a sort of Dalton Plan, but one based on properly designed assignments. We have thought of correspondence colleges as an alternative to schools, correspondence courses as an alternative to being taught: a scatter of experience here and abroad suggests the contrast need not and should not be so sharply drawn.

In the midst of the pressing inadequacies of our schools it is tempting indeed to turn to educational technology for salvation. 'Science,' said John Stuart Mill, 'takes cognizance of a phenomenon and tries to ascertain its laws: Art proposes to itself an end and looks out for means to effect it.' Thus technology is the art of science, its creative application the synthesis of elements derived from analysis into new patterns required for given ends. It is a reflection of the primitive state of the science of education that our picture of its complementary technology generally consists of gadgets for the classroom and not of whole systems of learning. The scale of intentions concealed within the single word 'technology' becomes apparent when we look, as we shall now, at educational broadcasting. It can be just a gadget, an occasional embellishment to class teaching; but it can also be substituted entirely for class teaching, offering an alternative system to the self-contained class in the self-contained school.

Any such extreme use of broadcasting we connect with thinly populated countries and with poor countries, with radio teaching in the Australian outback, and with mass education by television in the market place in rural Sicily or Samoa. With us, the BBC has been a model of modesty and caution, declaring its intention to be a supplement to and not a substitute for a teacher. Its earlier schools programmes exploited the peculiar merit of broadcasting – its ability to present the people, the events, the places in the news, more quickly and more vividly than a newspaper. But as time went by so the demand from teachers grew for something more predictable, sequenced, and complete. At first such series filled obvious gaps in a school's provision, for as the catalogue of expected activities grew ever longer, so more and more schools found themselves short of the skills and facilities required. When the three Rs were no longer enough, broadcasting helped with 'Movement, Mime and Music', with 'Starting French' and other novelties. But the distinction between supplying a subject that would not otherwise exist and offering a course in a subject that already exists is uneasy, varying from school to school. With a shortage of teachers in some normal academic subjects, or with subjects radically changing in content and approach, broadcasting finds itself moving from the peripheral and optional areas of the curriculum into the disputed core itself. A course as complex and complete as 'Maths Today' (which includes preliminary broadcasts for teachers, teacher's guides, and broadcasts and work-sheets for the children) shows television in a central place in the school curriculum.

But such direct teaching in a subject makes heavy demands on the time and resources available for schools broadcasting, limited at present to what can be bought for about a shilling in the pound of BBC revenues. A series in a major curriculum subject has to run regularly through the year. Further, if it is popular, a demand then grows for a similar course covering succeeding years of the syllabus. Everyone learns a subject like maths, but most schools run only to one or two television receivers: please then, can the programme be repeated at least once? Radio broadcasts, cheaper to transmit, cheaper to receive, easy to record, present fewer problems.

The necessary limits on national television transmissions are such that Local Educational Television Centres have now started to form.[5] Their programmes are transmitted by cables linked directly to schools. Cost, therefore, confines the area of transmission, making ETV an urban possibility for the present. The first centre was at Glasgow; Plymouth and now London have followed suit. With six channels, London can far exceed in transmission time the sum of all present educational broadcasting in this country. More courses and frequent repeats become possible. Glasgow, with a two-channel cable, budgets a repeat of each major programme four or five times a week. There is sufficient time too when the school day is over to give an advance screening of some future programmes, so that the teachers need then no longer be as unprepared as the children are for what emerges from the box. A local ETV station allows easier 'feedback' and permits greater involvement on the part of local teachers. Programmes of local interest can be screened. Special needs can be met. For example, the number of immigrant children who need instruction in English may scarcely justify a national broadcast programme,[6] the annual intake in any one school may be quite small, the special skill needed to cope with them not available. In such circumstances, local ETV courses can provide an irreplaceable service. London's station will in time serve schools with some 400,000 children in them, training colleges for 19,000 teachers, and 3500 students in further education establishments. In total it will be the largest of all single stations. If we want to see educational television exploited to the full, however, we need to look, inevitably, at Japan. Nippon Hoso Kyokai, which operates through 1000 local committees, has 370 educational television stations, 120 using colour, and holds an annual conference in Tokyo each year for 17,000 teachers.[7]

Television can be even more local than ETV: some schools in America have their own studio linked to a number of classrooms. At present it is a 'fun thing', no more. The snag is not so much the capital cost of the equipment, nor maintenance, nor even the running cost, but the problem of making programmes. Teachers found it hard enough to write Dalton-style assignments, adjunctive to books; producing a television programme is less familiar, and much more complex. You cannot rub out mistakes easily as you go along – it is a live performance. Unless recording equipment can be afforded, the product then disappears into thin air. Closed-circuit television in a school is a choice example of a contemporary ailment – the provision of 'hardware' without sufficient technical support, training or time to exploit its possibilities.

Of course, the tantalizing possibilities of closed-circuit television might seem less remote were teachers not misled by the high quality of public broadcasts. National networks establish expectations which infect educational television, although some recent research (reinforced by extensive experience on the Hagerstrom circuit in Pennsylvania) suggests that the 'talking face' approach, although less exciting for viewers and producers, may be perfectly adequate for most teaching purposes and a lot more cost-effective.[8] A further step towards the simplification, and therefore the credibility, of the medium for use within a school has been the development of a television teaching console that the teacher can handle entirely himself – even if at first sight it seems to require exceptional feats of co-ordination.[9] Despite such ingenuity, it remains the case that the cost and the labours involved in closed-circuit television are disproportionate to the requirements of a single school. It flourishes best in universities where finances are more ample, numbers larger, and mass lecturing commonplace.[10] In theory, closed-circuit television in schools might usefully save the wasteful duplication of instruction to parallel classes and multiply the effectiveness of a teacher with rare skills, thus easing our staff shortages;[11] in practice, unless a school is committed to extensive television teaching and fully equipped and organized to that end, it is hard to justify timetabling enough surplus time for the exacting task of programme preparation. If preparation time is allowed, then the cost argues for transmission to a larger constituency than a single school.

It is unnecessary here to dilate upon the impact of radio or television broadcasting. We have ample first-hand experience of it. It provides excitement in our lives, and at its best enrichment too. We know we can learn from a broadcast programme, but doubts begin to gather when we consider television as a means of regular direct teaching. How much of the total business of learning can be effectively carried on by television? Is the quantity sufficient to off-set the restrictions it imposes? Is it so superior to other media that it justifies the cost? Normally, of course, television is only a part of the whole process of learning. What benefit derives from mixing it with other media? For example, research based on the universities of Nebraska, Wisconsin and Michigan produced the surprising conclusion that 'correspondence study alone appears to produce better results than are secured when correspondence study is combined with television or motion pictures'.[12] The value of television presumably depends on the nature of the results intended:

We have no grounds for expecting people to perform better in a verbal test after seeing television than after receiving a radio broadcast. We might expect them to show greater achievement in tests based on the pictorial content of the communication alone. If, however, one eliminates all verbal, and perhaps most reasoning elements from a communication, or a test of achievement, one is confined within very narrow limits, and the use of a visual mode of communication may not often be justified.[13]

Plainly what we normally mean by 'learning' implies a process that is extended, active, sequential, ordered, considered. The written word serves rational and sustained argument better than speech can and far better than pictures, however initially stimulating these may be, or however useful to illuminate a particular issue. K. V. Bailey, Senior Education Officer of the BBC, has pointed out the difference:

The most appropriate and convenient way to make a detailed and analytical study of a range of documents is for the eye and mind to move at their own pace, and for students to transfer attention at will from one document to another for purposes of comparison and cross-reference. Educational broadcasting, on the other hand, and particularly television, is created by building into one intense but transitory experience a sequence of images, aural and visual, derived from a multiplicity of sources and conceived in a mode essentially different from that of the printed document. The type of attention which is brought to it by the learner is different in kind from the attention needed to follow the message of a book.[14]

It is, of course, precisely the rational and sequential nature of traditional learning that Marshall McLuhan rails against.[15] Television is a 'cool' medium; print is 'hot'. The terms are derived from jazz. The point of the comparison appears to be this: first, just as the listener to 'cool' jazz 'fills in' between occasional notes and beats, so the viewer must construct whole images out of a scatter of light points into a picture;[16] second, just as the jazz addict is wholly involved in the music, so too the television viewer responds emotionally, indeed subliminally, not at the shallow level above the neck-tie, but deep down, well below the belt. Charlotte Mason, as we have seen, thought it a singular advantage of learning independently from books that the method pre-

vented any undue invoking of emotions; but she lived in a less
fevered age. The peculiar power of film or television, combining
words, music, pictures in an artificial frame that excludes the distractions of the real world, makes these media marvellously,
sometimes dangerously, suitable for stimulation, but relatively
weak or superfluous for ordered and reasoned learning. As Ray-
mond Fletcher put it (though unfairly perhaps to books)
'Images open the mind to impressions. It is cold print that fixes
them.' [17]

This may help to explain why television has made so much
more progress in primary schools than in secondary schools.
Basic skills can be learnt by allowing a child to find his own path,
with a teacher's guidance, through discrete materials and experiences available to him, but in the secondary school, in most academic subjects, we require a boy to follow an externally organized sequence of work on which we may subsequently examine
him. The rational mode of learning bulks large – the kind the
'Gutenberg technology' suits. Thus, although some secondary-
school broadcast programmes are essentially self-contained (such
as music programmes), and others require only light follow-up
(an impromptu discussion, say, after a talk to sixth formers), any
attempt at direct teaching in a major academic subject quickly
extends to teachers' pamphlets, pupils' pamphlets, workbooks,
suggestions for exercises, and the like. As the part of printing
grows larger and the part played by the actual broadcast smaller,
the teacher begins to wonder if it is all worth it.

The cost is not to be measured in cash alone. As a start, the
teacher loses his treasured freedom to choose his own syllabus.
Then, unless the full text of the broadcast is published (print
again) or the programme pre-broadcast, the teacher does not
quite know what is coming. Unfamiliarity can be unnerving and
it may make effective follow-up difficult. Television tends to
come between a teacher and his class. It is a much closer substitute for teaching than, say, a book, and a much more glamorous
one. It takes over one of the most enjoyable parts of the teacher's
trade – the lively exposition of new material. Indeed, observation confirms that many teachers after a broadcast, whether from
doubt about its efficiency or from habit, run through it all over
again in their own words.[18] Above all, broadcasting imposes an

absolute lock-step, not only in its content but in its inexorable pace. The larger the receiving audience for a programme, the worse the danger that many will find the experiences described irrelevant and the speed of instruction awkward. The programmes in Glasgow ETV's French course, for example, run 'at the rate at which pupils participating in the national pilot scheme covered the work'. The familiar worries about the lock-step of the classroom apply, then, with yet greater force to broadcast teaching. The broadcaster cannot adjust as a teacher can to a particular class, and so far there has been no prospect of running alternative streamed broadcasts.

Such criticisms are not meant to deny television's educational role, only to try to define its probable limits in secondary schools. In a university, for example, collecting the more or less 'homogeneous ability level grouping' recommended for effective instruction from a single source presents no great problem.[19] Entrance exams are set in order to provide just such a working homogeneity. Secondary schools have to deal with a much more comprehensive range. There is no doubt of television's ability to entertain and absorb the young: it's the world's best baby-sitter. As such it merits a place in any educational budget but at secondary level, alas, only a small place. Indeed, television's astounding power, its ability to annihilate time and space, to encapsulate and emasculate experience, leads some to fear, as does Boorstin, that it may undermine our sensitivity to what is real and our will to cope with it.[20] The open mouth may lead to the slack jaw. Often the book, in using weaker images, prompts where television swamps, and by forcing us to animate dead symbols involves a more active, individual and complete version of the man than Marshall McLuhan would allow.

For all such philosophic doubts, we would not choose to be without those instructive and amusing scenes in foreign language television series, the superb productions of plays, those vivid expositions of recondite scientific mysteries, those informed discussions of everyday problems. But, pending some radical change in our concept of what secondary education is about, the stimulus television marvellously supplies will remain peripheral, however exciting, and the teacher and the book central.[21] It follows that where the book and teacher combination works least well

– for example, among those who cannot read, or whose verbal comprehension is far below their visual comprehension, or when teachers are unqualified or totally unavailable – then television has a role of particular importance to play.

In more ordinary circumstances, however, whatever our views of its proper place, the use of television is limited by the available broadcasting time (very little when set against the many subjects at many levels taught in secondary schools for many hours each week) and by the rigidities of timetabling which broadcasting imposes. These limits of quantity and timing will be eased when recording vision becomes about as inexpensive as recording sound alone, especially if there is an accompanying reform of esoteric copyright restrictions, ignorance of which – real or feigned – at present turns many a masters' commonroom into a smugglers' den. The cost of some video-tape recording systems is no longer wholly prohibitive for schools, and a much cheaper device is rumoured which will allow easy recording from a television receiver and re-play over it.

But the interesting feature of all such recording devices is that they make the process of broadcasting itself less important. Taped programmes are simply films using a different sort of projector. They might just as well be produced without ever being broadcast at all, and could be published like books. The BBC's Radio and Television Enterprises is an organization for promoting the secondary use of materials already broadcast, and at the Commonwealth Broadcasting Conference a recommendation was accepted that, whenever a company's Charter allowed, contracts should include a clause allowing the sale of commissioned materials never broadcast at all. For education, secondary use may then tend to become primary, and the publishing and recording departments more important than the transmission studios.

Herein perhaps lies the most significant lesson to be learnt from broadcasting. Bemused by the technical paraphernalia of transmission we have missed a more general point. *In order to broadcast we maintain people professionally to compose teaching materials for use in the schools.* Might such an arrangement of supporting centres be equally useful and justified if the materials were in permanent form and conveyed prosaically by post and van, rather than ephemera despatched through the air?

In television and radio we have examined a domesticated branch of educational technology: altogether less familiar is the possible role of the teaching machine and that ultimate in teaching machines, the computer.

The theoretical possibilities of the computer in education are extensive indeed.[22] For our purposes, we may consider three of its chief faculties: it can calculate, it can compare, it can present. Our model of the computer can be taken to consist of an arithmetic unit, a store and a terminal, all linked through a governing processor.

The very word 'computer' reminds us of its primary function of calculating at lightning speed. Instructions from the learner sitting at the terminal pass to the processor; this switches the arithmetic unit to appropriate activity and the result is presented at the terminal. In its store, the computer can hold great quantities of information. The particular item required by the learner can be summoned by the processor from the store and presented to him at the terminal. But the computer can, in addition, make rapid comparisons. A message from the terminal can be compared for common elements with a single item – for example, a correct answer – or with numerous items, the processor scanning them rapidly to pick out those with the required common elements. These powers of calculation, presentation and comparison can be combined in a complexity of ways that offer tempting prospects in education.

Since our concern is with methods of learning we need only glance in passing at the computer's use in controlling the plant and resources that make up the costly business of a nation's education. The computer can record pay-roll information and help with budgeting; register the movement of commodities used in schools and devise inventories; store statistics about children, teachers, buildings and income, thereby facilitating the planned use of resources. It can store children's scores on nationally administered tests, making allowance for variation in age, correlate the results with previous scores or teachers' ratings, take into account variations between different types of school. Thus, norms can be established bringing a fair measure of objectivity to an extremely complex situation.

The value of the computer in the business of education will serve as a reminder of how powerful a tool it can be. Plainly, instruction in its use will increasingly penetrate the curriculum of the secondary school. Indeed, the Royal Liberty School in Romford has raised funds to acquire its own computer. It is a magnificent enterprise, but not likely to be repeated elsewhere, for even when the machine is made available to other local schools the total costs are prohibitive. Less formidable is the sort of arrangement to be found in America at Phillips Academy, Andover, and some other schools, where a single terminal in the school is connected 'on-line' with a commercial computer on a time-sharing, rental account. Least costly of all is an alliance between a school and local industry for 'off-line' facilities. At Sevenoaks School boys learn 'Fortran', type their instructions on a computer programming desk (which costs £350) and send the coded tapes to the Marley Tile Company. These are processed free of charge on a sophisticated computer, using marginal, 'unemployed' time. Similar instructional use of the computers now being installed for managerial purposes by county authorities has been proposed.

But how can the computer serve the more general process of education in our schools and not just education in computing? A convenient division is conventionally made between computer-managed instruction (CMI) and computer-aided instruction (CAI). In *managing* instruction the computer helps a teacher with decisions about who should learn what, how, where, when and with whom; in *aiding* instruction it conveys appropriate information direct to the learner – in a word, it teaches.

One of our instruments for managing instruction is the timetable. To reduce complications we collect the units it deals with into bundles. The minutes of the day are bundled into forty-minute 'periods'; the content of successive periods becomes a 'syllabus' in a 'subject' for a whole year; the children are lumped into 'classes' of thirty or so for all (or almost all) their periods; the periods for a particular class in a particular subject are assigned

to one master. These bundles we assemble in a composite con-
tainer of appropriate, manageable size called a 'school'. Rough
simplicities of this kind have been dealt with traditionally
in a timetable constructed once a year by a senior master armed
with graph paper, a well-sharpened pencil and a clean rubber.
Such days we must now regard as primitive or golden according
to temperament, for each customary bundle in the timetable is
now coming undone.

We can best see the new complex timetable at work in America
where 'flexible scheduling' based usually on fifteen minute
'modules', team teaching, and a wide range of courses, has now
arrived in a number of large high schools. A further dimension
is added where the attempt is made to use the school over four
terms or 'quarters' in the year rather than three. In the high
schools in Atlanta, Georgia,

the curriculum developed for the four-quarter plan offers 710
courses, most of which can be taken out of any established sequence.
Students can now choose among forty-eight English courses of one-
quarter length, where previously there were only five year-long
courses.[23]

Yet even the 'one-quarter' course seems unnecessarily restrictive. At Brookhurst junior high school, for example, each child
is presented with his own shifting individual timetable every
day.

   In such circumstances the computer becomes an essential tool
for timetabling. Of course, someone still has to do a lot of
preparatory work. The computer has to be fed the requirements
and all the restrictions before it can present the possible alternatives. In composing a timetable the old way, the senior master
notices while pencilling in Latin for III alpha on Thursday afternoon that he has already got them down for a period of maths to
follow, and decides he is lining up rather a gruesome afternoon
for them – and for old Hardy who would have to take them, in
the notoriously stuffy Room 7, after a heavy morning's teaching
and immediately after lunch. But the computer, if it is to solve
such subtle problems, must be programmed in advance with the
necessary limiting conditions. More probably, a number of

clashes will be noticed on the early print-outs and the timetable will then be run through several times before the last of the foreseen, programmed criteria can be met. Even then, some subsequent alterations may have to be made locally – no easy task when the timetable is so complex, and when no one has that intimate knowledge of its details possessed by the master who has laboriously compiled it by hand. Despite these problems, computer timetabling, such as that pioneered in the appropriately named GASP project at Stanford University, seems practical and likely to stay.[24]

Altogether less convincing, however, is the attempt to carry computer timetabling beyond the GASP stage (which retains many of the conventional units like classes and annual syllabuses) to extremes of minute particularization in 'daily demand computer scheduling'. Leaving aside one's doubts about the educational advantages of such flexibility, the burden on a team of teachers who are supposed each evening to 'instruct' the computer about which children they want for this purpose or that on the following day is severe. Sometimes the 'demands' of teachers for certain children conflict. The computer duly says so; but the predicament is not discovered until the next day begins and hurried extemporization becomes necessary. But the real problem is not so much the timetabling of each individual, but checking that he is where the timetable says he ought to be. The larger the school the more difficult it becomes to deal retrospectively with absentees. The multiple re-grouping required to allow extensive choice between subjects, the anonymity of a large school, the administrative complexity that any attempt at devolution breeds, have led to the problem of 'internal truancy'. This exists even in conventionally timetabled, large comprehensive schools; when an ambitious programme of 'daily demand' is superimposed, then, as a disarmingly frank boy guide at Brookhurst Junior High revealed, opportunities for 'getting lost' become spectacular. Clearly, the computer can be set to play no end of complicated scheduling tunes: the doubt is our mortal ability to keep up with the dance.

There is a chore yet more burdensome than timetabling which a computer may help us with and one that affects us all – the chore of marking. The more conscientious the teacher, the more

time-consuming marking becomes. Whatever our doubts about
the use of scarce time for this purpose, secondary education runs
to a great deal of testing, correcting, and periodic marking as a
sometimes dubious measure of achievement, a recognition of
effort, a check on labour done, an assessment of progress in relation to expected standard, an artificial inducement. The rigours
of marking have been relaxed in many schools in recent years, but
so long as secondary schooling involves compulsory labour, so
long as it leads into competitive alternative occupations, marks
will presumably remain as a wage and a testimonial. Already in
America, and in some degree in this country, the computer is
being used for centralized public examining, and there is no
reason but cost why it should not handle day-to-day testing
within a school as well.

There are limits, however, on the style of testing possible. A
computer can compare any given answer with a model answer
held in store; it can act, then, like boys in a classroom being used
to mark one another's answers by reference to the correct version
on a blackboard. Such tests are often called 'one-word tests'.
Masters know all too well the problems that crop up the moment
any latitude in the wording of an answer is allowed. 'Please, sir,
can I give him half a mark for Elizebeth with an "e"?' 'Sir, Johnson's put "The Virgin Queen".' 'What about just "the Queen of
England", sir?', and so on.

A computer can be programmed to accept certain foreseen
alternatives, but cost sharply limits the number. If the computer refuses to accept 'Elizabeth' in a number of mis-spellings
or in various verbal disguises, it acts like (and is often criticized
for being) the most mechanical and stupid of martinets. There
are two ways of easing such rigidities: first, the computer can be
programmed to scan an answer for important elements only,
ignoring reversals in letter and word order or intervening letters
and words in a paraphrase; second, the permitted replies can be
limited at source. In the jargon, this process is referred to as
avoiding 'freely constructed responses' and using 'multiple
choice' instead. If boys taking the test do not simply guess at an
answer but have to choose between, say, (1) Mary, Queen of
Scots, (2) Queen Mary, (3) Elizabeth, (4) Titania, we shall avoid
complications over spelling and synonyms and paraphrases al-

together. We generally – and rightly – connect 'multiple choice' with petty routine and dull testing; but its use in skilled hands in some American College Board examinations, or in experimental papers in O-level biology, physics and maths (even of the more thoughtful Nuffield and 'new maths' kind) and now even in English, reveals the possibility of considerable subtleties. Few would think this sort of examining enough, but it may be useful as part of a whole which includes 'freely constructed' essays and other discursive answers. The increasing elaboration involved in trying to ensure fairness in the standards applied by one examiner and another, or one examining board and another, and, above all, the ominous pressure of the growing number of candidates, ensures 'multiple choice' and the computer a significant place in public examining, and, in time, in a school's internal testing too.

Although most boys see a test as an inquisition, a master may use it to discover not so much whether they have done what he set but if they understand it. In the light of his knowledge of the boys, he may decide, of those who fail, that one was careful but slow, a second had missed the point, a third had got there but had been careless. Ideally, these three 'failures' need different treatment: the first should be given less to do, the second needs a new explanation of the work, the third can be set to repeat it. Similar distinctions may be drawn among those who pass the test. Alas, a schoolmaster generally has time to do little more than set a required minimum standard for the whole class and to consign all who fail to dull repetition in detention until they satisfy or exhaust him.

Now, the computer could help with the task of setting alternative work to meet the varying needs of those above and below the average. Having marked the test, it could record each boy's scores, compare them with his past performance and show which boys' results were out of character. It could indicate just where each boy had gone astray. It could store information – what pages in what books – about suitable remedial work. This more sophisticated sort of computer-managed instruction is part of Project PLAN in Palo Alto, California. Special courses in maths, world history, languages, science and social studies are being compiled for children in the early high-school age groups by some forty full-time writers and thirty-five teachers on annual secondment.

Schools in thirteen districts in California, Pittsburg and New York have begun to use the courses. The children take tests roughly every fortnight; these are scored by a computer in Iowa City, from which the results, cumulative records and recommendations can be gathered on demand by the teachers. 'The program', says the director, Dr Flanagan, 'could function without a computer but it would be more expensive and less responsive.' Similarly, the IPI (Individually Prescribed Instruction) Project at Pittsburg has developed materials for elementary schools and hopes with the computer's help to guide each child along a path and at a speed appropriate to his individual needs.

But instead of 'telling' a teacher, on the basis of periodic tests and cumulative records, what this boy or that should do next, the computer might itself present each appropriate stage to the boy. When this direct communication occurs, computer-managed instruction gives way to computer-assisted instruction. At the simplest level the computer may take the learner patiently through simple routine *drill* and then present him with suitable tasks as *practice* in what he has learnt. A further stage is for the learner to *revise* with the computer so that from his results in a subsequent general test the computer can make a *diagnosis* and a *prescription* of an appropriate cure. The computer can then provide *tutoring*, presenting material in linear programme form, one frame after another, or vary the branch taken according to the feedback of answers it gets. Practice in routine problem solving can be greatly extended by *simulation*. Problem situations too complex and costly to establish in physical form can be represented on the computer and solutions tested which would otherwise be too time-consuming to attempt. In dealing with such simulations the computer can be used for all the necessary *calculations*. In addition the operator, when he has decided what facts and figures he needs to arrive at a solution, can cull them from the computer's store – a process called *inquiry*. Suppose, however, he has no specific problem and simply browses, then the computer assists in *exploration*.

Examples of the more complex elements in this hierarchy of the computer's potentialities occur in universities and in industry: can they be found in the schools? In America, the handouts certainly lead one to expect so.[25] Visitors are urged to see

CAI operated by Stanford University at the Brentwood School
in California. 'The Stanford–Brentwood Computer-Aided Instruction Laboratory is the first to be an integral part of a public
school' says the publicity sheet. But 'integral part' turns out to
mean that a special laboratory has been built which can cope
with only sixteen children at a time and requires the presence
of computer technicians and specially trained teachers. In its
earlier days exclusively, and still principally, the computer has
been used to conduct simple arithmetic drills. The child sits at
the terminal, and having identified himself, is presented with a
suitable problem teletyped on the paper before him. Add 17 and
26. If he answers 43 the machine assures him he is c-o-r-r-e-c-t.
Recent modifications enable the answers to be dialled. Alternatively, in certain problems, should the child type 'blue' when
'red' is right, the computer can play a pre-recorded tape: 'Pay
attention, now, you know very well that the blue cars have been
eliminated. Try again.' Similarly slides can be selected and pro-
jected on a screen or on a cathode ray tube which enables the
child to make answers by pointing with a light pen to the appropriate spot.

In a remedial reading programme, still confined to the CAI
laboratory in Cambridge, Massachusetts, a text for comprehension is displayed on a slide projector while related questions and
answers, normally of a yes/no kind, are answered on the teletype; or a word is presented on the teletype and the child tries
to select another with similar meaning from a given list. Simple
and attractive simulations have been tried out on 5th grade
children at for example, the Mohansic School in New York.
Project SEARCH (Sequential Enrichment and Accelerated Reinforcement programme for Children) aims to give compensatory education to infants with deprived backgrounds; but a
visitor from the Schools Council found both sad and unconvincing the sight of a three-year-old Negro child being fed, by
visual displays on a computer, with the ideas, vocabulary and
'experience' a middle-class child might derive from walks and
talks with his parents.

The difficulties to be surmounted if computer-assisted instruc-
ion is to spread in secondary schools are formidable indeed.
Computer hardware, however apt already for calculation or

management, is singularly clumsy for instructional purposes. The terminal (the man–machine interface) at present requires tedious, limited print-out, or the costly maintaining of an image on a cathode-ray tube, or photographing the image so that it can be seen on a slide viewer or turned into an emprint for the student to keep. These clumsy restraints may one day be eased by the plasma tube devised in prototype by Professor D. L. Bitzer in Urbana, Illinois. At the moment, moreover, the language of communication with a computer is very stilted. Usually it can accept only short answers in a closely defined vocabulary so that these can be matched with the models held in store. Colloquial speech is likely to present a problem for many years; even more intractable are the subtleties of intonation and facial message that qualify ordinary speech.

If, then, for the time being, the computer can sensibly be used for instruction only where the problems are such that the solutions are in the form of definite answers and not value judgements, and do not require a freely constructed response,[26] how large a part can it play in teaching in school, and at what price? Certainly at present the cost is very high. Actual estimates for hook-up to existing computers on a time-sharing basis range from 24 to 43 dollars an hour; a speculative estimate given to Dr Oettinger was for 7.50 dollars an hour [27] – but this excludes the cost of personnel, overheads, programmes and presumes a 'high-utilization' by students working on a shift system. Yet even the optimistic and strictly basic cost of 7.50 dollars an hour is much more than that adaptive, responsible, fully programmed, mobile gadget called a teacher costs, even in America. When the Radio Corporation of America generously offers computer link-up facilities at 50 dollars per student per year we have to bear in mind the 4 dollars per student per year spent on textbooks.[28] If the costs of the hardware oppress, so do those of the software, the animating programmes. For a computer is not a tool in the ordinary sense, adapted to a particular purpose, but as blank, and therefore as fundamental, as a piece of iron. Its function, its 'shape', as well as the details of its performance, depend upon the quality of the programme which guides it. Designing a programme is in consequence a skilled, lengthy and costly task. A working party set up by the National Council for Educational

Technology, with Professor J. Black as chairman, having compared the cost of conventional teaching with that of computer-
assisted instruction, and taken account of increasing salaries on
the one hand and falling computer costs on the other, concluded:

These figures suggest that for large systems, and for large systems
only, computer-based learning can be expected to become steadily
more competitive. Further, present trends indicate no sudden break-
through. Projecting the figures forward it is nearly forty years before the costs of large system computer-based learning are expected
to become equal to the general level of costs of conventional secondary school education for the lower forms [that is, up to the sixth
form].[29]

But it is not cost alone which makes computer-assisted instruction more immediately promising elsewhere than in the
schools. The use of the computer in advanced scientific and
technical education promises a prompt return in increased pro-
ductivity and wealth. Again, in further education the computer
may offer a style of learning scarcely less personal than the mass
lecturing and machine marking already the familiar lot of the
growing army of students. Above all, 'education' and 'instruction' more closely coincide in the years up to a first degree or
diploma than ever they are likely to in the school, where the purposes of education are numerous, confused and often conflicting.

When, therefore, we consider the use of the computer in the
process of instruction in schools we need to ask not just what
the computer is able to do but what it should be allowed to do.
The computer can keep detailed records of a child's progress
through a programme and of all his tests – but shall we then be
submerged in a blizzard of information, struggling to perceive
its drift; and ought everything to be taken down in evidence
against a child? Perhaps human forgetfulness is an essential part
of human hope, and human inefficiency an essential part of
human freedom. Again, the computer can 'individualize' instruction, allowing useful variations, impossible in the classroom, in
pace and course content – but is such 'individualization' spurious
and dangerous, if, like the 'personalizing' of motor cars, it is confined to selection among previously manufactured components?
The computer can handle instructional programmes which in-

clude a large number of alternative branches – but will the very high cost of producing such programmes tend to result in an undesirable lack of choice, a dangerous uniformity? The computer handles programmes constructed so that definite answers are possible, point by point – and in order to exploit it, shall we be tempted increasingly to apply those mechanistic views of learning already prevalent? 'It is not,' says Hannah Arendt, 'that Behaviorism is wrong, but that it might become true.' Is there a danger that we shall resort to a sort of academic artificial insemination – more efficient in its primary purpose, but without the redolences of love?

Yet it would be a pity to end this brief glance at the use of the computer as a machine for teaching with a dystopian wince. We can be confident that for some considerable time the computer in secondary education will be usefully and safely confined, by sheer cost, to the business of management – whether of the system at large, or of examinations or timetables or individual records – and, within the classroom, to practice in mathematical computation. The first intrusions into direct teaching are likely to be limited to the sixth form and to those subjects, such as maths for non-specialists and computer programming, in which the urgency of the need and the shortage of staff may make the computer a valuable ally quite soon.[30] For the rest any extensive general use lies in a far-off future.

For a picture of those days to come when computer-assisted instruction becomes commonplace we may turn to Oettinger's pamphlet *A Vision of Technology and Education*.[31] It is inevitably 'a dated vision', both in the sense that it needs a distant date set upon it, being 'a vision of technological possibility deliberately unclouded by economic or temporal realism'; and dated in that it is a projection of present notions, whereas the actual process of evolution will ensure that 'if the vision is to come true at all ... [it] will deviate radically from its present innocent state'. With these qualifications, here is what Oettinger foretells:

In the first tableau of our vision, we see that it is technically possible for sound, pictures and even objects stored at appropriate centers to be available with the greatest of ease and negligible cost at innumerable local points of access, first perhaps in schools, libraries or factories and only a little later, as seen from our visionary perspective, in every home. The cost of getting them there is one of the things that should give us pause, but potential means, safely short of involving extrasensory perception, are now at our command. Once this much is granted, an entirely new look at the means for education is possible....

In the next tableau we see individual consoles linked to the common information pool serving as the basic tool for virtually all formal education The key idea is that, by pushing buttons or otherwise signalling from a suitable terminal, a student has access to:

1. The catalogs of great libraries, hence access to their collections.
2. The catalogs of new video tape or film libraries, hence access to the collections which include recorded lessons on specialized topics (possibly in the manner of an illustrated encyclopedia) and also source materials such as records of significant contemporary events, of outstanding dramatic productions, of clinical recordings (perhaps of a difficult operation particularly well performed in a leading hospital) and so on.
3. Teaching programs of the kind already in widespread experimental use.
4. Tools to aid symbol manipulation and concept formation such as numerical and algebraic manipulators, dictionaries, thesauri, editing programs, etc.

The teaching programs give routine directions through the maze of materials.... The local teacher gives guidance, perhaps after having mastered the materials himself as part of a machine-aided program of continuing education. Indeed, guidance is all important since the individual has greater responsibility for his own education than he has had in the past; the teacher's role thus becomes far more humanistic and far less mechanical than it is now.

The manipulative tools are very important both for education and for research. At present, visual display systems are useful in helping men understand the results of experiments or calculations; they may be used by students of introductory differential equations to generate direction fields and thus to give immediate insight into the global character of the solutions to those equations; they may be used by research scientists, perhaps to make visible various proposed structures for complex organic molecules and to view these from arbitrary orientations and across arbitrary sections. Such tools enable the easy confrontation of model and reality, as in the visual superimpositions of calculated streamlines on those in a real fluid flowing around a real obstacle in a real tank. To those who have observed them, such confrontations have dramatic immediacy and perspicuity. There is here a means for expanding man's consciousness and giving him a new way of grasping ideas that is especially valuable where scientists must use intuition and complex calculations to study phenomena increasingly remote from what is immediately evident to the unaided senses.

The system we see also provides expert help for both ends of the ability scale. Special materials are available for the very advanced or the particularly slow.... Students who are now at the low end of the scale but who do have intellectual potential could be reached by the new techniques. Such students have been shown to respond well to individualization of education, especially when personal contact with a teacher keeps learning from being a fearful experience. The teacher, released from routine chores for guidance activities, can provide much more individual attention than now....

Such an approach fundamentally changes the entire teaching process. To the extent that teaching by rote is necessary, it can be handled by the programmed teaching devices incorporated in the system. But far beyond this, people can learn to use library resources of all types and can master the manipulative tools put at their disposal. The system helps them remember both the tracks they and others pursued while browsing and the problem-solving techniques they developed for their own individual purposes....

One immediate interesting consequence of these visions is that they leave no obvious intellectual need for the separation of children in grades or for other forms of lock-step. The child can progress through the system as rapidly as he is able or wishes to.

Another interesting feature of the system is that it relieves the school of what is the bulk of its concern today, namely the abstract and the verbal. The school may concentrate instead on the concrete, the social and the human ... the meeting, the rubbing and the blending of the individuals who must later take places as partners in society.... The school, free to concentrate on guidance and counseling, may also emphasize such concrete matters as laboratory exercises in the sciences or student productions of plays, poetry readings, and discussions of books in the humanities. Picture the student who has seen video lectures on certain physical principles presenting himself to the laboratory instructor and claiming that he is ready to perform a certain experiment. This is one of the points at which the teacher can check the student's progress since, if the student fumbles miserably in the laboratory, he can be sent back for further study at the machine. Furthermore, the student's progress might well determine the path of his future inquiries into the machine pool of knowledge. ...

The difference between being in and out of school is reduced since industrial plants have access to the same information as the education system. ... An easy flow back and forth between school and work is conceivable for people of all ages.

This electronic vision is startling in detail but strikingly familiar in general design. We have heard before this talk of freeing the learner from constant teaching, of allowing him to work at materials supplied while 'the local teacher gives guidance' and provides 'more individual attention than is possible now'. The materials envisaged, although handled with a new dexterity by the computer, are not strange – ordinary print, tape, films and 'teaching programmes of the kind already in widespread experimental use'. Such materials allow us to match varying requirements, including those of the 'very advanced or the particularly slow'. Gone is the necessity 'for the separation of children in grades or for other forms of lock-step'.

These ingredients are the very ones we have come across in differing measure in past and present attempts to modify class teaching. Their re-appearance in a futuristic vision may therefore appropriately end our browse through possible recipes for learning. This particular recipe did not work very well when it was first tried; that one does not quite meet our needs; much of a third lies beyond our present means. All the same, can we from among them concoct something practical, palatable and nourishing with which to feed the minds and spirits of children now?

Part Three
Resolution

Chapter Nine
Systems of Learning

We can conceive of a number of different systems of learning being used in secondary schools. Foremost among them is the teacher-based system familiar to us all in the classroom. Other systems already tried here or abroad are these: book based, book-and-boy based, assignment based, programmed learning based, correspondence based, radio and television based, computer based. At first sight, it seems a daunting complexity, but we may find the appearance of conflict between these systems misleading. The passionate exclusiveness of rivals may be a measure of a basic similarity, just as snobbery is most intense where differences between incomes are small. What essential elements have these systems of learning in common which distinguish them all from conventional teaching?

We can start by noting that whatever system is used in a school the teacher is assumed to be present. The most extreme exponents of programmed learning threatened to reduce the teacher to a cipher, but with regard to schools this was 1984 stuff and scarcely conceivable. Teachers are plainly of critical importance in caring for and about children; the inspiration, encouragement, control, guidance they provide matters profoundly. Further, no one but the teacher on the spot can perceive and supply the particular needs of a particular child at a particular moment. Neither the teacher's pastoral nor his tutorial functions can be replaced. When we talk about alternative systems of learning, then, we are asking only where, principally, the burden of *instruction* should rest.

A further similarity between most systems of learning lies in the resources used. A teacher in action is not just a fount of words. The most austere is likely to employ a blackboard and books. To these some teachers now add, from time to time, broadcasts, records, slides, film-loops, overhead projector transparencies, films. Indeed, the modern teacher, as he emerges in conferences and in articles, is expected to achieve prodigies of co-ordination, busking his restive audience like a one-man band.

The essential difference, then, between the familiar teacher-based system and the others we have considered does not reside in the simple contrast between 'chalk and talk' on the one hand and sophisticated media on the other; nor yet in the supposition that, whereas teaching requires teachers, programmed instruction, or teaching machines, even those as elaborate as the computer, dispense with them. We can begin to work back to the crux, the dividing point, through the words we habitually use. Thus, 'I am taught' by a teacher; but 'I learn' from a book (or a Dalton assignment, or a piece of programmed instruction, or a computer). Of course, 'I learn' also from a teacher and 'I am taught' by a book, but normally boys will ask 'who teaches us next period' and 'what do we have to learn tonight for prep'. The syntax reminds us that we have shifted from the passive 'I am taught' to the active 'I learn'.

For this sense of activity to be possible, the things I am learning from must be there when I need them. They must have some measure of permanence. Whether contrived or natural they must provide a collection of physically existing, relatively stable objects from which I can learn. On this essential common ground, improbably and doubtless to their mutual dismay, would stand Rousseau and Charlotte Mason, Montessori and Skinner.[1] Whether we are learning from raw nature or from the specially designed *kindergarten*, generously from books or efficiently from programmed instruction, we are learning from a material enviroment rather than being taught by the immaterial words of a person.

Yet although convenience may dictate that a learning environment should consist substantially of books and other materials, the objects in it can be diverse and certainly include children and adults, specific events and happenings, as well as timeless materials. *What matters is the learner's relationship to them* – whether the boy is normally cast in the active or the passive role, whether, with due guidance, he can move independently or is constantly led among his resources for learning, whether in general he goes to them or they come at him.

Translated into a secondary school, the difference is substan-

tial. When we are taught, pace, style, content, place, time, all become fixed. Because the source of instruction is impermanent,
because the teacher's words die away at once, we must be gathered
at fixed times in fixed places, be silent and still, to catch those
words, and no others, in the manner and at the speed at which
they occur. But the situation is changed if a teacher's words, and
those of some other teachers dealing with the same topic, are
recorded in print or tape or film. Since we might simply inflict
the recorded teacher, in place of the speaking teacher, upon the
whole class of children together, it is clear that the permanence
of learning materials is not in itself a sufficient condition of
greater individual freedom. But it is the necessary condition,
for when we use permanent materials, and only then, can we
ease the constraints of time and place, of uniform content, style
and speed of work, implicit in being taught.

Further, if children are to work more actively, then the objects in the learning environment must not only be permanent
but comprehensible. Reluctantly, even the most ardent exponents
of learning from the natural environment concede the need for
some interpretation. But here we must be wary. The ample, more
or less continuous interpretation of the world around us, and
of books describing that world, is precisely what we mean by
teaching. We shall be back where we started if the physical constituents of our environment have to be uniformly dissolved
into a teacher's words before we can learn from them. Generally it is the world and the books that must 'speak' to us, not the
teacher. For a shift from teaching to learning to occur, then, the
resources should, for the most part, not only be material and
accessible, but such that the learner does not need to be led
through them point by point by a teacher.

When we move from theory to practice we shall have to deal
not with stark extremes but with a continuum. Neither constant listening to a teacher nor entire self-instruction is a real
alternative. All the same, for the sake of clarity we can order the
muddle of arrangements for learning around two poles: at the
one we have a system in which everything is arranged to permit
children to catch the perishable words that fall from a teacher's
lips – books or other materials having an intermittent, ancillary
role; at the other we have a number of systems, varying in de-

tail, in which children learn chiefly from materials or from one another, directly and independently – the interpretation of the teacher having an intermittent if vital role. Systems of this sort inclde PNEU, Differential Partnership, the Dalton Plan, correspondence courses, programmed instruction and computer-assisted learning. All these are made from the same cloth frayed out into different threads or, in the case of the computer, over-laid with the dazzle of electronic millinery. For brevity we can group all these systems together and, since they rely on collec tions of learning situations and materials, call them 'resource based' or, alternatively, 'package based'.

If we use 'teacher based' and 'resource based' as our two polarities, where does broadcasting fit in? A broadcast can be an item of enrichment or a stimulus in either system, but our concern is not with broadcasts as a subsidiary part but with broadcasting as a principal method, a system of learning in its own right. As such, normally, it has the same evanescent quality as learning from a teacher. Boys have to be gathered together in groups at set times in set places to attend to what is said from a single source of instruction. Indeed, all the boys in each listening class in all the listening schools constitute an army in step, not just scattered platoons. We may ease this mass timetabling imposition by re-broadcasting the same programme quite frequently as closed-circuit stations do, but to release individual boys to learn actively we should need to record the course so that each can work through it at his own pace. Recorded radio and television broadcasts with accompanying printed materials have begun to appear on sale. They become at this point 'packages'. It matters little whether in the first instance such courses were broadcast or not. They might equally have been compiled as packages in the first place. The shape of broadcasting is varied, protean: it does not alterthe essential polarity of teacher based package based we have proposed.

When we try to assess the possible merits of resource-, or package-based learning, in the contemporary secondary school we run into a difficulty at the very start. PNEU, Differential Partnership, the Dalton Plan, correspondence courses, programmed instruction, computer-assisted learning – in the school context, all are rarities. We badly need some samples in ordinary contemporary use which we can examine.

In a way, the same difficulty applies when we comment on teaching. The impermanence of the spoken word ensures we have few actual samples. Each one of us in discussing teaching uses *his* assessment of *his* recollections of *his* assorted experiences and observations, all of which may coincide only very roughly with those of other people. Thus, some teachers may talk almost continuously; others may believe 'no impression without expression' and let children do much more. Again, some teachers may expound acknowledged truths; others may believe in a heuristic approach, encouraging 'discovery' by the boys themselves. If, then, we refer to conventional teaching as 'chalk and talk' we certainly underestimate the resourcefulness of some teachers, the subtlety and quietness of others. All the same, the way boys are arranged into classes and assigned to teachers, the day divided into periods and the school into teaching boxes, the sort of equipment manufacturers design and the textbooks publishers sell – these and other practical details reflect the supposition that the focus of attention and instruction in the classroom, the active leader of the group, is the teacher. We may use the customary 'chalk and talk' description of teaching as representing its tendencies, its characteristic excesses. Since an exact portrait of something so ephemeral and varied as teaching is impossible we shall have to get what illumination we can from a caricature.

It would be useful – and we shall later attempt – to pick out the characteristic excesses of a system of package-based learning, but whereas everyone can extrapolate, however uneasily, from an ample experience of teaching, we have no such riches to draw upon with packagery. Each of us is familiar with teaching but not with the same teachers. With packages the reverse is the case: few of us are familiar with learning from packages at all, but in discussion we are almost bound to refer to the same examples. Teaching is protected by vagueness and multiplicity, packagery exposed by preciseness and rarity.

Because available packages are so few, the method may sound esoteric and lead us to expect marvels. It may then come as a disappointment to find that a package designed for everyday use necessarily consists of very ordinary materials and employs very ordinary practices. It is not in its individual elements that a package is unfamiliar, only in their combination and use. Dismantled, it will seem as banal as the book elaborated and homework and projects enlarged. The difference is that in the classroom books enjoy little independent life, being the teacher's pale shadow, and homework and projects are brief, peripheral excursions around the central business of teaching. Intermittent and extemporary independent learning is as commonplace as extensive and systematic independent learning is rare. We are dealing with something not in the least peculiar in kind, only in degree; and something not in the least new in essence, only in extent.

The absence of suitable packages and lack of experience in using them was an embarrassment to the Swedes when they introduced compulsory comprehensive education in 1965. In the new unstreamed classes they soon realized conventional class teaching simply would not work. No teacher could pipe a tune to which all the members of a class of wide, unselected ability could march. This was especially the case in sequential subjects like maths, in which, by the middle years of secondary schooling, natural differences in boys' ability (or wish) to understand had such cumulative effect that the best and worst were strung out scarcely in earshot of one another. Independent work was therefore essential. Since existing books were designed for the old situation, the Swedish government commissioned Hermods, the correspondence college, to produce a new maths course – IMU – (in translation, Individualized Maths Instruction). Since contemporary examples of packages in use are so rare, it is worth examining in some detail how IMU works.[2]

The course is intended for thirteen to sixteen year olds in the new unstreamed *grundskola*. In some schools a teacher looks after his own class during two double periods of IMU maths each week: in others team-teaching in various forms has been tried. In one school I saw, for example, three teachers shared their burdens, moving the children for varying purposes between their classrooms; in another school two teachers and an aide looked after three classes working in the dining room. The course is set out in workbooks – text, problems, answers all stay together, only periodic tests being done on separate sheets. The text consists of diagrams and pictures integrated with the accompanying, simply written explanations. Each point is illustrated by numerous examples, reinforced by small exercises. About every tenth page there is a section entitled 'Test Yourself'. The boy does the test, checks his answers and enters his results on a record sheet. When he has reached the end of the workbook, the boy collects a tape, which, in conjunction with related illustrations, provides him with a review of the work he has done. To complete his revision he now does a 'recapitulation' exercise. This is designed to reveal whether a boy has understood the section he has completed, and to help him put right his mistakes. Thus, if a boy gets question 1 right he skips, say, to question 4; if he does not, he is referred back to certain important pages in the text, then tries questions 2 and 3 to see whether he has now understood it. If he is wrong again, he goes to the teacher for help. And now, with workbook examples, self-tests, revision, and recapitulation exercises all done, the boy asks for a 'Diagnostic Test' on the whole section. This is corrected by the teacher or, in the team-teaching arrangement, by the aide. Boys who arrive at the test at much the same time and reveal similar confusions can then be called together in a small group for conventional teaching, or they can be given individual tutoring.

The diagnostic test serves not only to discern a boy's past deficiencies but to show what subsequent diet will suit him. Each of the three years of the IMU course is divided into three modules which are each divided into three components (A,B,C). A diagnostic test comes at the end of each component and a grander version at the end of a whole module. In component A there are workbooks covering the same topics at two different levels of complexity, and in the components B and C the number of levels increases to four. Whenever a boy takes a diagnostic test the teacher will suggest the appropriate level for him to follow in the next component. Some boys, I was told, then try a harder level and a few an easier one; but the great majority, either at once or quite soon, found the professional diagnosis accurate and accepted it. There is also a component G containing materials for additional group activities and for remedial tuition. Figure 1 illustrates the pattern of the nine modules.

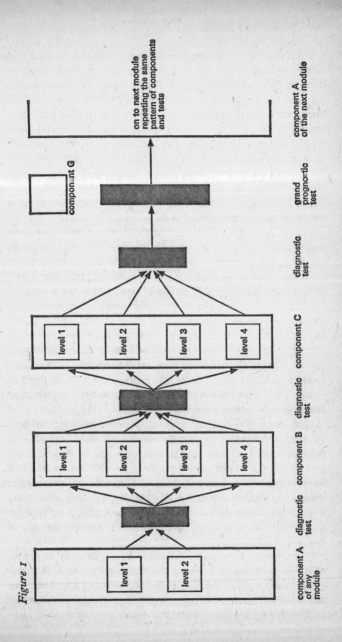

Figure I

component A of any module — level 1, level 2

diagnostic test

component B — level 1, level 2, level 3, level 4

diagnostic test

component C — level 1, level 2, level 3, level 4

diagnostic test

component G

grand prognostic test

on to next module repeating the same pattern of components and tests

component A of the next module

IMU materials have been painstakingly compiled, exhaustively field tested and carefully revised. They may be taken to represent package materials of a different order of sophistication (whether we welcome this or not) from PNEU or Dalton assignments or correspondence courses or published pieces of programmed instruction. IMU represents what the Swedes think necessary if independent learning is to work in secondary schools of a mixed-ability kind. The reactions of children and staff, which are now being evaluated, will provide interesting insights into this method of learning.

Yet to assess the method properly we shall need much more information and experience than the study of IMU alone can provide. For plainly, the lay-out of IMU in part reflects requirements specific to mathematics. In learning a foreign language, for example, the traditional approach, involving the cumulative, conscious mastery of grammatical structures might seem to lend itself to self-instruction of an IMU type; but if we accept the current belief in children learning the tongue, like natives, intuitively, through the pores rather than logically through the head, then who but the teacher (at best) can provide the necessary flow of foreign sounds in which they can so profitably bathe? Again, the stress is now on oral rather than written mastery: children should therefore practise speaking the language. If we transfer this to independent work, how, short of language laboratores everywhere, shall we avoid bedlam? And suppose we try packaging work in sciences, shall we run into intolerable difficulties in practical work – all those boys all over the place doing all sorts of experiments – and in such circumstances will the contemporary emphasis on real 'discovery' invite a specially glorious brand of chaos? Least of all will the detailed sequencing and close structure of IMU maths suit a subject like English, in which personal exploration and expression now are paramount, while formal, grammatical elements are placed firmly in the background?

If we intend to consider packaged-based learning as a possible, entire system of learning we shall need to trace its implications over a representative range of subjects.[3] And there are certain other variables of importance. How should the materials and methods used for independent learning be designed to suit differences in age? Is the lowest ability limit of those who might learn effectively this way much the same as with conventional class teaching, or is there a larger, perhaps differently constituted 'remedial' population?' What change in materials or media become necessary as we approach the 'remedial' limit? Many of the advantages of learning independently from packages, such as a more individual and fluid use of time, depend on their being available in a number of subjects simultaneously, but it may be the case that IMU maths is stimulating or supportable only because, at present, it is offset by other subjects taught conventionally. We need to discover what happens when learning from materials, a teacher being present, becomes the norm, just as learning from the teacher, materials being present, is the norm in our secondary school now.

These uncertainties faced the Nuffield Foundation Resources for Learning Project when it came to assess the possibilities of independent work in secondary schools. The Project's brief ranged widely over all possible ways of learning and all possible resources to implement them, but when, hesitantly, they began to examine the principal systems of learning, they found little was known about the package-based ones. No end of effort and money was directed into understanding and improving the teacher-based system: departments and colleges of education and the schools themselves were already busy at the task. Instruction by radio and television also had its established centres. Both the BBC and ITV were bound by law to consider the needs of schools and their efforts were reinforced by a growing number of local, closed-circuit stations. How different the situation with package-based learning. Published materials suited to secondary schools were fragmentary indeed, available experience slight. Indeed, in order to gather a sufficiently representative body of experience the members of the Nuffield team found they had first to compile materials themselves and test them in some schools.

Unlike Nuffield curriculum projects, they were not concerned with making 'definitive' new courses or publishing ideal examples, but rather they were undertaking a preliminary exploration of the problems and the possibilities of package-based learning in the context of the contemporary secondary school.

Earlier attempts at package-based learning had failed, and were almost extinct in the secondary school: programmed instruction had found more comfortable lodging in the tidy enclosures of industrial training; PNEU improbably continued but only in sequestered reserves; the Dalton Plan lived on in a few last relics. Those who now tried once more to design materials for extensive independent learning were plainly not doing something new and startling; rather they were part of an evolutionary process. Here was an old genus, successful in primary and tertiary education but weak at the secondary stage. What was it in the secondary school environment that proved so inhospitable, what features would a new mutation need to survive in it, and even, in time, to prosper?

Chapter Ten
Problems and Possibilities in Independent Learning[1]

The problems of survival affecting a package start at conception and birth. Remarkably few get written; fewer still published. In a free economy supply and demand interact. If there were a market in secondary schools for extensive courses designed for independent work then publishers would produce them. Equally, only when publishers produce them is a market likely to develop. For the time being, when we search for packages, we can read tantalizing descriptions of materials used in the past – out of print; or of materials designed for elaborate developments in the future – for experimental use only; or of materials evolved for specific local needs – unpublished.

Educational publishers are aware of a growing interest in independent study and some of them publish appropriate materials, in a fragmentary way, but the scale of what is required and the customary economics of publishing do not match. IMU maths illustrates the problem. Module I runs to 640 printed pages (plus a teacher's booklet). It is expected that an average child will cover three modules in a year. Roughly, then, a year's work requires some 1920 pages. Since the work is designed at differing levels, each boy does not have to wade through all those pages – only about a third of them. Small comfort this to the poor publisher. A choice of levels merely reduces the production run of any one booklet and increases his costs. No matter what economies we contemplate, in designing a package we shall arrive at something longer than the most generous textbook – even those volumes and ancillary materials put out by the curriculum developers. The reason is clear. If in the classroom a teacher were simply to read through the explanation of some process as it is given in a textbook it would take little time; it is the teacher's additions, the necessary repetition, the stressing of cardinal points, the additional diagrams, the extra examples, the parallels with everyday experience, the quizzing of boys round the room, the leading on from point to point – the reinforcement so necessary if a majority of children is to understand and to remember – that provide the staple of daily lessons. A self-instructional maths package like IMU has to incorporate a good deal of such elaboration, but in print. It is longer than a conventional textbook for the same reason that a novel is longer than the script of a play. Moreover, the material must be presented so that children, more accustomed to verbal than written communication, can follow it. It is not that the language required for effective communication is rare or difficult – a package like IMU does not reflect any esoteric skill – simply that things have to be spelt out carefully and amply. The striking feature of a package, especially in sequential subjects, is sheer length.

It is this that deters publishers. Length means cost, and if the package uses elements other than print alone – tapes or film strips – then the costs soar still further. Publishers have an honourable tradition of taking risks. Of course, they hope that some of their books will turn out to be bestsellers; but they knowingly publish others not at all likely to sell widely, and some, such as works of scholarship, which are in no danger whatever of making a profit. Thirty thousand new titles are published in Britain every year. A book likely to appeal only to a tiny minority can be priced accordingly, may be bought by libraries, or can entice customers over a period of years from the booksellers' shelves. It is not so with textbooks. True, a school bestseller, bought not by individuals but for whole age groups, can become an institution; normally, however, the publisher has to work within the closest of margins. The school market is potentially large but immediately mean. Prices must be kept low, libraries – research or public – offer no outlet, the book does not attract the browsing customer from the shelves but has to be sold directly by representatives, wearily and expensively, common-room by common-room. Occasionally a school publisher will indeed set off on some large and daring enterprise, but only if supported by a number of reliable items or armed with an authoritative badge. He can risk novelties because his list includes a few solid sellers, or print ample new courses devised by curriculum developers because he can brandish the symbol of the Schools Council or the Nuffield Foundation. How much more will he require support before he risks publishing something as unavoidably costly as a package.

Producing a package is awkward for the writer no less than for the publisher. A book may represent a year of the writer's life, but the capital cost of the equipment he needs – pen, paper, a typewriter – is negligible. For this reason, unlike other workers, he is not maintained and salaried while he labours, apart from a little in advance. But a package is a different matter altogether. With IMU, for example, the thousands of pages, diagrams and pictures, the recorded tapes, the differentiation of ability levels, the requirement of absolute lucidity, present a task without the attractions of pure scholarship or pure invention, and yet too costly and uncertain of a market to offer, in compensation, the assurance of profit.

One or two publishers aware of all this have taken to supporting a writer or a group of writers, as drug manufacturers support research scientists, while they engage on an expensive, long and hazardous task. The tradition of publishing, however, does not run this way. Advanced support is generally confined to assured best-selling novelists. In consequence most of the research and development in America or in Britain has fallen entirely or in part upon various foundations, and in Sweden upon the Government. School book publishing is one among many elements of the teacher-based system of learning which will need sizeable adaptation if a package-based system is used. As things are, published packages are certain to be few and far between.

One unfortunate result of the lack of choice among packages is that the few that exist have an air of prescriptive monopoly which mortally offends teachers, sensitive about their independence within their classrooms. This sensitivity is especially marked in England. When the Schools Council was established it proved essential to issue a declaration asserting the Council's intention to uphold 'the principle that each school should have the fullest measure of responsibility for its own work, with its own curriculum and teaching methods, based on the needs of its own pupils and evolved by its own staff'.[2]

This liberty, more complete than is known in any other country, takes several different forms: a teacher (with others in his department in a school) has, first, freedom to choose a syllabus; second, freedom to choose among alternative courses or textbooks embodying that syllabus; third, freedom to vary whatever course or textbook is chosen; fourth, freedom to create in effect a 'course' or 'text' of his own, spontaneously, by his teaching. How does a package affect these freedoms?

So long as packages are rare they must appear to lay down the law about the syllabus. So active have curriculum reformers been in recent years that it is hard to persuade teachers looking at packages that this particular madness runs to method alone, that it is not the message but the medium that matters, not the particular text but a translation which can be applied to whatever text is chosen. As more packages appear the apparent restriction on the freedom to choose among syllabuses will disappear.

So too will the inability to elect among different courses or textbooks embodying the syllabus chosen. Already in Sweden alternative maths packages to IMU have begun to appear. One is being written by teachers in a local authority; another – now the market has been created – is being sponsored by a commercial publisher. Choice is a matter of time.

If choice among syllabuses and among texts may be restored readily enough, the freedom to vary a text seems more dangerously threatened by the nature of the package itself. Let us look again at IMU maths as our prototype. There are booklets at differing levels of difficulty, places within each booklet where a right answer lets a boy jump over the next few sums and a wrong one sends him back over earlier pages in the text, additional material outside the main booklets for the least and most able, providing many alternative routes through the course.[3] But these routes are still contained *within* the course. There is a sense of being led along carefully trimmed, approved paths.

This sense of constraint is aggravated when one examines the validation methods that have been employed. Every line of the course has been tested and adjustments made in a steady approximation to a measurable ideal. Thus, in the IMU course, the materials have been painstakingly compiled and exhaustively field-tested. A preliminary study among teachers, university lecturers and businessmen established the aims of the course, which were then translated, wherever possible, into measurable 'behavioural objectives'. The first version of the course was then tried on seventy-five children and careful note taken of their difficulties. Any problem not correctly solved by 80 per cent of the children who tried it was rewritten. This second version was tried on 300 children whose progress was followed minutely, and a further 8000 whose opinions and suggestions – and those of 200 teachers – were collected periodically. Again modifications were made. The third version was then used by 11,500 children, of whom 3000 took part in an efficiency examination. At present the course has been revised five times and a detailed independent evaluation of the course and its effects on children and teachers has begun.[4] One has the impression that the course has come not from the end of a pen but the tip of a screwdriver.

But all this feedback has its own perils. Feedback has been hailed as bringing the scientific method at last to education.[5] It may prove a lasting blight. For at the end of all the detailed adjustment and all the evaluation a teacher hardly dares to make an alteration. Deplorably the human reaction to such perfection is far from friendly. As E. M. Forster wrote of the villagers in their dealings with Mrs Miniver: 'They listen to her saying the right things and are dumb. They watch her doing the right things in the right way and are paralysed.'[6] It will not do now to submerge teachers under omniscience as teachers in the past have so often submerged children. They will feel diminished and convey their resentment in a thousand small ways to those they teach. It is indeed an advantage that whereas teaching in the transient medium of speech is hit-and-miss, written or recorded instruction can be improved by revision, by what engineers call 'cut and fit'. Of course the writers of any course will want to improve it by revision, but there should be no attempt to turn a common-sense process into a vast and detailed statistical exercise, thereby oppressing men more by the dogmas of scientism than ever they were by the more easily questioned dogmas of assertion.

To combat this a teacher must be as free to vary a package as he is to vary a textbook, leaving out this item, amending that one, inserting fragments of his own. Since a package has physical form, it must be so designed that alteration is easy. Within limits set by confusion and cost, separate sheets or small booklet are to be preferred to bound volumes. Similarly tapes can generally be used more flexibly than records, separate slides than film strips. It may well be that the alterations made by a particular teacher to the basic package in some measurable way result in it being rather worse; that matters far less than the teacher's sense of being the master of the package rather than its puppet. Considerations of cost will tend to keep a package simple; so, even more imperatively, should considerations for the teacher's independence.

Yet when he uses a textbook such considered alteration is not the principal measure of a schoolmaster's contribution. He is free to make a running comment to it, to elaborate spontaneously and almost continuously by his teaching. If boys are to learn independently from the package itself, what happens to teaching?

A package like IMU is designed to be self-instructional; class-teaching, if not exactly forbidden, certainly receives no encouragement.[7] Instead the master has time and opportunity for tutoring individuals or small groups. Individual tutoring may occur casually from a boy's request for help or a master's perambulation round the room, or more formally at specified places in the course where a boy checks his progress with a master. Some things hard to explain in words are easily demonstrated – using a compass, for example. An entirely self-instructional course would require everything to be written out in prolix detail, designed to foil every conceivable misunderstanding. Jerome K. Jerome makes the point when he writes out his instructions for learning to roll the 'r' in French: 'Press your tonsils against the underside of your larynx. Then with the convex part of the septum curved upwards so as almost – but not quite – to touch the uvula, try with the tip of your tongue to reach your thyroid. Take a deep breath and compress your glottis. Now, without opening your lips, say "garoo".' Of course, where words becloud, a picture may help, but a human demonstration is best of all.

Such demonstrations, such teaching, may often with economy involve a pair or a small group rather than one boy alone. Sometimes the added number can be a positive advantage, as in a discussion or in conversational practice in a foreign language. If boys are in any case doing their independent work in pairs or small groups, whether from choice or because the course has been

written that way, then collecting groups is easy enough. Even
when the work is done individually, a piece of written work or a
test may reveal common shortcomings among certain boys, and,
as in IMU, the teacher can then teach them together. The Dalton Plan, as we have noted, involved children filling in a chart as
each unit was completed, so that their teacher could see at a
glance which among them were at much the same point – a process which made grouping fairly simple. A group is also particularly effective for teaching of a spontaneous kind. Teaching is
often at its best when a schoolmaster picks up some aside, some
matter of concern, and extemporizes around it. Permanent
materials have many virtues but lack this casual inventiveness.
It would be dull indeed if informal teaching excursions were
thought inappropriate to sober working through a package; they
are, arguably, the more readily justified in that those who do not
want to join in can get on independently with their work.

But in addition to these more intimate brands of instruction
there should be, in my view, some class teaching. The objection
to any class teaching when work is individualized is clear. If boys
are to be allowed to learn more at their own speed, then we can
help them as individuals, we may be able to collect a pair to teach,
or we may catch a group while it briefly coalesces at a given
point in the course, but the chance of teaching appropriately to
a whole class will be slight. What will fit into one person's
sequence will be an awkward interruption to another's. However,
the idea that class teaching involves an ordered progress through
the material to be learnt is a half-truth at best. No doubt the
master's own plan of work, or the one which fits in with the textbook he is using, will be set out in this structured way. What
actually happens is far less steady. The march along a Roman
way turns out to be a meander down a rolling English road with
rambles along footpaths, occasional cut-offs and frequent doub-
lings back. That's a most interesting question from Jones – it
raises a point in statistics that we wouldn't normally cover till
next year but. . . . That answer from Williams shows that he
hasn't got the foggiest recollection of division of fractions which
he was supposed to have learnt last year. So the whole class jumps
forward and back, follows this red herring, consumes that stale
fish. Equally if a master decides to intrude a lesson on boys work-

ing at packages the topic may be 'ahead' for some and 'behind' for others, or an amiable excursion for them all; but it confounds their progress through a sacred sequence in scarcely a more arbitrary fashion than is commonplace in class teaching.

And there are more orderly ways of including class teaching. IMU, in line with most American individualized work, is arranged for continuous progress. When at last the age-old shackles of the class are broken it is easy to run wild, especially in the sequential subjects. In my view, a more modest use of independent learning is generally prudent. For example, work can be phased. A teacher can set a span of time for a particular topic. He can initiate it with a class-teaching period and end it with one, the boys working independently between these limits. During the phase he may introduce a period or two of related material not dealt with in the package materials, thereby enriching the whole. Alternatively, a teacher may extract from a syllabus certain topics he reserves for class teaching, leaving others for package-based learning. He may keep specified periods on his weekly timetable for class teaching, or allow boys to learn from packages for some weeks and then use all his periods for a spell of class teaching. In Daltonized schools, work on the Plan occupied part of the day, not the whole of it; a subject could be part taught, part worked from assignments; and there were recognized arrangements for closing subject laboratories to permit *ad hoc* class lessons.

How many class periods to include when boys are learning from packages must be a matter for judgement, but there could surely be some. It is not simply that class teaching may be sometimes an efficient and economical way to explain something: it allows the variety, eccentricity, impulse, even accident the printed word prohibits. Print allows revision; what appears is deliberate. The gain lies in care, the loss in spontaneity. A Wodehouse may manage to preserve on paper the flavour of casual badinage: but the talent is rare and requires infinite pains. Written instructions in learning programmes in America often begin with 'Hiya', encourage with 'You're doing swell' and end with 'Well done, wasn't that fun' or something equally friendly and arch.[8] Such gratuitous, universal chumminess is most familiar to us in broadcasts to schools. Small children may innocently submit to it but for those more adult the pretence of familiarity is merely patronizing. Like wild flowers brought indoors, spoken words look wrong when potted into print.

As words in a conversation have their own style and merit, so too do words in a classroom. The history I was once taught at school is now mostly lost in a haze, but I remember vividly a lesson on the Peninsular War given by a master who leant toward order rather than inspiration. That day the dull text or the dull faces suddenly aroused him to frenzied extemporization. Apparently the Peninsula is made up of mountains and rivers. Anyway, some Marshal of Napoleon's, whose name I have forgotten, kept trying to get from France down to Madrid, toiling up and down the mountains and wading wearily through the rivers. Meanwhile Wellington had set up camp behind the lines of Torres Vedras in Portugal whence, taking time off every now and then from his foxhunting, he would nip along the valleys and catch the French on the flank or cut off their supplies. Apparently these strategic concepts, so obvious to the master, had not lodged any more clearly with us boys than with that dim-witted Marshal. Desperate, then, to drive his point home the master had some of us scrambling north and south, over the tables, down on the floor, up over the next row, while other boys dashed across the room between the tables, east and west as it were, showing how Wellington had used the geography of Spain to his exclusive advantage. Such was discipline in those days that the lesson managed to stop short of total riot: but somehow in the hilarious mêlée, the outlines of the Peninsular campaign lodged in my head, and in others' I suspect, with unforgettable, surrealistic clarity.

Questions about the value of such information belong to curriculum developers. What is relevant here, in our look at teaching methods, is that it came across marvellously in class teaching. It would be singularly undramatic packaged into print. The essential quality of the lesson would not fit into any Trump team-teaching category – 'large group instruction' is a carefully staged performance; small group seminars place their emphasis on student-led discussions; in individual tutoring such extemporization would, from repetition, die the death of a thousand cuts. It belongs to that strange, intimate, theatrical world of the classroom, in which, from time to time, a lively audience triggers off some happy flight in the master, or a dull audience forces him to a performance that surprises him and them. There is a special brand of didactic inspiration that belongs to the master as class teacher, not to the master as gossip or friend or tutor or chairman in discussion or lecturer, nor yet to his words in print.

In deciding how much to teach, a master must strike a balance between alternative benefits. If he teaches too much then the lock-step re-appears and he has too little time for individual or small group tuition; too little and the boys may get bored – and so may he. Many of the best schoolmasters have the instincts of artists who, having seen some rare beauty or some subtle truth, are anxious to communicate it. The pity is that their audience is captive, if restive, and that lessons, which might be admirable if they were events, become a perpetual grind, the longest running show of them all. But it will not do to banish entirely the pitch from the platform because, at its best, there is a vitality, a vividness, a directed force in teaching which no other medium quite duplicates. Too much formal teaching in the past should not be counteracted now by proposing none at all.

In sum, in the vexed matter of the teacher's freedom, we may conclude that time will mend the shortage of packages and so restore in considerable degree the freedom to choose between syllabuses and among differing texts. By making up packages from discrete replaceable pieces, by encouraging alteration, we can retain the schoolmaster's freedom to modify the text or course. The teacher's words are also a valuable component and should not be excluded from the package. Some class teaching can remain and more tutoring than ever. All the same if boys are to work more independently, then what they work at must for the most part have a permanent – if alterable – form, and that necessarily implies a reduction in the teacher's holding forth. For a teacher, then, using a package is not like wearing his own skin, nor is it incarceration in the programmed-learning suit of armour; rather it is like putting on a suit of clothes – very convenient, and even if ready-made, given a nip here, a tuck there and a period of wear, it can become comfortable too.

If we accept that for the teacher the package intrudes in some measure on a treasured (if sometimes exhausting) freedom to create the course thirty boys in his class are to follow, from the boy's point of view the compensatory gain in freedom is considerable. Ideally, of course, the teacher is responsive to a boy's needs; and so he might be if he did not also have to get through a syllabus and, worse, cope with thirty boys' needs at a time. Unavoidably, he has to lead more often than respond, taking all thirty to look together and compulsorily now at this, now at that. His freedom to choose just what is done is matched by their bondage to his choice.

A package in a secondary school, like the teacher, has thirty boys in a class to consider. If boys are to work more independently they must generally know what to do next, otherwise there will be a time-consuming chaos of 'What do I do now?' The teacher may with advantage be involved in giving guidance to all children at certain key points in the package, but if he is too heavily implicated he will have too little time left for tutoring the individuals who need help and for teaching small groups. In some subjects this means the package will have to prescribe detailed sequences of work; in others, children can manage happily for longer periods between the points where guidance is needed. But even when children are working within the prescribed framework at least they can choose among alternative routes and travel along them at their own pace.

The one and only sequence the teacher sets can be represented as 'freedom' only because it is never written down; the sequences in the package, however numerous, seem, in contrast, tiresomely detailed and sometimes a little absurd. But just as the freedom of the citizen is not best served when the law can be made up on the spot, so the boy has more liberty when the teacher abdicates his absolute power and generally uses recorded law.

But how much freedom should boys, being young, be given? Secondary schooling is, as we have seen, a highly artificial process. The curriculum we inflict upon children reflects our adult consensus of what is the most useful common ground for most adolescents to tread in preparation for a bewildering variety of future occupations. Unavoidably, to some of them, schooling is a sort of oakum-picking. Their *real* choice is not to be at school at all, or being there, to while their time away in company with their friends, to work a little and to dream a lot, or having tried one thing to drop it and skip to another. For them no amount of choice between options, no elaborate attempt to help them pursue their own interests can do more than usefully mitigate perpetual necessity. Boys are free only when we are prepared to turn every activity into a hobby. When children are small we may cheerfully assert of the few who resist encouragement that they will learn when they are ready to: it is a far riskier proceeding when their schooldays are running out. The higher up the secondary school, the more sharply the anxieties of parents and the demands of employers impose artificial requirements and standards on boys. Because of this, whatever the learning method used, the job of motivating the majority of boys, of persuading some, and finally, when necessary, compelling the remainder, is the ineluctable lot of the schoolmaster.

All the same, a shift from constant teaching to more independent learning may help to improve the relationship of master and boy on which so much of motivation depends. A class of boys has to be still and silent so that a master can be heard: there is not the same need for minute points of order if boys are working independently. The constant fretting needed to keep thirty lively boys attentive in their desks, like a circus ring of lions perched uneasily on their wooden boxes, diminishes. If we replace teaching a whole class largely by tutoring individuals or small groups, then there is more opportunity for personal understanding and concern. Further, when there is a package to be worked through the schoolmaster is less clearly cast in the role of the force-feeder. At least for the children reasonably keen to get on, or anxious to get through an exam, the materials become the visible enemy, the teacher an ally in the necessary struggle to defeat them.

It is fecklessly optimistic, however, to expect package work to suit everybody. In adopting a more independent way of learning in a school we have to ask both how completely the lock-step is to be broken and also for how many. The further we go along each continuum the greater our complexities, especially over pastoral care. The least able and willing boys when presented with even a small measure of independent work, and the majority of children when given a lot, may require a degree of support and guidance that few schools can reasonably provide. The Dalton Plan allowed a boy for part of each day to choose what subject he tackled and for how long – at once it became essential to give him a daily session with a form master or tutor to ensure he was using his time effectively. Those schools in America which have moved towards 'continuous progress' invoke more and more people as aides – or a computer – to keep track of who has got to where and needs what, to support and guide individual children through the maze. In particular the least capable and the least willing children can find independence a confusion and a burden. Some may well prefer the familiar classroom pattern – conversational, relatively undemanding, secure.[9]

We can discern, then, an ascending order of ways in which a package may be used. First, a package may be used by a teacher under close supervision; all the children then do the same thing at much the same time – a near lock-step but with less verbal teaching. Second, a package may be used part-time, the teacher covering certain topics in the conventional way and the materials the rest. Third, a package may be phased, the boys working independently at varying materials but all within the same general topic. Fourth, when packages in a range of subjects are available they can be used in the Dalton manner. In this, although the work to be done by a class in any subject is phased over, say, a month, a boy is allowed for part of each day (or for a day or so each week) to choose how he distributes his time between subjects. Provided minimum requirements are satisfied in all his subjects, he is free to put his emphasis where he likes and may, when his stint is finished, work beyond normal school subjects and requirements. Fifth, a teacher or team of teachers may allow all boys, or certain individuals, to work freely through the packages at unrestricted, individual speed – what is called continuous progress.

Within these broad differences, possible overlaps and variations are many. Closely controlled class use of package materials at one extreme and continuous progress at the other are likely to prove best for a minority of children, a middling position for most, but there is no one right way. Packages permit, they do not require, radical change. Their use, just as their content, allows for teacher variation. The aim should be not a new orthodoxy

but a genuine choice, for until package courses exist, any shift
away from class teaching is possible in theory but extremely
difficult in practice. Once the choice is there, then how many
boys move how quickly how far in independent learning is a
matter that must rest with local judgement.

We have seen that the opportunity a package allows to break
the lock-step of the class can be seized upon all too greedily. The
term 'individualization', used in America and in Sweden to describe the new freedom, contains another trap. To be totally free,
it seems not only should we refuse to march in step; we ought
to walk alone. But a boy working in solitary style in his carrel
reminds one disturbingly of a battery hen, and elaborate learning consoles made up from screens, dial access, wireless communication, and so on, still cast the learner as an anchorite. Such
solitary austerities may work with adult learners; they are not
likely to appeal for long to boys. Individualization needs to be
qualified.

Another objection than tedium applies to an excess of individualization. Children learn from one another. They are not
often given the chance in class teaching: mutual aid at present
is generally confined to laboratories, to occasional project work,
to illicit combines in homework and to out-of-school activities;
but in recent years, with competitiveness going out of favour,
group work has become more frequent and fashionable.

It is possible to welcome the impulse and yet have grave doubts
about the usual outcome. Theorists about group work refer to
the 'hidden agenda'. By this they mean the unspoken complex of
relationships, the oblique and subtle jockeying that goes on between individuals before a group as a whole can function effectively. When there is nothing to be done a group can be a cheerful forum for gossip, but when it has to organize itself to work
then too often noisy who-does-what wrangles generate in which
the aggressive and extravert dominate the rest. It can be argued
that learning to get along in, to learn from, a group is a vital
part of education. And so it is. It may belong most naturally,
however, to the playground, the dinner table, the home, the
street, where action and discussion arise from genuinely shared
interests. Tasks or topics set to groups in class seldom achieve

any such vigour or point or direction, and group discussion artificially contrived seldom proves a useful way to learn unless subtly directed by a skilled chairman, normally the teacher himself. Some teachers have indeed developed considerable expertness in arranging group work, but it is far from easy.[10] Those making packages may have the time to prepare group work with the care its success demands.

It is presumably anxiety about mass conformity in contemporary society which leads some to stress individualization, and others participation in a group. Somehow the compromise of the pair does not arouse much interest – a pity because, as a learning unit, two has much to recommend it. As a start less careful planning is needed for work in pairs than for work in groups because the threatening shambles is smaller, and, as Norman MacMunn showed, it is relatively easy to compose work specially for a pair. When it is a matter of who does what a pair can usually make decisions more quickly and a lot less noisily than a group and more easily arrive at an acceptable speed of work. In a pair a tentative suggestion is less exposed to possible ridicule. A teacher can alter partners to arrive at viable pairs more readily than adjust the complex of relationships in a group. In a pair both partners are usually actively involved; in a group some children quickly become passengers. Question and answer between a pair can provide useful reinforcement of what is first learnt from materials in a package. Charlotte Mason's words echo here: 'As knowledge is not assimilated until it is reproduced, children should "tell back" after a single reading or hearing.' It is a species of testing which boys from time immemorial have found best done with a friend. The partner who thinks he has grasped a point can profit from trying to explain it, no less than his neighbour from receiving such personal if inexpert tuition. (The teacher and tests can always provide a final check on accuracy.) A schoolmaster is reputed to have said: 'I explained something to the class and they didn't understand. I tried again and still they didn't understand. The third time I understood it.'[11] This element of clarification through teaching and questioning may explain why small pieces of research in recent years have indicated that a pair of children of dissimilar ability may constitute an effective learning unit for both the more and the less able partner.[12] In this way does old cheating become new learning.

There is yet another reason for using a boy's neighbour as a 'resource for learning'. For reasons of its economy, its power, its convenience, a major part of a package is likely to consist of print. Literacy becomes a key factor. The number of those wholly illiterate is small – under 1 per cent of the adult population, and in secondary schools probably not very much larger. But, as Keith Gardner has recently pointed out, this is only the tip of the iceberg.[13] He estimates that some 25 per cent of children leaving school at 15 'cannot read well enough to make sense of a newspaper, let alone a Government form or a hire purchase agreement'. Gardner compares this kind of literacy with the ability of the average Englishman to read a French newspaper: he may be able to get the gist of the news but misses nuances of language and meaning and quickly gets bored; 'he cannot really read good French, he can only identify words'. However imprecise the definition, however uncertain the extent of this sort of semi-literacy there is no doubt at all of it being a major hindrance to academic learning, even of the present largely aural and passive kind: in independent work from materials it is a formidable barrier. A boy living in a twilight of literacy turns most naturally to a more capable friend for assurance that he has understood some written instruction or caught the gist of a passage. Paired work is invaluable for such children.

A package, then, may deliberately include group work and paired work. More important, however, is the general attitude of the teacher using the package, whether he encourages competition or co-operation. For however individual a course may seem on paper, many boys if given the chance (and often when officially denied it) gravitate together for collaboration and for company. Both by deliberate design or simple consent, the characteristic excess in package work of being too ruthlessly individualized can readily be avoided.

In present circumstances a boy is generally taught in class and then works individually (more or less) at homework. What place does homework have if boys are already working independently during a substantial part of their time at school? If boys are working at differing speeds, setting a single homework task for a whole class becomes distinctly awkward. It might still be set in some item outside the package. Similarly if, as a variant to package work, a teacher has elected to teach a given topic in the conventional manner then he can follow it with a conventional homework. For the most part, however, homework simply becomes a continuation of the work being done in the package. As such it becomes less easy to check exactly what has been done by whom on any particular night. Whether this becomes an issue depends on if homework is regarded as an extension to learning or merely as a means of keeping boys occupied in the evening. The extensive tests surrounding the development of IMU in Sweden showed that those working on the course spent far less time on homework than those in the control group and yet covered the same material on the syllabus. It is important to remember that independent work is much more exacting than sitting in a desk being taught – hence the groans when homework is set, hence Charlotte Mason's insistence that schoolroom hours should be sharply curtailed if children worked by her method. To retain a full stint of homework on top of package work is to invite a schoolboys' strike (conscientious schoolboys already work hours that would exhaust their parents) or at any rate intervention by the NSPCC.

The problem is no less severe for the teacher. Independent work generates testing, correcting, marking, whether done at home or in class. Marking is already a burden and a frustration. By the time it is done and the boys' books returned, the subject is dead: few profit from the careful corrections. The alternative of 'Swap papers and we'll mark it now' is a singularly wasteful use of class time. Fortunately, putting children into an artificial 'form order' at regular and frequent intervals is not now a widespread practice in comprehensive schools. None the less, even if the labours of detailed marking can generally be reduced, taking proper notice of what thirty boys of secondary school age can accomplish when working independently can be a major burden on the teacher. There is after all no better way of preventing a lesson generating any tangible product than for a teacher to hold forth: forty minutes gone and (praise be) nothing to show for it. More freedom for boys can easily mean still heavier chains for teachers, few of whom would willingly trade the role of lecturer for that of examiner.

It becomes essential, therefore, in designing packages to exploit every reasonable means to keep correction to a minimum. In some subjects there are useful alternatives to written work as an end-product of learning – class discussion, drama, exhibitions, making tape recordings, map work, diagrams, and so on. Telling back may substitute quite often for writing down. Where informal testing seems useful then one boy in a pair can help another. Multiple-choice intelligently used can make self-testing much more accurate and lighten the task of the master when he decides to administer a test. Certain parts of a course lend themselves to linear programmed instruction techniques – response, answer, correction coming close together; in other parts self-tests and quizzes can lead a boy on unchecked and unmarked to appropriate branches. Thus in IMU, whether a boy skips a section or works through depends on his answers in a test he corrects himself, the teacher's formal corrections being confined to less frequent examinations. In sequential subjects each page constitutes a milestone so that, given periodic built-in tests to check understanding, a boy's place provides in itself a partial measure of progress. A master's time can properly be devoted, therefore, more to helping a boy on his way than in a fret of marking. Further, when the teacher's energies are not so much absorbed in instruction he has far more opportunity for noticing informally how individual boys are getting on. With package work formal assessment of the traditional kind can reasonably be less frequent.

We should now look at some of the logistics of using packages – handling, storage, equipment, and the like. The teacher's words – our principal source of instruction at present – are transitory; not so the package. It has the advantage of physical permanence, and the curse. It is likely to consist chiefly of text and pictures in print. To keep, say, a thousand children busy for a year, how many sheets of paper will we use? The quantities are awe-inspiring. A year's work in IMU maths runs we have seen, to about 1920 pages, each child needing about a third of that total. The Nuffield Resources for Learning Project, trying out the effect of five subjects in package form, assumed that each child would use an average of ten pages (five sheets) per subject per week. That would yield: 5 (subjects) × 5 (sheets) × 1000 (children) × 35 (working weeks)=875,000 sheets in a year. The sum does not bear multiplication for a whole school system. Plainly, paper consumption needs watching carefully.

A closer look at the problem fortunately makes it less alarming. In the first place, 1000 children already eat through several trees a year in the form of the textbooks, duplicated materials and exercise books which the packages largely replace. Certain parts of a package can be used by more than one boy in more than one year. Choice means that not everything has to be available in full number; so does difference in working speed. As for storing the paper, bookshelves and filing cabinets remind us that an astonishing number of pages can rest neatly in a small space. As a further encouragement, printing is surprisingly cheap. A run of 10,000 copies of a 32-page booklets, 7 × 5 in. by reprographic off-set litho, stapled, paper-bound, delivered by a jobbing printer, costs about sevenpence a copy. Electronic stencil copying of an original followed by subsequent local duplicating is scarcely more costly. Neither in production cost nor in handling and storage does the printed part of a package constitute a very serious problem.

But what other resources do we need beyond paper, however imaginatively and generously used? All the forward-looking literature about education, many conferences, the advertisements in the journals, promote the advantages of new audio-visual equipment. The variety of hardware is ample and many schools are quite well equipped, but there is a general complaint that such equipment is grossly under-used. Of course, schools are not mass-production factories, with every bit of equipment perpetually employed in churning out copies of an identical product. There is no more reason to expect visual aids to be in constant use than all the wall-bars in the gym or all the books in the library. All the same, such aids are expensive, potentially a great asset, and their under-use a cause for concern.

Some wonder if it's the rarity of the equipment, shared and stored away, that accounts for its neglect by teachers. A new school I saw in a suburb of Stockholm had a liberally equipped audio-visual store set in the midst of each group of four classrooms, but the results remained singularly disappointing. It is not just a matter of getting the right equipment and the right class at the right time in the right place. More complex is finding the material to show. What is commercially available, the software, generally covers only a thin scatter of topics in any one subject, and the teacher has little time to prepare his own. It is the disproportionate effort required to animate any single teaching period with audio-visual materials that deters most teachers. 'Chalk and talk' and book may be less vivid, but they are also less obtrusive and less complicated to set up; they allow quick response to mood; they do not break down at the most maddening and embarrassing moments. In present circumstances, audio-visual aids are no daily diet of teaching: they are reserved for infrequent banquets. It is one of the merits of a package that by building appropriate materials – within limits set by cost – into the course, it can animate audio-visual equipment now gathering dust.[14]

The more elaborate and expensive audio-visual items must, of course, be used principally by a teacher; a more obscure problem is the place of audio-visual aids for direct use by children. Audio-visual equipment, at present, is designed as part of the teacher-based system of learning: it enlarges, elaborates, colours the lessons given to a class. The emphasis is on the high quality necessary for mass viewing or mass listening; the cost of each item can be high because it is being shared by thirty children. If we shift to package-based learning a different sort of equipment is needed. Volume and definition need match only a single pair of eyes and ears; the cost must be low enough for several of each item to be made available. At the moment such equipment exists only as a spill-over from the home entertainment industry, some of it thoroughly suitable, a lot of it lacking features needed for classroom use; most of it – because individuals spend more cheerfully on their own pleasures than rate-payers on education – still too expensive. For example, by chance, the entertainment market provides suitable viewers for looking at home-made slides; but the cassetted tape-players at present available lack precise place-indicators, have an extravagant appetite for batteries, and are still too expensive for sufficient distribution among children working at packages.

Not only economic but human consideration should deter us from a proliferation of machinery when a package is used in a classroom. In certain subjects, however, the argument for the ample use of the tape-recorder and the tape-player is very strong indeed. We have glanced already at the problem of marginal literacy. In subjects like science and maths where the amount of reading is limited, the pairing and grouping of children and the ample use of drawings may go far to make printed materials sufficient for independent work (though more varied resources may still be desirable): but in English and social studies the amount of reading is far more extensive. A tape and an accompanying script then become a powerful help to an uncertain reader.[15] Even for those who are fluent, acres of print can be exhausting and a tape a most welcome variant. Moreover, as the radio so vividly illustrates, sound does more than merely instruct: the human voice, music, everyday noises – these can marvellously evoke strange times, strange places, strange lives, both to move us and to delight. Not only listening to tapes but making them can be stimulating in literary subjects and especially valuable to those least able to express their ideas on paper. As for foreign languages, there is no need to dilate on the importance of recorded sound there. The pursuit of perfection has, unfortunately, made the recorders, the earphones, the console that forms a full language laboratory so costly that the height of ambition for most schools is to possess just one; and dogmas have sprung up to explain why, after all, it is a good thing that each child's share in its use should be so slight. At the moment, in most subjects, when children hear recorded sound it comes from an expensive tape recorder played from the dais by a teacher. In a more independent style of learning we shall need, as it were, bicycles for everyone to ride a lot, not a Rolls-Royce for periodic jaunts. The single piece of equipment most imperative if independent learning is to spread is a small, portable tape-recorder, cheaper to buy and cheaper to run than those at present on the market.

The use of audio-visual equipment is one element among many in which the design of the package is affected by cost and by school budgeting practice. The use of packages tends to increase certain items of school expenditure – teaching materials and equipment for example – but it might save on others, such as wasteful use of graduate teachers in small sixth forms. The snag is that, in the earlier stages, packages are likely to be handled in ordinary classroom circumstances, constituting simply an increase in present costs; savings follow only when there is a commitment to package materials on a substantial scale. Further, school expenditure is not subject to 'virement', that is, it is allocated under specific headings. In state education a headmaster makes decisions about children freely, about staff quite extensively, about money scarcely at all. Items are separately categorized and ceilings fixed. In the column marked 'materials' a package simply appears as a sizeable extra for which special permission must be sought. There is no question yet (though Somerset and Oxfordshire have made moves in this direction) of a headmaster choosing how, say, £5000 in his budget might be spent on whatever mixture of extra staff, non-teaching aides, equipment, materials, will suit his school best. Some virement is essential if new methods are to spread.[16]

When it comes to packages, extra costs are immediate and clear, savings delayed and obscure. We can see this in the case of school building. Smaller schools even though comprehensive might, if serviced by packages, offer a satisfactory range of subjects, especially in the sixth form. We might thereby reduce the need for expensive rebuilding into large comprehensives. Unfortunately the saving cannot be estimated because the costs are so tangled. Each locality differs. The cost depends on what brand of comprehension is chosen. It is hard to tell how much of comprehensive re-building is simply displacement, advantage being taken to re-group when shifts of population or a rising birth-rate or raising the school-leaving age would in any case require 'roofs over heads' expenditure. Nor is it at all clear how much of the total theoretical cost of comprehension will actually get spent. In 1926 the *Hadow Report* urged that there should be separate schools for adolescents rather than all-age schools. Some local authorities began to build in line with the recommendation. By 1944 the principle was embodied in an Act of Parliament and all local authorities drew up plans. But in a number of areas the change was still not complete when comprehension came to make it unnecessary.[17] Some all-age schools, stolidly keeping their children well past the statutory limit of eleven, will now appear in the fashionable guise of 'middle schools'. In this way much of the costing of an educational change in England turns out to be paper costing. In practice, every school building tends to go on being used to the limit of, some would say well beyond, its working life. Costs for new building appear in the estimates, in reality, 'temporary' arrangements in existing buildings continue for years.

A similar complex, when using packages, of visible present increase and uncertain future saving occurs over staffing. In 1968, less than 1 per cent of total expenditure on schools went on books; on all kinds of teaching materials the allowance for each child in a secondary school was set at £5 0s. 3d.: the cost of teachers per child was just under £90. This reflects the degree to which secondary education is 'teacher-based'. For their leisure we encourage boys as individuals to learn from books, but in the classroom we insist they learn as a group from the teacher. Clearly, a marginal saving in a boy's share of teaching would permit a dramatic increase in learning materials – a 5 per cent saving on the one side would finance a 90 per cent increase on the other. In Sweden it is estimated that IMU (including in-service training and additional payments to teachers) results in an overall *saving* of 16 per cent over conventional teaching when a team of two teachers and a teacher's aide is used for each group of ninety children rather than three teachers.[18] Whereas teachers qualified to teach in secondary schools in maths, science and certain other subjects grow increasingly rare, the experience of America and Sweden is that willing and competent aides are legion among those women to whom a job limited to school hours and school terms is particularly attractive. The official union resistance in this country to unqualified people in the classroom, theoretically absolute, seems in practice to be a question of definition. So long as our model of the classroom is of one person *teaching* a group of children it is essential that the solitary teacher should be trained. But keeping track of what is being done by children working independently, seeing that materials are there when needed, carrying out reprographic chores, running tests of a routine kind and recording scores – such jobs can be handled for a teacher or a team of teachers by someone less well qualified academically. If teaching consists less of instruction and takes on, in part, the colour of work done in a laboratory (hence the Dalton Plan use of the term), then the function of a laboratory aide or assistant becomes separate and unobjectionable. All the same I think packages in this country are likely to be used principally by individual teachers with their own classes; any attempt to tie package learning to team teaching is over-ambitious if not mistaken. No saving from using aides should therefore be counted on.

Yet other factors confuse the attempt to draw up a financial debit and credit account in using packages. For example, the cost of a package will be affected by how elaborate we make it. Economy creates a pressure to cut out every merely pleasant variation, every extra illustration, every additional tape or slide. And yet at some point, cumulatively, such omissions may leave a dismal and ineffectual thing, repellant especially to less willing children.

Again, the price of a package is affected by how long it is expected to last. The IMU course consists of workbooks the children write in: the life of each copy is therefore one year. It seems a vast increase in cost over normal textbooks – until one discovers that in Sweden textbooks too only have a life of one year, being given, by law, to children to keep. With us the official survival rate of textbooks is now six years and the cost, amortized over that period, is consequently very low. So long a life is out of the question for the kind of package we have envisaged – made up of short booklets such that they can easily be altered, added to, substituted for by the teacher. And, of course, cost is greatly affected by the length of the printing run. Many of the overheads, such as the salaries of those who write and design the packages, remain unaltered whether the market is five hundred or five thousand children.

In a commercial enterprise, estimates of cost are set off against reasonable expectation of profit. If we could show that learning from packages resulted in distinct improvement in boys' enthusiasm for school, in their acquisition of skills or knowledge, in their growth in greater independence, in concentration and self-discipline and so on, then even a substantial extra cost would be easily justified. Alas, as we shall see, there are hopeless complications in comparative evaluation of whole systems of learning applied over sufficiently long periods to children of differing age, ability, temperament and background. The economic justification of packages has to rest on something less contentious than an assertion of their ultimate educational worth.

There seems nothing for it but to take a thoroughly gloomy view and to see what the cost then comes to. Thus, John Vaizey, Keith Norris and Eric Hewton,[19] in a detailed study shortly to be published, have costed a number of alternative methods of instruction including learning packages of the sort produced experimentally by the Nuffield Resources for Learning Project. They have assumed no educational benefits from using packages (nor any loss), and no compensatory savings in re-building or in staff whatsoever. Things remain as they are and packages are extra.

For writing the packages in five subjects – English, maths, general science, social studies, French – they have allowed a salary cost equivalent to one teacher in each subject (plus that of a co-ordinating director and of secretarial staff) for each year's work produced. All ancillary costs in producing, receiving and using the packages have been included. Suppose costs are spread over 5000 users – and the textbook market normally reckons, of course, on much larger printing runs – the total cost of education in a secondary school would then rise by 2 per cent per child; at 10,000 copies the increase is 1·5 per cent.[20]

The increase is substantial but not prohibitive. It is considerably less than the cost increase required in individual subjects by some recent curriculum reform movements – and this, be it remembered, is all cost added without any subsequent and consequent savings. Package-based learning is not, then, impossibly expensive, which is as well, for the years in which education expenditure has been allowed to rise far more steeply than the gross national product are not likely to return.[21] When in the future we look back upon the next few critical years we are likely to find that the history of education has been written principally in a ledger.

With the order of magnitude of the costs of packages established and some idea of how packages might work within the secondary schools, we are now equipped to speculate about who should produce them.

We can order the possibilities in a scale from most to least local thus:

1. A schoolmaster composes his own package.
2. Teachers in a department in a school make packages for their own use.
3. A university department of education or college of education or teachers' centre or some organization established by a local education authority compiles packages for use in the area it serves.
4. Teachers, as writers, in central organizations – such as those for broadcasting or correspondence education or those set up specifically for curriculum development or supported by publishers – produce packages for national publication and sale.[22]

We could give each of these possibilities – and others – a mark in turn for probable speed of production, a sense of participation, probable quality of production, ease of co-ordination between contributors, probable degree of realism and effectiveness, cost, and so on. But I fear any detailed exercise of this sort at a time when we are still exploring whether learning from packages is worth pursuing at all is like discussing whether unicorns should have curved or straight horns. We had better avoid such niceties and confine ourselves to major considerations.

First, we must remember we are talking about packages and not just ordinary teaching materials; second, we are thinking of package learning as a *system*, not just an occasional variant in a single subject; third, we are considering what may work in everyday circumstances, not what heroes and enthusiasts can manage. For these reasons it is misleading to generalize from the remarkable achievement of individual schoolmasters. Similarly, although members of exceptional departments in good schools may have compiled packages over the years, such an achievement in one subject alone will not answer our need. We may well admire curriculum materials produced in co-operation at some local teachers' centres, but we can draw no assurance from this that detailed, closely co-ordinated materials, amply illustrated and varied, such as we require for extensive independent learning, could similarly be produced.

For my part I cannot believe a package-based system – as distinct from occasional pieces of work in particular subjects – will develop from, little less be sustained by, willing but burdened schoolmasters in their spare time. Of course it could be argued that learning from packages is novel, that once schoomasters have seen the light they will set about producing them. But I do not believe the idea of preparing work for independent learning to be novel nor the task expert – lack of time, not lack of vision, has been the bar. Because packages did not exist, because we could not produce them ourselves without herculean labour (for they are far more burdensome to compile at secondary than at primary level), we have put the notion of independent work from materials out of our minds. The problem, in my view, is not lack of willingness nor conservatism in a majority of teachers, but occupation and pre-occupation. The first essential for setting up a package-based system of learning is time, which means money. At the start (it can be tapered off later) the minimum is the equivalent of one teacher's salary for each year's package in each subject, plus ancillary services.[23] Short of this we shall not achieve the necessary 'critical mass' to get the method going.

Just how that one teacher's salary is best used is a matter of detail. One full-time writer per subject has advantages (a committee of one, growing expertness), so has several part-time writers per subject (diversity of experience, interaction). If the writer or writers in a particular subject are based on one school they have easy communication with colleagues and amply opportunity to try out materials with boys they know; if full-time writers are gathered in one place they suffer fewer distractions and learn from colleagues struggling with similar problems in other subjects. Rather than one teacher's worth of time over a succession of years, it may be better to have more but for a shorter period – maximum thrust for take-off, and so on.

However defined, the main teacher-writer or writers should certainly draw upon other colleagues ready to make contributions to the total package. The many experienced and capable women who leave teaching while they raise their families might well find adding small sections and variants to a package a possible and pleasing task. A department of education or college of education, in conjunction with a local education authority, would be a particularly good focus for co-operative enterprise in package-making. A pair of suitable students might, under supervision of a tutor, be allied with a local schoolmaster in producing, improving by observation, and helping to administer pieces of package material for a class. Over a period of time such bits of packagery might accumulate into a useful local bank of materials. Such an exercise would add a further welcome touch of realism to teacher-training and enable would-be teachers to make a practical contribution during their long training, in the way that doctors and nurses contribute during theirs.

Yet no matter how inclusive we try to be, the number of participants writing or compiling a package will certainly be substantially smaller than the number we hope, for hard economic reasons, will use it. Participation is only complete when one man, or a small group, produce materials for their own use. The moment we move beyond this narrow circle we have to distinguish between participation in making the original, basic package and participation in modifying or adding to it.

For with the coming of teachers' centres the general argument for local participation has entered the educational world. It is altogether admirable that such centres should disseminate ideas and supply local needs. When it comes to originating curriculum materials it is excellent that teachers so inclined should use the teachers' centre as the focus of their activity. There may be, for example, gaps in what is published and purchasable which they want to fill. But there are sometimes implications in local originality which need care. Flintshire materials for Flintshire teachers is a rallying cry of considerable force but, except in local history and environmental studies, it may have little to do with the quality of the materials. It is this after all which matters to the children who use them. Some teachers may actually feel more free in choosing what they want off the shelf, thereafter modifying it, than in belonging to a local group making materials in committee. Nor is this to be thought somehow less creative. It is a matter of temperament. Some teachers like to be in at the beginning; they want to make things from the raw materials; to them a textbook or any given course is a species of enslavement. Other teachers are perfectly happy to start with something partly fashioned and then to improve it; they never feel enslaved because it never occurs to them to be so.

In practice, no matter how locally a package is produced, participation in making the initial materials is bound to be limited unless we keep going back to square one. Let us take the most local of all situations – the school itself. A teacher produces a package and uses it with his classes: when he leaves the school are the materials to be put away, the children to revert to ordinary teaching, until his successor has time to enjoy a sense of participation in making his own new package? A department in a school sets about making packages in vigorous participation: will not a newcomer simply have to fit in to what they have already decided on and done?

To worry unduly about where the package originated is in any case to miss the point that the ingredients supplied are not the final dish, little less the whole meal. The intention is that the teacher and the children should have an active hand in the concoction. The real focus for originality and participation is the classroom. The teacher can alter and add to the package in written and recorded form, and he can mix in his verbal contributions by periodic teaching of the class and in tutoring small groups and individuals. Children can 'alter' the visible package by choosing among options (sometimes adding, with the teacher's assent, their own), by contributing to paired and group work, and, as Charlotte Mason urged, by finding their own relevancies in the material available, dwelling on and elaborating what interests them in a way class teaching does not allow. In sum, the basic package, supplied and examinable, is not to be mistaken for the real and final package in the classroom. To set that down would require a variorum edition in many volumes.

If package-based learning is to be established, what is needed, following the feasibility studies of the Nuffield Resources for Learning Project, is an extended trial. In my view, the best centre for such a purpose would be a university department or college of education, or a substantially expanded teachers' centre, in each case acting in consort with a local education authority and servicing teachers in surrounding schools. Should independent learning prove satisfactory then doubtless at all the points on the suggested scale of producers, from the most personal to the national, package-making would follow. We might then hope for a mixed economy in producing the materials for package-based learning similar to the present mixed economy in producing teacher-based materials. Something of this sort has begun to develop in Sweden following the success of IMU. The fire needs a lot of attention at first but once it is burning properly it creates its own draught.

Yet in another and more important sense, package making is a mixed economy from the start, for if independent learning is to survive and thrive in secondary schools, this time it will need to avoid both the total reliance on local voluntary labour that marked the Dalton Plan and the perfectionist product-engineering approach that marred programmed instruction. A package needs to be sufficiently complete to start with and should then promote extensive local alteration and addition. It will succeed best when it stimulates the activity of teachers and children, a pot egg that sets the hens laying.

Chapter Eleven
Making Judgements

When something new is proposed we naturally want to know if it's better than what we have got. We see some attractive novelty we're tempted to adopt, but our glimpse of it has been superficial, the views we have heard partisan: can't we find some convincing evidence to guide us? Every innovation costs more, in money or effort or both: what profit can we confidently forecast to persuade our colleagues the expenditure is worthwhile? And if we ask them to abandon habits given sanctity by time and experience, what can we do, by way of compensation, to invest the new practice with instant authority? Change, then, makes us crave certification: not mere personal opinion but Science shall speak.

Alas, when it does so, its voice proves uncertain and seldom carries far. Research findings – as opposed to the popular report of them – almost always turn out to be Delphic in their obscurity, their cunning qualifications, their non-commital nature. The oracle is impressive indeed, not least for those countervaling complexities which allow us to be more convinced than ever of our private intents. And then, from time to time, some priestly disagreement, some transparent absurdity, reminds us that the imposing tones we hear are not the voice of God but those of fallible mortals armed with primitive tools trying to solve the darkest riddles.

Lee Cronbach defines evaluation as 'the collection and use of information to make decisions about an educational program'.[1] Such a definition finds place for many forms of investigation – the assembly of facts, classroom observation, interviews, the examination of documents and so on. In practice, however, the force and prestige of evaluation lies not in such diverse, descriptive elements but in deliberately contrived experiments with measured results derived from batteries of tests. 'Measurement specialists,' says Cronbach, 'have so concentrated upon one process – the preparation of pencil-and-paper achievement tests for assigning scores to individual pupils – that the principles pertinent to that process have somehow become enshrined as *the* principles of evalution.'

The dominant model of evaluation derives ultimately from experiments in the physical sciences.[2] Quintessentially such experiments run: take a thing; do something to it; see what happens. When the 'thing' is not one of many identical, unchanging objects the model has to be modified. It then becomes: take two or more representative samples; place them in identical circumstances; introduce the innovation into one sample; now study th difference between this 'experimental' sample and the other, the 'control'. Experiments of this sort are familiar, for example, in animal psychology. The same model imprints attempts at the 'summative evalution' of innovations in education.

For scientific evaluation to work at least three conditions must be fulfilled: first, the innovation we're testing must be distinct and controlled; second, at the start and during the experiment we must be able to discount, or account for, any difference in our 'identical' samples other than those we have deliberately induced; third, we must agree what changes matter and be able to assess them. Suppose we try to apply classic summative evaluation to resource- or package-based learning, how shall we fare in meeting these criteria?

The innovation we're testing must be distinct and controlled, for only so shall we know what it is we're assessing. If a student reads many books and attends only a couple of lectures we recognize that he has learnt in a different way from the student who attends many lectures and reads only a couple of books: but how many books and how many lectures enable us to describe one of the two systems of learning 'book-based' and the other as 'lecture-based'? Legal battles have been fought to establish the definition of a sausage. We all know it is a mixture of minced meat and breadcrumbs, but in what proportions? Unless the limits are established how shall we guard against the sausage we buy turning out to be a bread roll in disguise? No court of jurisdiction penetrates beneath the skin of educational practices, stating their proper mixture of constituents and fixing an informative terminology.

Indeed such is the flux and uncertainty of educational practice that small shifts of emphasis get fixed and pinned down, described as unique and special objects. The uninitiated then marvel at

strange discoveries: yet when these are at last examined, how disappointingly ordinary they all seem. We discover we've been guilty
from our earliest years, when giving tests to children, in having
'behavioural objectives', in a dissolute way; innocently we've
forced boys to lisp 'overt responses', willy-nilly, to our questions;
when assessing the proper contribution to our ultimate ends of
the parts of our course, we've indulged ourselves in 'systems
analysis'. In education, it seems, familiar objects, impressively
labelled, like the bones of a goat displayed as the relics of a saint,
achieve unexpected sanctity and miraculous force.[3]

In the bouncing days of programmed learning there appeared
indeed to be a clear and exact product to test. Soon, however,
increasing sophistication led researchers to discover what teachers
had always known, that the surrounding conditions of learning
mix with formal instruction into innumerable compounds of
varying strength and effectiveness. Chief among such surrounding conditions is the teacher himself. In the case of the sort of
'resource-based' learning we have described, the confusion is
still more extreme, for the basic 'package' does not aspire to the
stability of a 'programme' and the teacher's contribution is not
merely implicit, in the kind of relationships he has with the
children in his care, but explicit, in that he can modify the
'package' as he thinks best for them. Some teachers may take
the package neat, others alter it greatly – and among those making
alterations some may strengthen, others weaken it. Some teachers
may put in quite a lot of class teaching, others scarcely any – and
among those who teach, some will stimulate, others depress.
Then there are different ways of handling the package: some will
permit 'continuous progress', others will prefer instead to 'phase'
the work to be done – and for those who phase there's a choice
among alternative methods. Some teachers may decide that children should, in general, get on with their work alone, others will
reckon that paired or group work is better – and these must
select among different ways of arranging groups and controlling
their activities. And so on.

As if the set of variables within 'resource-based' learning were
not problem enough, if we attempt any comparison with
'teacher-based' learning we shall be faced with another set of
variables. Although we talk about 'class-teaching' as though it

were a uniform object, we know well enough, of course, that it is a portmanteau term stuffed with the extremes of human divergence. Moreover the variables in resource-based and teacher-based systems confusingly overlap, since 'resources' include the teacher and the teacher uses 'resources'. Our innovation, then, is neither stable in the experimental samples nor is it very distinct from what's going on in the control samples.

In sorting out the particular effects, singly and in combination, of such sets of variables, summative evaluation often swells to vast dimensions. Research organizations, computer-assisted, laboriously plod through interminable studies. In Sweden, for example, the evaluation of IMU maths begun in 1968 will not end till 1972; parts of the study so far are based on the second, parts on the third version of the course. Meanwhile events have already overtaken the evaluators: a fifth version of the course is in production and a number of earlier deficiencies in text and method which the published report will reveal, have already been rectified on the basis of experience, common sense and debate.

At the other extreme less thorough investigators, desperate to achieve some manageable simplification, often display the Senna Pod Syndrome, the signs of Artificially Purifying the System. They cope with the threatening confusion by laying down precisely how an innovation is to be used. In independent, resource-based learning, for example, it's tempting to say: 'Here's a package of materials; don't alter it; have every boy study entirely on his own. Then we can see if it works.' Privately we may think it more sensible to let teachers alter the materials and to use them in a variety of ways to suit boys' needs, but how on earth is anything so vacillating to be tested? Thus, teachers in America testing 'programmed learning' as an alternative system to conventional teaching, painfully decided that they shouldn't say a word to any child, whatever his perplexities, for fear of fouling up the experiment – otherwise, presumably, with a copy of each programme evaluated, there would need to be a copy of each teacher.[4] The programmes, they felt, had to stand as pure as an unshaded lamp on a deal table. In their rectitude these teachers proved some familiar truths about inducing boredom but little about the value of programmes used in normal school conditions.

We can, of course, sensibly maintain the fixed distinctiveness of an innovation in brief experiments – learning a particular concept from programmed text, say, as opposed to an ordinary book: but we cannot in this way treat whole systems of education because they're made up of many different elements in shifting interactions. Whole systems are complex and flexible in their very nature and it's phoney to rig them otherwise, whether by laying down precisely what the mixture of elements must be or inflating one element, however characteristic, into an entirety. Evaluation must somehow contrive to embrace this complexity if it's to have any real value.

A second condition for classic summative evaluation is that *at the start and during the experiment we must be able to discount or account for any difference in our 'identical' samples other than those we have deliberately induced.* The problems of initial sampling are so familiar that they need not long delay us here. Broadly, we have to choose between deliberate and random sampling. When samples are deliberately compiled, we need to agree what qualities are relevant in making up our parallel lists, and confident in the tests we then apply.[5] Should we match children in our samples in terms of intelligence or attainment or willingness or what? In teacher-based learning, quick oral comprehension is a highly significant indicator: in resource-based learning reading comprehension may matter much more. Of course many different indicators may be dealt with in a multivariate analysis. If, however, we then leave each item distinct we may produce a report too complex to be influential; if we try dangerously to conflate the items on some general, comprehensive scale we shall have to make impossible decisions about the proper weighting of each component. The easier alternative of random sampling, alas, has snags as well. Common experience confirms that the application of entirely neutral factors can result in lop-sided groups. Classes divided by the alphabet, teams chosen by birthdays, turn out to be hopelessly unequal. Of course, if the sample is sufficiently large then all the variables conveniently cancel rather than compound one another – only by looking down enough corridors of distorting mirrors can we reckon to make out the correct image at the end; but the commitment to large numbers is in itself a serious constraint, forcing the evaluator, for the severest practical reasons, to confine himself, in over-whelming degree, to simple tests capable of being processed.

Let us suppose, however, that satisfactory initial samples, 'experimental' and 'control', have indeed been established: our next perplexity is to keep them equal. The task will be easy in proportion as the experiment is brief. Yet if it is *too* brief our results will be compromised by the 'Hawthorne effect' – the tendency of almost any experiment to have beneficial results simply because it happens to be new. This is a more serious problem in educational than in, say, medical research for reasons Cronbach describes:

In testing a drug, we know that valid results cannot be obtained without a double-blind control in which the doses for half the subjects are inert placebos; the placebo and the drug look alike, so that neither doctor nor patient knows who is receiving medication. Without this control the results are useless even when the state of the patient is checked by completely objective indices. In an educational experiment, it is difficult to keep pupils unaware that they are an experimental group. And it is quite impossible to neutralize the biases of the teacher as those of the doctor are neutralized in the double-blind design.

Yet suppose we protract the experiment to diminish the Hawthorne effect, then in any long experiment – as the evelution of a whole system of learning must be – we must somehow account for the cumulative effects of all significant influences for otherwise it won't be the results of the innovation alone we assess. Recent research reports have made us more aware than ever of the multiplicity of influences bearing upon a boy's academic performance: one emphasizes the paramount importance of parental attitudes, another the expectations of the teacher, yet another the boy's whole social milieu.[6] So multiply compounded is he, that the Germans with their habit of explanatory words should have one for 'boy' long enough to develop a perspective. All these factors will, over the period of an experiment, differently affect different boys in different samples. We cannot sensibly discount these powerful extraneous influences: but are we able properly to take account of them? [7]

And what about the third condition for summative evaluation, *that we should agree what changes matter and be able to assess them.* Unless we know our objectives and have appropriate measuring rods to apply, how shall we tell whether we're making progress of the right sort, and how much of it? This need for explicitness, though its origin is earlier,[8] has been publicised in Mager's influential handbook, *Preparing Educational Objectives.*[9] When instruction is given, the teacher or the writer of the materials being used should, Mager insists, list his objectives and state what changes in the student's 'terminal behaviour' (that is, what exemplification of skill, knowledge, attitude or insight) will be used as a measure of how far the 'behavioural objectives' have been accomplished.

This emphasis on a more precise definition of our vague instructional aims has great value: but it has inherent dangers too. The anxiety to achieve solid results, duly totted up and precisely figured, may all too easily lead to those things that can't be counted coming not to count.[10] Examples of this tendency in other spheres are not hard to find: thus, preoccupation with traffic flow – a measurable benefit – has led to the rape of many country towns; and financial gain – easily accountable – has justified the fouling of our environment. Our profoundest senses may object to what is done, but what weight can we give to their gratification? If measurable objectives come to dominate the classroom, what place will the casual, the unexpected, the merely pleasant retain; and against some 'efficient' method of instruction what attention will be given to our fears that, in an immediately unproveable way, a boy's long-term emotional and intellectual growth has been stunted? In the past, we have accused public examinations of distorting education: children concentrate on what's marketable; teachers stuff them with concepts and words beyond their digestion ('inert ideas' in Whitehead's phrase); things easily regurgitated and examined become the unhealthy staple of school diet. Won't Magerite formulae, naïvely and widely applied, even more strongly lead to the dominance of what is measurable?

The answer given nowadays by evaluators is that the list of objectives for a course of instruction should include *all* objectives, not just the measurable ones. Bloom's celebrated *Taxonomy of Educational Objectives*[11] provides a long catalogue indeed and includes many elusive and subtle goals from both the 'affective' and the 'cognitive' domain. But the mere inclusion of such elements, among the objectives of a course, doesn't solve the problem. Such is our predeliction for figures rather than opinion that those objectives we know how to measure, although they may be only a small and relatively unimportant part of the whole, achieve a wholly disproportionate status and weight. In these circumstances evaluation is not really 'summative' at all, but dangerously selective and partial.

Such complexities explain why full-scale scientific validation is so rare, expensive, complex and slow.[12] Yet anything less does not begin to stand up to serious scrutiny. We generally come across bits of validation one at a time; an unsubtle researcher, a bold propagandist, may then make categorical pronouncements on the basis of slender findings. It is only when we review several parallel studies that the primitive quality of most 'scientific' evaluation becomes apparent. Three brief anthologies of research will serve as examples. The first is about the effects of unstreaming classes; the second makes comparisons between different ways of teaching a topic; the third deals with a really simple matter – just one element in programmed instruction:

From the 1920s through the 1950s researchers, mainly from the university education departments, conducted many enquiries into the efficacy of grouping by ability: some in secondary schools, some in primary; some involving a few pupils, others many. Some came to definite conclusions (for example, that slow learners learnt better on their own); others came to the opposite conclusion (slow learners were inspired to higher achievements when taught together with bright children). Most however came to no definite conclusions.[13]

By far the largest category of research is that of 'relative effectiveness' studies, in which the performance of students instructed by television has been compared with the performance of others instructed directly, or face to face, by a teacher in the usual way.... The vast majority of these studies revealed 'no significant differences' in measured performance between students.... It is interesting to speculate on the reasons.... Some people have suggested that the measuring instruments are not sharp enough to detect differences which may exist.... Another hypothesis is that many studies have dealt with comparisons of complexes of variables which tend to cancel each other, while still other experiments were concerned only with single variables which in many cases are not sufficiently potent to produce significant differences in learning.[14]

One of the points prominently advocated by the Skinner–Holland school of programming is the need for active, overt responding (such as composing or writing an answer, making a vocal utterance, etc.) on the part of the learner. A number of investigators, however, have failed to obtain significant differences between response modes (Stolurow and Walker, 1962; Lambert, Miller and Wiley, 1962; Widlake, 1964) while others have variously found in favour of the overt mode (Williams, 1963; Cummings and Goldstein, 1962; Eigen and Margulies, 1963) and still others have obtained differences on a test of retention – sometimes overt responders being better (Krumboltz and Weisman, 1962) sometimes the covert (i.e. reading) responders (Goldbeck and Campbell, 1962).[15]

From this flurry of contradictions, of claims, counter-claims and claims qualified to extinction, one begins to wonder whether the function of educational research is to answer questions or to ensure that those contentious souls who might have fought with bare hands can instead belabour one another with clubs. 'Have at thee! A Krumboltz, a Krumboltz!' 'Ho! villain. A Goldbeck (1962) for your pains. . . .'

Yet, this does not mean that less attention should be given to educational research, but more. The task is as important as it is difficult. One investigator, in comic despair, suggested his report should be subtitled 'or why researchers into infant behaviour should be Oriental metaphysicians'.[16] The problem is no less when the infants are larger. It is not the researchers' fault but God's that their subject matter is so hopelessly complex.

Not only are the answers given by educational researchers attempting a 'scientific' evaluation often uncertain and contradictory: the kinds of answer they can hope to give are limited and easily misunderstood. Suppose that independent, resource-based learning really could, somehow, be evaluated, many teachers might still find the result disappointingly unreliable, even misleading. Why is this so?

In everyday discussion we cope with the nebulous and amorphous shape of things, the flux of particular incidents and transient states, by transmuting our over-all impressions into generalizations. A teacher may be well aware that individual boys exhibit the oddest inconsistencies and vacillations from day to day and still say, 'John's willing and hardworking'; he will know that within any group of boys every sort of attitude and opinion is to be found and still declare, 'Boys much prefer to be taught than to have to work things out for themselves.' Because we all use generalizations in this way ourselves we know instinctively that they are more fragile and uncertain than they sound. We accept them as representing the speaker's considered views, at least at that time, in that context; and we then discount what he has said according to our assessment of him and our own experience.

Educational researchers make general statements too, but in a statistical form so far at odds with our normal usage that we do not know what status to accord them. The statistician, too, has to capture the incoherence of the real world in generalizations: but he embalms the flux for eternity in rigid posture and imposing stare, so that some beholders are unduly overawed, others too completely repelled, and most bewildered. Suppose, to take a simple case, the outcome of an experiment is represented in a Gaussian, normal distribution curve: the curve itself is an approximation of particular results which, as one Swedish statistician has poetically put it, 'flutter like a butterfly around the curve', and each of these particular results represents the butterfly caught, killed and transfixed at a particular moment in time. In short, statistical statements, however subtle, involve telling lies about a series of real exceptions in order to encompass an abstract rule: they mislead in particular in order to illuminate in general. The statistical 'maps' which result have value to planners but offer little guidance to the daily traveller. So Olympian is the height from which mortals are viewed on the statistical scale that they dissolve into masses, and individual features important at ground level shrink into invisibility.

Herein lies the critical difference between research into physical and into human affairs. It is not that physical scientists provide real answers and social scientists merely statistical answers, for contemporary physics has revealed that the Newtonian scheme gave only a blunt general approximation to the particular world of quanta and relativity. Truths in the physical sciences are statistical too. If countless particles could give tongue doubtless they would protest at the crude, lumpish view of a uniform material universe we find adequate for our daily purposes. The Memoirs of a Mesotron would reveal a rakehell existence composed of 'uncertainty relations', 'metastable and excited states', 'fleeting equilibriums' and 'various kinds of degeneracy'.[17] However, when the social scientists produce stable, lumpish, statistically valid views of *us*, then our imprisonment in, our intimate awareness of, the world of human micro-particularity, relativity and change, prevents their findings being either convincing or of everyday value. If all our sciences can cope only with truths in the mass, truths of a general statistical kind, truths useful to planners, then the large truths of the physical scientists are useful and reliable because in relation to the dizzy, explosive sub-atomic world of matter we are all Gullivers: but when social scientists make their large pronouncements we see them with the canny eyes of Lilliputians.

This genuine problem of scale and not some wanton conservatism may explain the resistance of particular teachers to innovations which have proved to be of general value in large-scale tests. Whenever anything new is proposed in education nowadays, the chilling word that greets it is 'evaluation'. How will its effectiveness be measured? The question is easily and sensibly asked: but, in addition to remembering the daunting problems of worthwhile evaluation, we have to add the gloss 'evaluation for whose, for what, purpose – for the planner dealing in gross or the individual dealing in units?' Piaget's work may properly guide the designer of learning materials to be used by large numbers of children, Bernstein's findings justify the government instituting compensatory pre-school education;[18] but even such distinguished research can do no more than offer occasional insights when we deal with individuals or small collections of children. A statistical generalization about any group encloses a wide range of individual differences, and we never know whereabouts the particular child or collection we are dealing with fits. In its current state of development educational research cannot bridge the gap between 'we know from statistical evidence that this innovation works' and 'you can make this work in your class'. We are still far from a science of education, which is to say a body of generalizations that enables us accurately to predict individual results.

What stage has the science reached? About that of Voltaire, perhaps, who having set down his Laws of Fire, prudently added a last law that the others didn't always work.[19] Or perhaps we inhabit what the physical scientists, in disparaging retrospect of their origins, would call the world of magic. The magician believed, as does the scientist, in a more or less fixed chain of cause and effect, and he, too, tested reasonable hypotheses by experiment in order to achieve reliable manipulations of nature. First do this and then that, precisely, and the crops will improve, you will fight better, the sick man will be cured, the rain will fall. To become scientifically effective, however, the magician needed either an exact knowledge of the actual process of change (not just the act and the outcome) or alternately some means of isolating the variables in rotation so that he could know the particular result of each particular part of the act.[20] Without such knowledge, any individual success or failure might be the product of endless possible combinations of circumstances. Similarly in education our ignorance of the process in the brain called 'learning' is almost complete, and in all but the simplest experiments we cannot prevent the complex of variables shifting and weaving inextricably. You can, Voltaire assures us, kill a flock of sheep with the right magic incantations – accompanied by a sufficient dose of arsenic. The trouble is that in education we're never quite sure which is which.

Because human complexity defeats the most skilful attempts at classical 'scientific' evaluation, another less forbidding style of evaluation has begun to develop. It is a style at once more modest and more ambitious: on the one hand it doesn't aim at the authority and the high level of generality that characterizes science; on the other it tries to deal with real, whole situations, not just those parts amenable to scientific treatment. Such evaluation relies less extensively upon the application of validated tests, more upon various evidences, derived from observation, questionnaires, interviews, informal conversations, psychological tests, examinations, diaries, documents.... all of which is a codification and sharpening of the multiplicity of ways in which, in ordinary everyday practice, we try to assess whether some innovation is likely to suit us. In such evaluation, as in life, oddities and side-effects may prove particularly illuminating: in scientific evaluation oddities get lost in statistical composites and side-effects excluded because they're not listed in predetermined objectives. Inevitably, evaluation of depth and of a personal kind can be applied to few cases, whereas scientific evaluation draws its strength from many: but an impressionist painting done from life may convey an understanding of the whole class of objects to which it belongs no less well than a classical study done chiefly in the studio, a composition of abstracted fragments into a universal archetype. Or perhaps a parallel for the two styles of evaluation lies in the distinction between 'science' and 'natural history'. One is reminded of Sir Julian Huxley's pleasure (following his celebrated study of the Redshank) at 'having made field natural history scientifically respectable again. It was so for Darwin but later more attention was given to laboratory experiments as against straightforward observation of animals' habits in Nature'.[21]

An exploratory, more open style of evaluation is particularly apt when we scrutinize – and the difference is critical – not separate items of instruction but whole systems of learning. When we design instruction in a given concept or short series of concepts, when we look for the most efficient way to transmit bits of necessary information or training in a given skill, then we can legitimately confine ourselves to limited, behavioural objectives, those which can be clearly stated and scientifically evaluated. We can pause from worrying about souls while we teach solutions to simultaneous equations. But when we are considering whole systems of learning, applied over a number of years and over a range of subjects, we dare not ignore remoter aims, however nebulous and controversial. The 1944 Education Act enjoined us to care for the spiritual, moral, mental and physical development of children. Unfortunately, this order of priority exactly reverses ease in measured, scientific evaluation.[22]

The contrast drawn between the 'science' and the 'natural history' of evaluation need not, of course, imply exclusiveness. In theory – and actually in some large-scale studies – both modes may be used: in general, however, limits of time and energy and money tend to force researchers to employ one mode or the other.

The trouble is that the 'scientific' mode, being more powerful, is often used when neither the subject nor the available resources make it appropriate. The reason is often, in the broad sense, 'political': experimenters want proof; decision makers of all sorts – international agencies, national politicians, senior civil servants and such – require hard evidence to justify grants of money. Anyone anxious to improve education is likely therefore to be ambivalent towards scientific, summative evaluation, thinking it a bit of a goose but capable of producing golden eggs. Its partial truths and convincing lies provide essential arguments. Certainly, the best of those engaged in the evaluation business seem well aware of current limitations in their intricate task, and persist in spite of derogation from colleagues in easier and older disciplines. Mistakes in so formidable an undertaking are understandable; so, too, the scientific caution, the tiresome jargon which makes almost every research paper read like a translation. It is pretentiousness alone we may justly object to. When a distinguished Reader in Education declares: 'teachers who ignore research are like farmers who go on growing potatoes without finding out about fertilizers',[23] his analogy is grossly misleading. Its presumption lends colour to the scathing comment of Jacques Barzun, Dean of Social Studies and Education at Columbia University: 'Human capacity is more varied than educational researchers know, though their methods ensure that they shall never find this out.'[24] Those of us who would gladly be guided by evaluated certainties (if we knew they applied to us) and would cheerfully apply reliable fertilizers (if we could be sure they were appropriate to our needs) must contrive to manage a little longer without them.

The present gap between research and daily application is such that teachers generally turn for help to those in the same boat with them, all awash in a vast sea. Professors who grandly philosophize the aims of education flash over in aircraft; those who evaluate its practices nose beneath in submarines. Doubtless from above and below they can distinguish better than we who teach the fundamental forces of weather and current that affect us: but our main anxiety is to stay afloat and make some sort of progress, guided, if must be, by ancient stars. We wonder how others in similar straits are getting on. 'Have you tried to row facing forwards?' we shout above the racket of the elements; 'No', comes the answer, 'but paddling with your feet over the stern helps' ... and we suspect that the academics, secure from the daily fret of wind and wave, have forgotten what it is like to feel a little seasick all the time.

Chapter Twelve
What Hopes?

The argument of this book is that we should test independent learning thoroughly as an alternative method to teacher-based learning in our secondary schools.

Attempts have been made in the past to base a school's whole régime on independent learning, to allow boys to move within a learning environment of resources and events (what we have called 'packages'). Some such experiments – notably the Dalton Plan – seemed set for permanent success, but they faded away. We need to find out whether we can now get independent learning to work over a comprehensive ability range and on a substantial scale. Such an investigation is particularly worthwhile because independent learning would ease a number of the problems that plague us at present in secondary education, confounding the attempt to establish a workable system of comprehensive schooling.

If a more independent style of learning from packages were in operation, just how would it help us? Certainly it would alleviate some of our staffing difficulties. Packages can be used effectively by those who may be excellent with children but relatively inexpert in a subject or in its latest developments. As a means of providing in-service training, packages parallel the newly developed curriculum courses. These, however, are designed for mediation by a teacher, and often require that he should be more expert and more busy than ever, whereas a package is designed essentially for direct use by the child with less frequent interventions by the teacher. Packages may partly compensate, then, for the ominous shortage of teachers well qualified to teach the rarer skills.

Further, whereas extempore teaching demands a fully qualified teacher, once packages have a more significant role in learning outside help for the teacher can increase. This might consist of teachers in training or in retirement acting as contributors or adaptors of materials, or of para-professionals, assisting with tutoring, or of untrained aides handling materials, scoring tests, keeping records and the like.

The shortage of suitably qualified teachers is an acute problem above all at sixth-form level. All-through comprehension, desirable in so many other respects, tends to scatter A-level groups previously concentrated in the grammar schools. Further, the range of desirable A-level subjects, and of sensible combinations among them, steadily grows – not to mention the demands of those new sixth-formers who want courses outside traditional A-level confines. The Swedish *korrespondens-gymnasium*, and those thousands who plough through correspondence courses in more solitary conditions, are a demonstration that packages can be especially effective for boys of sixth-form age.

The anxiety of almost every secondary school to have its own sixth formers pushes us (if there is to be sufficient concentration of boys and graduate teachers) towards having large schools. So does the wish to provide in the main body of the school a variety of courses to satisfy the needs of a comprehensive intake of children and also to prepare for a wide range of subjects in the sixth. In all this smaller schools are awkwardly placed. Packages would help considerably to increase the variety of fare available in such schools. Smaller schools might still fall short of what the largest can offer, but many parents and children would willingly sacrifice a measure of specialist facilities for less travelling, a greater chance of composure, a more human scale. Serviced by packages smaller schools, though comprehensive, could become educationally viable. Small schools linked to a resource-supplying centre would be like those small grocer's shops that now link together in bulk-buying groups – a very good alternative to the supermarket.

The considerations which make packages useful to small schools apply yet more strongly where children suffer too many schools or really have no school at all. Charlotte Mason reminds us how independent learning can help them. Some such children are scattered in remote places abroad; others are in hospital; yet others are home-bound through illness or because they are 'school-shy'. Sometimes children although regularly at a school miss a lot of normal teaching. The cause may be their illness, or a teacher's, or the intrusive demands of a special talent, such as music. For them independent work is in varying measure unavoidable and materials imaginatively designed for the purpose would be a godsend.

Packages greatly ease, though they do not require, a greater measure of unstreaming. So long as classes of children learn chiefly direct from a teacher the argument for making those classes as homogeneous as possible is strong. At present variations in subject content and in pace occur between different classes, not within them. Unfortunately, set on a certain track, a child tends to stay in it, adjusting efforts and hopes to what is expected. While the snags of streaming are now well advertised, it does not follow at all that unstreaming by itself is enough or even better. In America the slow pace of an unstreamed class stifles the more able; in Russia the brisker pace results in constant pressure on the less able. If put into an unstreamed class and then taught the usual way, the less able child may well feel more bewildered, exposed and depressed than ever. Any worthwhile attempt at varying content and pace within a single class or group depends on suitable materials for more independent work being provided.

The range of varying ability and interest in an unstreamed class is such that not merely a difference of pace but a choice of alternative topics and activities within a subject becomes essential. Such choice might well appeal strongly to children in a streamed class as well, giving an increased sense of personal involvement. Packages provide such a choice.

Packages can also help towards a more active and, hopefully, a more responsible attitude to learning. They thereby reduce the present contrast between secondary education and both primary and higher education. Whether we like it or not, children of secondary school age are less docile and modest than they used to be. The habit of an active participation in what they do, rather than a passive attention to what they are told, is not likely to be put on and off, like a coat, as they pass through the classroom door. Ordered acceptance, on which our habits of class teaching rest, is a waning asset, but a move to anything less sedentary will prove exhausting indeed unless the teacher gets material support of the right sort. At present too much energy and money goes into bricks and mortar and into hardware. Often the proliferation of opportunities is merely an embarrassment, an added strain, a further widening of the gap between what imagination conceives and frailty allows. Period after period, the schoolmaster stands exposed and alone on stage, forced to put on too many performances, the only source of an often unpalatable curriculum, concocting what to do next to keep thirty or more adolescents busy. It would help to have sensible things for active children to get on with. Packages are designed to this end.

If we do not find a way to support teachers in the classroom by providing materials for children to use, our comprehensive schools will, I fear, be far more impressive for their plant and equipment than for what goes on inside them. This is a particularly bad time to project on a comprehensive scale a system of learning so exclusively dependent on an ample supply of qualified teachers, yet there is every sign that comprehension is going to be what went before writ very large, and that we shall merely plod down the same road that other countries have taken before us. We should aim to do better.

We began this book with a glance at the widely different aims spatch-cocked together in our notion of secondary education. A boy's spiritual, social and physical education have concerned us in this book only incidentally: our focus has been classroom instruction. We have assumed that at the secondary stage we shall continue to insist on children learning things that we adults think important for them, whatever their views. This restriction is an important and an awkward one. Much more radical and progressive proposals are possible if we avoid it. The puzzle is to decide, within the *real* limits – not assuming a sudden transformation in adult attitudes to schooling or a miraculous draught of extra teachers or of cash – what can be done to ease the rigidities of timetabling and teaching in that part of the school day when free expression and free exploration, self-expression and self-exploration give way to imposed requirements. What prosaic, practical help can we give to those teachers who think it wise to let the boys and girls in their care move, some a little, some a lot, out of the conventional class unison, towards

a greater independence in learning? I believe packages will provide the help they need.

In the above list of problems in secondary education which
packages may help to ease, each item is a fair one, but the total,
I fear, may seem too imposing. Our school arrangements are
permeated by the expectation that children are to be taught in
classes: alter that expectation and the effects are many. In the
same way a headache is common to all sorts of illnesses: cures
for headaches therefore list, perfectly justly, their contribution
to almost every complaint in the medical manual; but then mere
aspirin begins to sound like the elixir of life.

In education the claims of reformers tend to be especially
grand. Books on education ought to be smudgily printed on
blotchy paper with plenty of misprints as a constant reminder of
what we are really dealing with. Montaigne complained: 'When
I hear a builder puff himself up with such grand words as
pilasters, architraves, and Corinthian and Doric cornices, I at
once seem to see the palace of Apollidon – though all he is talking
about are the paltry pieces of my kitchen door.' I am particularly
worried lest anyone should suppose that packages are something very special. The kind needed in our schools, should, on
the contrary, be familiar and ordinary – what a good teacher who
wanted his children to work independently would himself do if
he had the time.

Packages of the kind we have described, intended for local
modification and supplementation, will become different in
each classroom. In this they differ essentially from distinct,
scientifically perfected pieces of programmed instruction by
book or machine or computer. In one classroom they will play
a dominant part in the over-all business of learning; in another
a somewhat smaller part. These children working from packages
will be allowed to rush forward largely on their own; those will
more frequently need check and support. The aim of the packages is to allow children a greater independence in their learning
and thereby to permit a changed relationship in the classroom;
but how far, how soon, for how many is for the teacher to judge.
Clearly we cannot advertise anything so various and elusive as
a panacea. It is just as well. In practice change in education is,

and should be, very slow. Schools are usually credited by parents with remarkable powers of shaping children. Such a belief is a measure of their affection and their hopes. Teachers in reflection sometimes suppose great benefits or great evils to result from each small change they make. Were it really so our responsibilities would be intolerable. Mercifully children display to a remarkable degree what the eighteenth century called 'bottom' – a basic stolidity derived from experiences which occurred before or lie outside the secondary school. To expect that a shift to package learning or any other system will achieve critical changes in children is merely to invite disappointment.

In particular a change in the method of learning alone will not in itself cure the problem of motivation. Many adolescents at their studies must feel as we would if forced to attend numerous lectures on the Sumerian tablets. We have examined earlier in this book why we teach adolescents a number of subjects, and details within those subjects, the purpose of which is obscure to them. Our passion for equality now impels us towards giving everyone the same thing, the complexity of society towards giving everyone everything. Early maturity makes adolescents restive sooner, prolonged schooling makes them restive longer. In the long run I believe we shall have to re-think the current practice of giving everyone as long a period of schooling as possible at the start of their lives with provision only for spare-time supplementation thereafter. For the time being we must not be surprised, although we change our method of learning, if the more recalcitrant adolescents still find school incomprehensible. The converted Jew in H. O. Sturgis's *Belchamber* 'instead of not attending the synagogue now stayed away from the church'.[1] At best we may hope that the number of reluctant boys will be reduced in that packages will at least allow more choice and make schooling less servile.

We have noted 'bottom' in boys as a factor which makes the effect of change less remarkable than enthusiasts expect, but 'bottom' is by no means confined to boys – teachers have it amply. In new maths, discovery by discussion with the teacher easily erodes into one-way teaching. 'The Socratic manner', observed Max Beerbohm, 'is not a game at which two can play.' Paul Brandwein writes of new American science curricula:

It is curious to note how the educational community changes its words but not its deeds; thus 'learning by doing' is replaced by 'learning through discovery', 'the discovery method' or 'the problem-solving method' by 'inquiry'. Yet observations will show that in the majority of high schools, teachers of science lecture 80 per cent of the class time, and that the laboratory time is given over to 'doing experiments' with equipment laid out in advance, hence the results are postulated in advance. Yet teachers and administrators will assure the observer that the new curriculums (PSSC, CHEMS, BSCS and the like, are being used and 'inquiry' is the mode of instruction.[2]

Teachers of modern languages in Sweden using the direct method believed, in pursuance of official policy, that they were providing their charges with ample opportunity to practise speaking the language. A stop-watch study revealed they did so for less than 8 per cent of the teaching time.[3] We should not assume that *plus ça change plus c'est la même chose* applies only in these two subjects or only in foreign countries.

This tendency of teachers to return to what is most familiar is the source of breast-beating at many conferences of administrators and innovators. Why don't the new ways 'take'? Doubtless for reasons as various as the nature of the teachers themselves. Chief among them I would list an *excess* of publicity and persuasion – too many popular articles and programmes on television. A slower individual absorption of some innovation offers more lasting prospects. For such steady dissemination, we need detailed books, word of mouth explanations by practising teachers to other teachers, and above all in-service training on a less derisory scale than at present in England.[4] Steady local support is another prime necessity. Often when innovators, reinforced by the mass media, fret and agitate, they do indeed succeed in getting quite a lot of teachers to try something. They achieve a flurry of interest. Education committees vote initial grants to try the latest innovation, to buy the necessary equipment. Being so open-minded, indeed far-sighted, is ground for congratulation. But *continuing* grants out of current revenue for servicing a change when its gilt has rubbed off is altogether less rewarding. The teachers, without the resources the originators enjoyed, find they simply cannot persist without risk of prostration.

When it comes to something as fundamental as a change in the acutal system of learning it would be better by far not to start at all than to make the attempt without a proper calculation of the resources needed, a determination to do the job thoroughly. Better the old ways than a muddle of old and new, neither done properly. In practice the essential alterations seem less a matter of large sums of money than of intentions, attitudes and organization, but the implications of independent learning on any scale larger than an experiment is at present a matter chiefly of surmise. Innovations can be made to stick on to existing institutions when experimental pressures are applied, often peel off when the pressures are lifted. What can be made to work in miniature often presents unexpected intricacies when extended.[5] What is needed next, then, is a shift from feasibility study to sustained trial, from model to working prototype. All that can safely be said at present is that independent learning has a renewed relevance in the context of the contemporary comprehensive school, that the potential benefits are substantial, that the change looks manageable, the prospects good.

Because a more independent and active style of learning is no new aspiration I have been conscious in writing this book of the amiable ghosts of a number of predecessors, finding special pleasure in the company of Charlotte Mason. And at my shoulder I have felt too the less cheerful presence of a certain Cadman. A commemorative tablet on the tower of St Mary the Virgin in Shrewsbury reads:

> Let this small Monument record the name
> Of CADMAN, and to future times proclaim
> How by'n attempt to fly from this high spire
> Across the Sabrine stream he did acquire
> His fatal end. 'Twas not for want of skill
> Or courage to perform the task he fell;
> No, no, a faulty Cord being drawn too tight
> Hurried his Soul on high to take its flight
> Which bid the Body here beneath good Night.
>
> February 2nd 1739

How the spirit of Cadman warns us of the need to take a few tentative hops on the ground and jumps from modest heights

before we launch out; and to check, double-check, each item,
to consider every detail we can foresee! These careful prelimin-
aries completed, the time comes, as I think it has done once more
with independent learning, to try a bolder leap, a longer flight.
Shall we find this time that we can fly?

Appendix: Nuffield Resources for Learning Project

The Nuffield Foundation set up its Resources for Learning Project in 1966. Rapid changes and growing expectations in education on the one hand, and a continuing shortage of resources on the other, emphasized the need to study how schools might take the best use both of teachers' skills and of new developments in method and equipment.

The Consultative Committee of the Resources for Learning Project is made up of the following members: Chairman, Dame Margaret Miles (ex-Chairman, A. L. C. Bullock); Sir Edward Boyle, Miss J. D. Browne, G. Taylor, Sir Ronald Gould, J. Stringer, Dr M. Young, Professor B. Morris, Lord Bernstein, Dr D. A. Pidgeon, Sir William Alexander, Sir William Houghton, H. J. Edwards, Dr A. H. Halsey, G. Caston, R. A. Becher, B. W. M. Young, R. Sibson, G. Rogers.

The Co-Directors of the Project are: I. McMullen, L. C. Taylor and Professor J. Vaizey. Members of the team are: M. Armstrong, J. D'Arcy, Miss D. M. Diamond, Mrs E. A. Hardman, J. Hare, Mrs P. Pestell, Mrs M. G. Roberts, Mrs E. B. Tidy (Primary Adviser).

Administration of the Project: Miss S. D. Watson, Miss R. Y. Lovegrove. Secretarial Staff: Mrs P. Jenkins, Miss P. Marsh, Mrs S. Rutter. General Assistance: Mrs G. M. Ward, Miss J. Thomson. Miss C. O'Keeffe.

Graphics: G. Wilson, A. Baron, Miss R. Pearson and K. Cowan, under the direction of F. Gluck and R. Inglis of the Hornsey College of Art.

Economic Studies: Professor J. Vaizey with K. Norris and E. Hewton of Brunel University.

Curriculum Resources Development Project, Leicester: Director – Miss E. Garnett (in association with County of Leicestershire and City of Leicester Education Authorities).

In various studies the Project has had substantial support from the National Council for Educational Technology, the

Inner London Education Authority, and the Centre for Educational Research and Innovation (part of OECD). Its work has depended on the co-operation of numerous schools, university departments, colleges of education, educational publishers and research organizations at home and abroad.

Notes

Chapter 1

1. See *Young School Leavers*, Schools Council Enquiry no. 1, HMSO, 1968.

2. Henry Adams, *The Education of Henry Adams*, Constable, 1919.

3. Douglas Pugh, 'Victim of role inflation', *American Journal of Teacher Education*, March, 1961. Reprinted in N. Beckner and L. Dumas (eds.), *Readings from Secondary Education*, International Textbook Co., Pennsylvania, 1968.

4. The authors of the *Plowden Report* write: 'We have considered whether we can lay down the standards that should be achieved by the end of the primary school but concluded it is not possible to describe a standard of attainment that should be reached by all or most children' (*Children and Their Primary Schools*, Report of the Central Advisory Council of Education (England), 2 vols., HMSO, 1967).

5. Edward Yeomans writes of an 'integrated-day' primary school: '... the sounds of activity seldom require damping down: everyone is talking; some are hammering at a bench (outdoors if possible); children are getting out apparatus or putting it away; highly spillable substances, such as soap suds and poster paints, are being poured and carried, sometimes spilled, always mopped up without fuss; and through it all there is a sense of the utmost serenity and purposefulness' (*Education for Initiative and Responsibility*, National Association of [American] Independent Schools, 1968, p. 21).

6. See W. D. Wall: 'While there is some positive correlation between abilities and interests it is surprisingly small. You have to dig deeper to discover if an expressed interest is superficial or not. Manifest interest is an extremely dicey index of what you

ought to be doing' (*Adolescents in School and Society*, National Foundation for Educational Research, 1969).

7. See Frank Musgrove: 'Since the late nineteenth century the advanced industrial nations have made two unprecedented demands on the school for normal children: the first is to provide for an economic redundant juvenile population; the second is to provide for more protracted opportunities for young people to explore themselves. ... The curriculum to which educationalists have ascribed a variety of subtle objectives has been a structure of activity to fill the time ...' (quoted in a review entitled 'Curriculum objectives', in *Education*, 22 November 1968).

8. J. B. Conant, President of Harvard, urged 'a common core of general education which will unite in one cultural pattern the future carpenter, factory worker, bishop, lawyer, doctor, sales-manager, professor and garage mechanic' (*The Comprehensive High School*, McGraw-Hill, 1967). It sounds a tall order.

9. Thomas Hughes, *Tom Brown's Schooldays*, Nelson, 1930, p. 64.

10. A. N. Whitehead attacks these developments: 'Let us now ask how in our system of education we are to guard against this mental dry rot. We enunciate two educational commandments: "Do not teach too many subjects", and again, "What you teach, teach thoroughly"' (*The Aims of Education*, Mentor Books, 1949, p. 14).

11. Jerome S. Bruner, *The Process of Education*, Harvard University Press, 1965, p. 33.

12. That the prime intellectual function of education is the 'initiation' of all children into various time-tested 'disciplines' has been strongly argued by R. S. Peters. See his *Authority, Responsibility and Education*, Allen & Unwin, 1963, and his published lecture, *Education as Initiation*, Harrap, 1964.

13. Quoted by Anthony Chevenix-Trench, 'The public schools', in Peter Blander (ed.), *Looking Forward to the Seventies*, Smythe, 1968, p. 76. Compare Sir Alec Clegg: 'As I see it, the job of education is to strengthen the young mind rather than to

fill it.... The job is similar to that of the dietician who knows how to produce muscle and bone and fat from the food resources at his disposal. Unfortunately, we do not yet know how physics is converted into compassion or the classics into humility' (quoted in J. Stuart Maclure, *Curriculum Innovation in Practice*, a report on the Third International Curriculum Conference, Oxford, HMSO, 1968, p. 25).

14. Three 'modes' of examining are practised. Mode One is the traditional, familiar style, of papers set on a syllabus decided by the examiners and marked by them. Mode Two allows a school to propose its own syllabus for approval and, at modest cost, to be examined upon it. Mode Three similarly allows local syllabuses but in addition permits internal assessment of the candidates' performance, subject to the official external examiners' 'moderation'.

15. Sarah Fielding, *The Governess*, 1749.

16. See *Language, the Learner and the School* by D. Barnes, J. Britton and H. Rosen, Penguin Books, 1969. 'Both the teams of investigators, in 1966 and 1967, all of them experienced teachers, when asked what their sharpest impression of the [recorded lesson] materials had been, first mentioned "passivity" ' (p. 26).

17. See Brian Jackson, *Streaming: An Education System in Miniature*, Routledge & Kegan Paul, 1964, p. 101, table 33, 'Twenty-eight teachers of eleven year olds in ten streamed schools'.

18. Matthew xxv, 24.

19. Herbert Thelen describes an experiment in matching up staff and children according to their preferences (*Classroom Grouping for Teachability*, Wiley, 1967).

Chapter 2

1. The difficulty of education prophecy is well-illustrated by a glance at the 1961 edition of the official University Central Council on Admissions booklet *University Entrance: The Basic*

Facts. With evident alarm this forecasts student numbers mounting to '170,000–175,000 by the early seventies' in 'twenty-nine' university institutions. In fact that figure was reached in 1965–6, and there are now fifty-four university institutions. If the 'early seventies' be taken to mean, say, 1973, then present estimates would require that forecast to be raised almost exactly 100 per cent. See 'Briefcase', in *Education*, 10 April 1970.

2. *Statistics of Education 1968*, vol. 1: *Schools*, HMSO, Table 45.

3. Department of Education and Science, *The Supply of Teachers*, Report on Education, no. 51, HMSO, December 1968.

4. The figures for wastage are given in Table 24 of *Statistics of Education 1967*, vol. 4: *Teachers*, HMSO. In writing that over 40 per cent of those so expensively trained are lost to teaching within ten years, I have taken the figures of wastage of all qualified women teachers for 1966–7, adding wastage 'under 25' and '25–9' – the actual figures being 17.0 per cent and 24.0 per cent respectively. Parallel figures for men are 9.7 per cent and 9.5 per cent. The concept of wastage in the statistics is that of wastage from maintained schools. Transfers to other sectors of education count as waste. Table 25, however, gives revised figures for 1967 which correct this and other anomalies. It is not quite the same as wastage, but it is instructive to see that, in 1967, 17,396 women in the age groups 'under 25' and '25–9' entered the profession from whatever source and 10,455 left it – that is leavers as a proportion of entrants was 60 per cent approximately. For men comparable figures were 7413 and 1943, or roughly 26 per cent.

Anne Corbett writes that 'one in three non-graduate men teachers leave the profession within 7 years and 3 out of 4 women within 5 years' (*New Society*, 20 November 1969).

5. This estimate is given in *The Demand for and Supply of Teachers 1963–68*, ninth report of the National Advisory Council for the Training and Supply of Teachers, HMSO, 1965.

6. Table 8 in *Statistics of Education 1968*, vol. 1: *Schools*, HMSO, gives the numbers and proportion of the age group fifteen to nineteen in schools in 1967. Table 3 in *Statistics of*

Education 1967, vol. 3: *Further Education*, HMSO, gives the numbers in grant-aided or independent further education institutions on full-time courses.

In estimating future numbers it is necessary to shift from fifteen to nineteen to sixteen to nineteen, since it is expected that all fifteen year olds will compulsorily remain in school after 1972. I have taken the DES estimate of 30 per cent in the schools and have presumed that if the voluntary staying-on rate is expected to increase from 21·7 per cent to 30 per cent in schools, then a similar increase from 4 per cent to 6 per cent might be expected in full-time courses in technical college. That gives a total of 36 per cent. Reasonable optimism in a matter so speculative justifies, I think, a more generous figure of 40 per cent.

Sir George Pickering prints a table, compiled by P. H. Karmel, which shows the proportion of the fifteen to nineteen age group in full-time education in various countries (*The Challenge of Education*, Penguin Books, 1967, p. 51). We hold a very modest place in the league.

Taking account of part-time further education is exceedingly difficult since it varies from casual entertainment to serious vocational study. However, the Latey Comittee reported that, of all seventeen year olds, 13·8 per cent were receiving full-time education at school, 3·6 per cent in all other institutions, while 16·5 per cent took part-time day and 16·3 per cent part-time night courses (*Report of the Committee on the Age of Majority*, HMSO, 1967).

7. See Jonas Orring, *The School in Sweden*, National Board of Education, Stockholm, 1967, p. 86. Dr Orring writes: 'Parliament decided in 1964 on the dimensions of the gymnasium (guide line approximately 30 per cent of each year group) and continuation school (approximately 20 per cent) systems. It is not only possible, but highly probable, that these figures will be exceeded, and it is surely realistic to reckon with about 35 per cent of each year group in the gymnasium and 25 per cent in the continuation school in the early seventies. Both these types of school, however, are selective-entry schools. Planning for the vocational school at least over the long term, is based on an intake of 30–35 per cent of each year group.

'These figures need not mean that 90–95 per cent of each year group, i.e. in practice all pupils, go straight from the nine-year compulsory school to further studies. All types of school, but above all the vocational and continuation schools, will surely be taking a number of older pupils who have already undergone another form of education or are concerned to continue their formal education after some years of employment. The previous view that about 85 per cent of each year group of sixteen year olds will continue their training immediately on leaving the nine-year compulsory school still seems realistic.'

8. Worse, in December 1969 applications for college of education places for October 1970 were running 13 per cent below the comparable tally the previous year – in the case of men 20 per cent down. 'In particular it is the constant decline in the numbers wishing to specialize in maths and science which is causing the Clearing House, and many of the colleges, serious worry' (*The Times Educational Supplement*, 19 December 1969).

9. Reported in *Education*, 14 March 1969, p. 341.

10. *The Shortage of Mathematics and Science Teachers in Schools 1970*, Report of a working party, chairman Professor Nevill Mott, sponsored by the Royal Society and the Council for Engineering Institutions, Royal Society, 1969.

11. *Report of the Committee on Manpower Resources for Science and Technology* (chairman Lord Jackson), HMSO, 1966.

12. The actual figure is 0·83 per cent according to the *Report of the Educational Publishers Council on Schoolbook Expenditure*, Publishers' Association, 1970. The figure is much lower than in other European countries. Similarly the period schoolbooks are expected to last – eight years before 1970 and six years now – is longer than in any other Western European country.

The Association of Education Committees and the National Book League have certain agreed standards of expenditure on schoolbooks: in 1967–8 only 10 per cent of local education authorities met the 'reasonable' standard set for secondary schools. (The current percentage, in a period of financial shortage, is expected to be below 10 per cent. This compares with 70 per

cent of local education authorities meeting this standard eight
years earlier.)

13. See Norman MacKenzie, Hywel Jones and Trevor Payne,
Audio-Visual Resources in Sussex Schools, Centre for Educational Technology, University of Sussex, April 1969. An abbre-
viated version appears in *Journal of Educational Technology*,
January 1970. A study, confined to West Sussex, by John Vaizey
and J. Sheehan for the Nuffield Resources for Learning Project
in 1967 parallels the above study, and concludes. 'The important
thing is that the one markedly scarce resource in the schools was
library books.'

Chapter 3

1. The figure of twenty years is arbitrary. The Introduction to
Statistics of Education 1968, vol. 1: *Schools*, says: 'The Education Act of 1944 provided that primary and secondary education
should be in separate schools. After twenty years and many millions of pounds of investment in new secondary school buildings,
this reform has been virtually achieved.' In Leicestershire every
child is now in a comprehensive school, fifteen years after the
original decision to go comprehensive was taken.

2. *Evening Standard*, 7 October 1969. The response to subsequent questions makes one doubt, however, if the implications
of comprehension were at all well understood by those questioned.

3. This was the situation as reported by the Department of Education and Science in December 1969. The 'all *or part* of their
areas' is a very important qualification. *Comprehensive Reorganization Survey*, Comprehensive Schools Association, 1969,
states there are now 1350 comprehensive schools but adds that
until there are three times this number 'there will have been no
meaningful comprehensive reform in Britain'. Some schools,
labelled comprehensive, are optimistically described as such, being heavily 'creamed' by local grammar and direct grant schools.

4. The figure for the number of children in comprehensive
school in January 1968 is given in Table 1 of *Statistics of Education 1968*, vol. 1: *Schools*, as 604,428 out of 3,092,950 in all

secondary schools. The most recent estimate, however, is 26 per cent: see Anne Corbett, 'Comprehensives: the tally', *New Society*, 12 February 1970.

5. See Anne Corbett, 'Comprehensives: the tally', *New Society*, 12 February 1970.

6. Letter from Roland Earl, Chief Inspector, London Borough of Sutton, in *Education*, 25 October 1968, p. 491.

7. At present the National Survey covers only the primary school years. The rate of moving may well drop from the present 7 per cent when the children in the sample reach secondary school age. Should it do so, it would suggest that variations in the local provision of education and extreme differences in syllabuses between schools may act as a brake in the mobility of labour in commerce and industry. In the United States 20 per cent of the population moves every year.

8. Although 'eleven to eighteen' is the most popular *single* brand of comprehension, Robin Pedley says that 20 per cent of reorganization schemes involve transfers at nine and thirteen, and 32 per cent envisage transfers at sixteen (*The Comprehensive School*, Penguin Books, rev. edn 1969). Thus all-through comprehension on the one hand and all sorts of tiering on the other are about evenly balanced.

9. Figures as given by the Department of Education and Science in August 1968 (personal communication).

10. See Jonas Orring, *The School in Sweden*, National Board of Education, Stockholm, 1967, p. 119, Table 2. I have stated the position conservatively since in academic subjects a majority of Swedish children over nine are taught by university graduates – all of them additionally trained to teach.

11. W. E. Egnar, 'Sixth-form dilemma', *Education*, 1 November 1968, p. 523.

12. I am grateful to the Chief Education Officers of East Sussex and of Somerset for permission to use their calculations. They

should not, of course, be taken to mean that either county intends finally to adopt a universal all-through comprehensive pattern.

13. Quoted by T. E. B. Howarth, *Culture, Anarchy and the Public Schools*, Cassell, 1969, p. 58.

14. *The Times Educational Supplement*, 28 February 1969, gives the figures for 1966 as 42 per cent and cites *Where?* (published by the Advisory Centre for Education, Cambridge) as its source.

15. Robin Pedley, op. cit. The euphoria is more marked in the first, 1963, edition than in the revised, 1969, edition. A statement of the contrary case is to be found in Robin Davis, *The Grammar School*, Penguin Books, 1967.

16. Rhodes Boyson, 'The essential conditions for the success of a comprehensive school', *Black Paper Two*, Critical Quarterly Society, 1969. Dr Boyson is Head of Highbury Grove Comprehensive School.

17. See 'Expanding numbers, declining interest', *New Society*, 5 June 1969. This is a report on M. D. Shipman's study 'Participation and staff–student relations: a 7-year study of social change in an expanding college of education'. A study of a large comprehensive school giving a more hopeful picture is J. B. Mays, 'Inside the big school', in *Schools of Tomorrow*, Longman, 1968. An American study by R. G. Barker and P. V. Gump, *Big School, Small School*, Stanford University Press, 1964, strongly emphasizes the virtues of the small school for a child's social education.

18. *Sixth Form Opportunities in Inner London*, Inner London Education Authority, Report 951. Working party under the chairmanship of E. W. H. Briault, December 1968.

19. Geoffrey Wansell in the *The Times Educational Supplement*, 3 October 1969, refers to a survey by Desmond Lee 'now circulating in Cambridge'. Mr Wansell reports the survey as saying that 'only 24 per cent of British sixth forms are big enough to allow their pupils a minimum chance of getting the necessary academic qualification to get to university. This corresponds to there being, according to the survey, only one school in four with a sixth form of 120. 45 per cent of boys schools, 66 per cent of girls

schools, 71 per cent of mixed schools have sixth forms of less than ninety.'

20. The Q and F proposals emanate from the Standing Conference on University Entrance and the two Schools Council joint working parties on sixth-form curriculum and examinations.

21. At present of children in the highest ability band (the top 32 per cent) in the Inner London Education Authority area, 17·5 per cent attend fifty-five grammar schools, 14·5 per cent are spread among eighty-eight comprehensive schools.

22. Alison Trufitt reporting in the *Evening Standard*, 19 June 1969, writes: 'The comprehensive heads admit that if "non-viable" A-level groups of less than 5 pupils were to be eliminated only twelve out of London's eighty comprehensives could continue with A-level work.'

23. A good description of the sixth form as a means of learning is to be found in Frances Stevens, *The Living Tradition*, Hutchinson, 1962, especially chapter 4.

24. The Open University may incidentally stimulate activity at this pre-university level. Thus three series of BBC broadcasts, combined with National Extension College correspondence courses plus tutorial support, began in spring 1970 as preparation for Open University work.

25. J. W. B. Douglas, *The Home and the School*, MacGibbon & Kee, 1964. Dr Douglas, on the basis of his very careful longitudinal study, finds that 'Grammar-school places are awarded at the age of eleven to 51 per cent from upper-middle class, 34 per cent from lower-middle class, 21 per cent from the upper-manual class, and 22 per cent from the lower-manual class amongst children of the same ability' (p. 47).

26. Article by Julienne Ford in *New Society*, 10 October 1968, and her *Social Class and the Comprehensive School*, Routledge & Kegan Paul, 1970.

27. T. G. Monks, *Comprehensive Education in England and Wales*, National Foundation for Educational Research, 1968. An editorial review in *Education*, 25 October 1968, quoting the

NFER study, says in the first year in a comprehensive school 8 per cent of children moved up and 7 per cent down; in subsequent years the movement was never more than 3·4 per cent. This includes any movement within streams and not just movement in and out of the 'academic' block, so it is not comparable with movement between different sorts of school in the tripartite system. At the time of this NFER survey very few of the schools were unstreamed at any stage.

28. Michael Armstrong and Michael Young, *The Flexible School*, *Where?*, Supplement 5, Advisory Centre for Education, Cambridge, 1965.

29. Reported in *Teacher*, 4 April 1969. J. C. Baker, *Streaming in the Primary School*, National Foundation for Educational Research, 1970, supports this view, finding streaming socially harmful and academically irrelevant at the primary stage. A handful of middle schools are now unstreamed, but it is almost impossible to find a genuinely comprehensive school which practises unstreaming over the age of thirteen. The one or two comprehensive schools that claim to practise unstreaming over the age of thirteen turn out to use a lot of 'setting' in sequential subjects (which is the atomization of streaming) or, being severely 'beheaded' schools, deal with a relatively narrow ability range.

30. Nils-Eric Svennson, *School Differentiation and Scholastic Achievement*, Almqvist & Wiksell, 1962.

31. I am grateful to Dr Urban Dahllöf for permission to quote from a draft version of his *Ability Grouping, Content Validity and Curriculum Process Analysis*, University of Gotheborg, 1969. It is likely to be published soon in this country.

32. Robin Pedley reports that 24·5 per cent of eighty-one schools in his sample were either totally unstreamed or unstreamed in most subjects during the first year. A further 13·5 per cent were partially unstreamed (*The Comprehensive School*, Penguin Books, rev. edn 1969).

33. Quoted by George Taylor, 'Management in education', paper written for the Peers Working Party of the National Council for Educational Technology, 1968.

Chapter 4

1. See Harvey Swados, 'The myth of the happy workers', in Eric and Mary Josephson (eds.), *Man Alone*, Dell, 1962.

2. See James Koerner, 'The American high school', *Where?*, Supplement 14, Advisory Centre for Education, Cambridge, 1969.

3. G. Cawelti, 'How high schools innovate', *Nation's Schools*, April 1967.

4. For a recent brief exposition see J. Lloyd Trump and Harold S. Davis, *Planning a Team Teaching Program*, Educational Research Council of America, 1968. Quotations that follow from Lloyd Trump are taken from this work.

5. See K. Lovell, *Team Teaching*, University of Leeds Institute of Education, Paper 5, April 1967.

6. See Douglas Barnes's research report 'Language in the Classroom' in *Language, the Learner and the School*, by D. Barnes, J. Britton and H. Rosen, Penguin Books, 1969. He concludes that teachers unwisely and wrongly assume that 'our pupils are able to make sense, in terms of their own experience and language resources, of what we say to them.' He emphasizes (pp. 20–46) the great extent to which the questions asked in class tend to be 'closed', requiring answers of a filling-in-the-blank kind – disturbingly similar, in fact, to the routine completion of partial phrases so common, and so much criticized by teachers, in linear programmed instruction.

7. G. O. M. Leith, 'Survey of programmed learning', *Visual Education Year Book 1966*, National Council for Audio-Visual Aids in Education. See also his *Second Thoughts on Programmed Learning*, National Council for Educational Technology, Occasional Paper no. 1, 1969.

8. Title of a chapter by W. Curr in G. O. M. Leith, E. A. Peel and W. Curr, *A Handbook of Programmed Learning*, University of Birmingham Press, 1964. Mr Curr's conclusion is that programmed learning used for 'easy and speedy communication of basic materials' would not so much eliminate teachers as free

them for more worthwhile relationships with pupils and 'help to prevent the teacher himself from becoming a machine' (p. 18).

9. David Evans describes attempts to use programmed instruction in a much less familiar role – that of trying to 'teach' productive (i.e. divergent, creative) thinking ('Programmed for creativity', *Education*, 19 September 1969).

10. J. N. Hook and William H. Evans, *Individualised English*, Follett, 1964. The cards have been adapted and put into book form by Denys Thompson and Michael Marland, *English for the Individual*, Heinemann, 1967.

11. I am grateful for the opportunity to see an early, unpublished draft of Doris M. Lee's paper, 'Programmed learning in schools', University of London Institute of Education.

12. See S. N. Postlethwait, J. Novak and H. Murray, *An Integrated Experience Approach to Learning*, Burgess, 1964.

13. B. Frank Brown, *The Non-Graded High School*, Prentice-Hall, 1963. Brown has also contributed a chapter with the same title in Ronald Gross and Judith Murphy (eds.), *The Revolution in the Schools*, Harcourt, Brace & World, 1964.

14. J. C. Flanagan, *Design for a Study of American Youth (Project Talent)*, Houghton Mifflin, 1962.

15. See Jack V. Edling, 'Programmed instruction in a continuous progress school', in Wilbur Schramm (ed.), *Four Case Studies of Programmed Instruction*, Fund for the Advancement of Education, New York, 1964. Glen Ovard of Provo University has guided many of the school's developments and written numerous pamphlets on continuous progress.

16. See J. C. Flanagan, 'Individualized education', Address to the American Psychological Association, 1968.

17. See Robert Glaser, *Adapting the Elementary School Curriculum to Individual Performance*, University of Pittsburg Press, 1967; C. M. Lindvall and J. O. Bolvin, *The Project for Individually Prescribed Instruction* (the Oakleaf Project), University of Pittsburg Press, 1966; and Anthony G. Oettinger, *Run, Computer, Run*, Harvard University Press, 1969, pp. 140 et seq.

18. 'More than a quarter of all Americans – about 55 million – are now involved one way or another in the educational process, in which almost $35,000 million a year is invested' (*Teaching and Learning*, United States Information Service, 1970, p. 3). (The current Russian claim is one person in three.)

Chapter 5

1. Throughout this chapter I have used 'Russia' as the more familiar term where, technically, 'the Soviet Union' would be accurate.

2. For a remarkable evocation of the journey see Vladimir Nabokov, *Speak, Memory*, Penguin Books, 1969, pp. 113–15.

3. Part of an anonymous poem 'The International' in an anthology of Russian writing edited by R. G. Davis-Poynter, *For Freedom, Theirs and Ours*, Panther, 1968.

4. I heard this argument put forward by the Vice-Chancellor of York University in a speech at a meeting of the Headmasters' Conference, at Cambridge, 1967.

5. Except in mathematics. The case for special provision for the outstandingly academically gifted, especially mathematicians, is trenchantly put by Lord Snow, 'Kinds of excellence', Inaugural Clayesmore Lecture, Clayesmore School, 1969.

6. As translated and quoted by Nigel Grant, *Soviet Education*, Penguin Books, 1964. Of a number of studies I read in preparation for visiting Russia, this seemed to me particularly reliable and illuminating when checked on the ground.

7. See Mervyn Matthews, 'Class bias in Russian education', *New Society*, 19 December 1968.

8. See Bryan Thwaites, 'Mathematical education in Russian schools', *Mathematical Gazette*, vol. 52, 1968, no. 382. Also Report of the President, *Educational Testing Service Annual Report 1964–5*, Educational Testing Service, Princeton, pp. 47 et seq.; and B. R. Vogeli, *Soviet Secondary for the Mathematically Talented*, National Council of Teachers of Mathematics, Washington, DC, 1968.

9. See Joslyn Owen, 'Mid-term in Moscow', *Education*, 13 September 1968. Every Russian teacher is required 'to devote one day in each six-day week to in-service training'.

10. See David Bonavia's article on an elementary school in Georgia, *The Times*, 28 May 1969. In this school children were 'taking an active part in determining what and why they wanted to learn, and checking and correcting their own exercises ... to see whether the traumas and anxieties caused by marking systems could be overcome without reducing the incentive to learn.' Teachers were encouraged 'not to be afraid of stormy classroom scenes as children vie with one another to solve problems on the blackboard. ... Children were encouraged to develop their critical standards by correcting the work of others as well as their own. Checks showed that they were further advanced in knowledge and analytical ability even than the children in the class above, who were being taught by traditional methods.'

Chapter 6

1. I have taken this phrase from the title of Kathleen Nott's excellent *A Clean, Well-Lighted Place – A Private View of Sweden*, Heinemann, 1961.

2. Kathleen Nott remarks: 'The Swiss commit suicide more frequently than the average, but other nationalities seldom ask them why' (op. cit., p. 11). The Swedes seem to be particularly outspoken about their social problems; they thereby provide ready ammunition for their critics.

3. See Torsten Husén, *Problems of Differentiation in Swedish Compulsory Schooling*, Svenska Bokförlaget, Stockholm, 1961, for an account of the debates and commissions leading to comprehensive reform in Sweden. Also Rolland Poulston, *Educational Change in Sweden*, Teachers' College, Columbia University, 1968; and Torsten Husén and Gunnar Boalt, *Educational Research and Educational Change*, Wiley, 1968.

4. For a brief summary see Torsten Husén, *The Relation between Selectivity and Social Class in Secondary Education*, Pergamon, 1966.

5. The best brief account of the reorganization of the school system is that of Jonas Orring, *The School in Sweden*, National Board of Education, Stockholm, 1967.

6. Details of present curriculum structure can be found in Orring, op. cit. For information about intended changes I am indebted to Bo Holmberg of the National Board of Education.

7. See the Swedish National Board of Education series, *Short Research Newsletters*.

8. The inquiry was by Dr Broden and entitled *Glesbygdgymnasium* (the gymnasium in sparsely populated areas). 'Neither significantly better nor significantly worse' is a correct representation of the *over-all* findings. I am told that unfortunately a number of teachers felt they ought to do more direct teaching than was recommended by Hermods and the results were less satisfactory. Where Hermods' recommendations were followed, the results were substantially better than with traditional teaching.

9. Individualized courses at the secondary school level include IMU in maths (a three-year course completed), UMT in German (first year completed), SAG in history (sixteen plus, first year completed). In the investigatory stages: UME in English, UMRE in religious education and ethics, *Young Today* in civics (in a very wide, 'general studies' sense). Also SISU for remedial work in maths, reading, writing, and SMD for deaf children.

10. In Sweden graduate teachers (i.e. virtually all those in secondary schools and gymnasiums) belong to a single union of graduate professions which includes all doctors, magistrates, and so on. A teachers' strike, in consequence, carries a far greater threat in Sweden than in England. A curiosity of the strike was that, with Government encouragment, most schools stayed open. Certain children were voted as 'teachers' and continued with appropriate parts of the syllabus (not, for example, experimental work in science). They were often privately advised by the teachers on strike, anxious as always that their charges should not suffer. One of the seniors was elected chairman of the school, and, with a committee, had over-all control. In all this, the activity of SECO, then a minority pupils' union, led to its establishing a

strong claim as representative of schoolboy and schoolgirl opinion. This is reflected in grants from the government and local authorities and in recent official proposals – not yet agreed by the union – for joint teacher–parent–pupil councils in every school.

11 At first this was rather desultory. It is now being thoroughly organized. Thus the Delta programme of inservice training in maths includes television broadcasts on the five official days, plus radio broadcasts – available and also for sale on tape at teachers' audio-visual centres – and a Hermods correspondence course. Satisfactory completion of the training results in a certificate. By this means the Swedes intend to change their official maths syllabus from 'old' to 'new' maths in a carefully phased operation over the next three years.

Chapter 7

1. See John C. Greene, *The Death of Adam*, Iowa State University Press, 1959.

2. Comenius, *The Great Didactic*, 1632, quoted in W. Kenneth Richmond, *Readings in Education*, Methuen, 1968.

3. Both in *David Copperfield*.

4. I have a treasured copy of this work. The most accessible source of all the quotations that follow, from *Home Education* and other works, is Essex Cholmondeley, *The Story of Charlotte Mason*, Parents' National Educational Union, London, 1960.

5. Compare *Language, the Learner and the School*, by D. Barnes, J. Britton and H. Rosen, Penguin Books, 1969. Douglas Barnes's research into classroom practice reveals that 'the failure to demand active involvement of the pupils *has gone hand in hand with a failure to demand they verbalize their learning*, that is, that they use language as an active instrument for reorganizing their perceptions. It is not that there is too much language, but that it is not fulfilling its functions as an instrument of learning. Rather, *language is seen as an instrument of teaching*' (italics in the original) (p. 66).

6. At Scale How, Ambleside. This training college includes a school. Such an arrangement is normal in America, Scandinavia

and many other countries. To our detriment I believe, it is extremely rare in England.

7. Quotations throughout this section from Norman MacMunn, *The Child's Path to Freedom*, Bell, 1921 (an extensive revision of the 1914 edition), and *The MacMunn Differentialism: A New Method of Class Self-Teaching*, W. H. Smith & Sons, 1914.

8. See chapter 2, 'George Moberly', in F. D. How, *Six Great Schoolmasters*, Methuen, 1904. Boys at Winchester are still allowed officially when doing their classical preparation to 'go over' it with another boy.

9. See Norman MacMunn, *The Things About Us, and a Few Others. A Book of Simple French Conversation. In two volumes to be used by alternate pupils*, Bell, 1914.

10. Quotations in this section are from Helen Parkhurst, *Education of the Dalton Plan*, Bell, 1922, and *An Explanation of the Dalton Laboratory Plan*, Dalton Association, 1926. The latter is a brief summary of various practical problems in using the Plan.

11. Introduction to C. W. Kimmins and Belle Rennie, *The Triumph of the Dalton Plan*, Nicolson & Watson, 1932.

12. For example, the Freinet System in France. See Celestin Freinet, *Les Techniques Freinet de l'école moderne*, Librairie Armand Colin, 1964.

13. Edward Yeomans, *Education for Initiative and Responsibility*, National Association of American Independent Schools, 1968.

14. Arthur Harrison, who used the Dalton Plan for many years as headmaster of Marlborough House Preparatory School, Hawkhurst, surmised, in conversation, that the Plan's ultimate demise in his school resulted from the sharp increase in competition for places in public schools in the early 1950s.

15. N. Ognev, *The Diary of a Communist Schoolboy*, Gollancz, 1928. The year referred to in the extract is 1923.

16. Quoted by Sonia Jackson, 'When the parent becomes teacher', *The Times*, 19 March 1969.

17. The conventional classroom has advantages over any sort of 'workshop' situation when it comes to impressing visitors. The children appear attentive; certainly they are quiet. If we could amplify the visions and internal dialogues going on in their heads, we might be submerged in the Bedlam: as it is we can admire unhindered the teacher's excellent performance, and the teacher can catch, undistracted, the echo of his good intentions. When the children perform it is usually in the context of some model supplied by the teacher. Matters run flat counter in a 'workshop'. Dialogues are no longer internal, nor movement entirely suppressed. The noise is unfamiliar and to adults disturbing. And the work we watch is, for the most part, not the polished performance of the teacher, or its close shadow, but the varied, unduplicable, messy effort of individual children.

18. An excellent account is by Lawrence A. Cremin, 'Progressivism in American education 1876–1957', *The Transformation of the School*, Vintage Books, 1964.

19. For numerous indexed references to Dewey's vigorous criticism of developments in progressive education, see Cremin, op. cit.

20. The sharp reversal of direction was signalled in the bestseller by R. Flesch, *Why Johnny Can't Read*, Harper & Row, 1955. Numerous attacks on the lack of rigour in American education followed. In fact, America's falling behind at this stage of the space race was due to an inadequate allocation of resources to the space projects – a deficiency since rectified with dramatic results. As usual, education was blamed.

Chapter 8

1. See S. A. Rayner, *Correspondence Education in Australia and New Zealand*, Melbourne University Press, 1949.

2. Rodolphe Töpfter, whose 'picture novels' greatly impressed Goethe, was a teacher and urged the use of closely integrated pictures and text for educational purposes. See Neil Rackham, 'Comics versus education', *New Education*, September, 1968.

3. Jenni Gunby and Brian Jackson, *Correspondence Courses in Schools*, National Extension College, Cambridge, 1967.

4. An excellent brief introduction to the subject is Borje Holmberg, *Correspondence Education*, Hermods-Nki, Malmö, 1967.

5. See D. J. Holroyde, B. Webster, W. Beaton and E. W. H. Briault, 'Local systems', in R. Postgate (ed.), *Educational Television and Radio in Britain: Papers prepared for a National Conference organized by the BBC and the University of Sussex*, BBC Publications, 1966, chapter 5.

6. Suitable programmes are now being put out by the BBC, using a time unsuitable for reception for normal school use but possible for recording onto tape.

7. R. Postgate, op. cit., p. 130.

8. But Father John Culkin speaking to the Senate Sub-committee on the 1967 Public Broadcasting Act contrasted the average of $80,000 per half hour spent on commercial television productions and the $150 per half hour spent on educational broadcasts in America.

9. Development work by Tony Gibson of Goldsmith's College.

10. See D. J. Holroyde (ed.), *Television at the University of Leeds*, National Committee for Audio-Visual Aids in Education, 1966.

11. See the final report of the *Warblington Experiment in Closed-circuit Television 1962–65* County Education Officer for Hampshire, 1965.

12. Holmberg, op. cit., p. 26.

13. Dennis McQuail, 'The preparation and exchange of information', in R. Postgate, op. cit., p. 232.

14. In R. Postgate, op. cit., p. 168.

15. Besides Marshall McLuhan's numerous works, see Sidney Finkelstein, *Sense and Nonsense of McLuhan*, International Publishers, 1968.

16. See Marshall McLuhan: 'Hot media are, therefore, low in participation and cool media are high in participation, or completion by the audience.... The TV image offers some three

million dots per second to the receiver. From these he accepts only a few dozen each instant from which to make an image. ... The TV image requires each instant that we "close" the space in the mesh by a convulsively sensuous participation that is profoundly kinetic and tactile, because tactility is the interplay of the senses' (*Understanding the Media – the Extensions of Man*, Routledge & Kegan Paul, 1964, Sphere Books, 1967).

17. 'Cold print' can also 'open the mind to impressions'. See Keats's ode, 'On first looking into Chapman's Homer'.

18. For the difficulties of teachers in successfully following up broadcasts, see K. V. Bailey and Helen Coppen, 'Training of teachers in using television and radio', in R. Postgate, op. cit., pp. 165–80.

19. See reference to Dr Kumata's research in Postgate, op. cit.

20. Daniel Boorstin, *The Image*, Penguin Books, 1963.

21. See *Learning by Television*, Ford Foundation Report. 'If something happened tomorrow to wipe out all instructional TV, American schools and colleges would hardly know it was gone.'

22. In this section I have drawn extensively on various papers and publications on computer-based learning systems issued by the National Council for Educational Technology: 1. *Report of a Working Party on Computer-Based Learning*, Chairman, Professor J. Black, 1968; 2. *Computer-Based Learning Systems*, report of a feasibility study by a team directed by I. McMullen and K. M. Hill, 1969; 3. *Computer-Based Learning: A Programme for Action*, proposals of a group chaired by Professor J. Vaisey, 1969.

23. Reported in *Time Magazine*, 15 August 1969.

24. See *School Scheduling by Computer: The Story of G.A.S.P.*, Educational Facilities Laboratories Inc., 1964. Also, for the SSSS computor scheduling at Stanford University, see R. M. Bush and D. W. Allen, *The Computer in American Education*, Wiley, 1967.

25. The contrast between official publicity and reality is frequently drawn with telling effect in Anthony G. Oettinger, *Run, Computer, Run*, Harvard University Press, 1969.

26. *Computer-Based Learning Systems*, p. 14 (no. 2 of references in note 22).

27. Oettinger, op. cit., p. 180.

28. Oettinger, op. cit., p. 191.

29. Even so, for their calculations, Professor Black's working party used 1000 hour use per year for costing conventional teaching and double use (2000 hours per year) for CAI. Such double use of plant presumes a radical change in existing school arrangements and the solving of many consequent problems.

30. These are the recommended areas, as far as secondary schools are concerned, of the National Council for Educational Technology study team (see no. 2 of references in note 22).

31. Anthony G. Oettinger, *A Vision of Technology and Education*, Harvard University Press, 1966, reprinted in *Run, Computer, Run*, op. cit.

Chapter 9

1. Both the essential similarity and the fundamental difference persist in their successors. Nowadays, both neo-Skinnerites and Montessorians find themselves jostling in the same narrow territory of individualized/independent/packaged/resource-based learning. For education technology has long since disowned the gadgetry, programmed learning the confining dogmas, with which they were once associated, and of the 'systems analysis' they now espouse as good an example as I have yet come across is, improbably, the Montessori (secondary) School in the Hague. So harsh are the financial stringencies, so pressing the habits and expectations inside and outside the secondary school, that, ground down between such base practicalities, wholly different intentions emerge in unexpected similar practices. For neo-Skinnerites individualized materials, by-passing the teacher (a source of 'noise' or 'static') permit the machinery of the world to be beamed directly and efficiently into childish heads: Montessorians hope that such materials, quickly dealing with essential matters and allowing rest from constant teaching, will leave a child more time for his own private agenda. Yet this divergence doesn't show if we simply examine short pieces of instruction:

it emerges only in the long term, in the pervasive key and tone, in the surrounding conditions of learning, in the tendency of the one, within limits set by the subject, to persist until they have tooled their courses to the closest tolerance, of the other to stop at the loosest acceptable fit. For between those who want to leave as much as possible open, personal, unresolved, and those whose instinct is to Kinsey all creation, there remains a final enmity.

2. A brief description is now available in English. See *Some Facts about IMU*, Hermods, Malmö, 1968.

3. In order to cover a sufficient age and subject range in the investigation of independent learning, the Resources for Learning Project found it necessary to get suitable materials specially written. Some of these materials are being and others may later be published. They are as follows: *Initial Reading* (five to eight year olds) – materials collaboratively produced in Coventry schools under the direction of Mary Cox and Muriel Summerfield of the Coventry College of Education; *Environmental Studies* (nine to twelve year olds) – by Colin Kefford, published by Blandford; *Biology* (secondary, years 1 and 2) – by Don Reid and Phil Booth at the Thomas Bennett Comprehensive School, published by Heinemann; *Mathematics* (secondary, year 1) – translation of modules 1 to 3 of the Swedish IMU text; *English, Maths, Social Studies, Combined Science, French* (secondary year 3); *Economics* (sixth form) – by Christopher Giles (the 'Manchester Project'), published by Ginn.

Chapter 10

1. This chapter informally reflects the experience of the Nuffield Resources for Learning Project during an extended feasibility study into the design and use of packages in various subjects for various ages. At a later stage a fuller handbook is intended. In such a handbook, the inclusion of varied samples of packages will be appropriate: here I have used the Swedish IMU course (shortly to be translated) as my single detailed exemplar, pointing out where its design is not appropriate for other subjects. I chose IMU because it is the most fully developed and tested

package to be found anywhere. And if sometimes my comments are critical, I should make it clear that, in my view, its merits far outweigh its defects which are, in any case, debatable, natural in pioneer work and open to remedy.

The first three modules of IMU are being translated into English and tried out in some English and Irish schools in a joint project involving Hermods, the originators of IMU, the Swedish National Board of Education, OECD, the Nuffield Foundation Resources for Learning Project and the Ministry of Education of the Irish Republic.

2. It should not be assumed that a prescribed syllabus is synonymous with tyranny. Such prescription is the practice of the United States, France, Sweden, Denmark, Ireland, Australia, New Zealand, and many other democratic countries.

3. *Some Facts about IMU*, Hermods, Malmö, 1968, asserts there are more than ten million alternative routes.

4. See L. M. Jivën and C. Öreberg, *Didakometry: Preliminary Plan for Investigating the Effects of a System for Individualized Mathematics Teaching*, School of Education, Malmö, 1968.

5. See Denis Rowntree, 'Beyond programmes' in *The Times Educational Supplement*, 24 May 1968. 'In effect programmed learning has brought to teaching the hypothesis-testing procedures of "scientific method".'

6. E. M. Forster, 'Mrs Miniver', in *Two Cheers for Democracy*, Penguin Books, 1965.

7. *Some Facts about IMU*, Hermods, Malmö, 1968, p. 6. 'The majority of the teachers and some of the students considered the students' motivation could be still further stimulated if individual tasks could be replaced from time to time by group activity.' From 1965 some schools therefore combined IMU with team-teaching and included periodic lessons to a big class assembly.

8. This practice reaches its nadir with computer programmes in which, when the child has identified himself (number 0-376-421 or whatever), he is then greeted with 'Hello Johnny'. Herman

Kahn counts this as one of the machine's virtues in 'Impact of the friendly computer', *The Times*, 9 October 1969.

9. Among their number N. Ognev: 'Dalton hangs round my neck like a bag of corn. Whatever I do I am constantly reminded of the tasks that haven't been prepared. Either maths or natural history or diagrams. There is no time and no place for work, and there's even less time for reading and skating ...' (*Diary of a Communist Schoolboy*, Gollancz, 1928).

10. See G. Barrington Kaye and Irving Rogers, *Group Work in Secondary Schools*, Oxford University Press, 1968.

11. The story appears in a rather different form, attributed to a professor of physics, in Jerome S. Bruner, *The Process of Education*, Harvard University Press, 1965.

12. See the report by Roda Amaria of research at the University of Birmingham in *New Education*, November 1968. An extended experiment at Sevenoaks School in 1963 in which boys learnt French in dissimilar pairs, their results being compared with parallel forms taught in the traditional way, indicated that paired learning held considerable promise, but neither the experimental design nor the size of the sample justified firm assertions.

13. Keith Gardner, 'State of Reading', in Nicholas Smart (ed.), *Crisis in the Classroom*, Daily Mirror Books, 1968. Compare J. C. Flanagan, *Design for a Study of American Youth (Project Talent)*, Houghton Mifflin, 1962, in which only 7 per cent of 9th graders (fifteen year olds – when compulsory schooling in most states ends) and 25 per cent of 12th grades (end of high school) '... were able to answer half of the questions based on typical paragraphs discussing national issues in *Time Magazine*'.

14. Not so the other media. In some American schools the library has become a multi-media resource centre. Similar, if slighter, provision is planned for some new schools over here – an alluring prospect but wasteful. For, plainly, the great majority of books are relatively inexpensive to buy, store, maintain, utilize; no special equipment is needed to animate them; they may be easily and quickly browsed through. None of this applies to materials in the new media. Their cost and complexity means that they cannot sensibly be bought, like books, on the principle

that someone will doubtless find them useful some time. The careful selection and co-ordination of collections in a few topics – what we have called in this book the compilation of packages – becomes economically essential. It is human time that LEAs need to budget for, as a first priority, not buildings and equipment; otherwise we shall merely substitute costly multi-media attics for our present repositories for books.

15. Tobin, Biran and Waller have done measurements of the improvement resulting when poor readers can work from materials on a tape-recorder rather than in print. See M. J. Tobin, 'An overview', *Visual Education*, April 1969.

16. 'It appears to be much easier to buy relatively expensive equipment than it is to find money for the materials it needs to be effective as a means of teaching or learning. The situation arises in part because equipment is often financed out of special or capital funds while materials must be paid for out of exigent capitation allowances' (Norman Mackenzie, Hywel Jones and Trevor Payne, *Audio-Visual Resources in Sussex Schools*, Centre for Educational Technology, University of Sussex, April 1969).

17. In 1965, when the Department of Education and Science circular on comprehensive reorganization was published, there were still 225 all-age schools. See *Statistics of Education 1968*, vol. 1: *Schools*, HMSO.

18. Borje Holmberg and Curt Öreberg, in *IMU Mathematics: From Analysis of Objectives to System Introduction*, Centre for Educational Research and Innovation, OECD, 1969. In calculating the saving from large class organization the teacher–pupil ratio is taken to be $1:38$. Observations showed that because an aide carried out many routine activities, teachers in a large class spent 82 to 90 per cent of the lesson in individual and group instruction, whereas in an ordinary classroom actual teaching time was 62 to 73 per cent. 'Despite the fact that there are more pupils per teacher ... the effective teaching time per pupil is not reduced.'

The saving of 16 per cent reflects in part the substantial salary difference in Sweden between a qualified teacher and an unqualified aide. The difference would be smaller in this country.

19. All of Brunel University. The study is assisted by a grant from the National Council for Education Technology.

20. The base used to calculate this percentage increase is the full cost listed in the educational budget – approximately £200 per annum per boy. Arguably only the instructional costs should be used as a base (in which case the percentage increase would be larger) but it is difficult to know where, and sometimes how, to draw the line. The total costs provide at least some secure, unequivocal ground.

21. At present education absorbs about 6 per cent of the gross national product. Sir William Alexander wrote in *Education*, 21 March 1969: 'In the last ten years the cost of education has moved from just over 800 million pounds to over 21000 millions per annum. On a simple extrapolation, we have to face the fact that the education service, if the trends of the past ten years continue, will need 3000 millions by 1974/5 and perhaps 4000 millions by 1980' – which is an estimated 10 to 12 per cent of the gross national product. In this connexion see also Stuart Maclure, *Learning Beyond our Means*, Councils and Education Press 1968.

22. The list of examples given below is not meant to be exhaustive. It merely represents the range of *unpublished* package work being done in England.

Some impressive packages – that is, materials which envisage independent learning by boys as a normal and central method of learning – have been produced by teachers, essentially for use in their own schools. For example: at Kibworth High School, Leicestershire, in maths (and previously chemistry); at Sevenoaks School, Kent, in technical studies and art; at Carshalton High School, Surrey, in maths; at Abbey Woods School, London, in English. At Bushloe High School and the Manor High School, Oadby, in Leicestershire, and the Sheredes School in Hertfordshire, individual and group assignment work is now the predominant mode in almost all subjects – as it has been for many years in the surviving Dalton Plan secondary schools like Bryanston in Dorset and the Rosa Bassett School, Streatham.

Examples of materials designed chiefly for independent work

and produced by teachers at a centre for use in a number of schools include: first-year humanities 'Man and his environment' at the Oxfordshire Curriculum Development Communications Centre, Director, J. Hanson; mathematics on USIS teaching machines in Surrey schools, led by Kenneth Gray; mathematics materials used in schools in the Tunbridge Wells area, chiefly devised by Bertram Banks; some 'learning sets' for sixth forms from the General Studies Centre, York University, Director, R. Irvine Smith.

Details of published courses – chiefly of a programmed instruction kind – are given in P. Cavanagh and C. Jones (eds.), *Yearbook of Education and Instructional Technology*, Cornmarket Press, 1969.

23. H.M.S. Collingwood, the Royal Navy training establishment, has some 250 instructors, of whom fifty are engaged full time or part time on creating instructional materials.

Chapter 11

1. Lee J. Cronbach, 'Course improvement through evaluation: an article by a doctor', *Teachers' College Record*, pp. 672–83.

2. See M. D. Jenkinson, quoted by S. Maclure in *Curriculum Innovation in Practice*, Report on the Third International Curriculum Conference, HMSO, 1968, p. 40: 'My quarrel is that because the emprirical method has proved so effective in scientific inquiry, we in education have allowed this to influence us too exclusively. The current magic lamp in education is "research". ... Educational evidence which is not labelled "research" or does not present evidence in what is often a pseudo-scientific manner, is usually suspect. Yet I would suggest that pragmatism, the method of evaluating things on their palpable effects, should more often be the basis of educational judgement.'

3. Like the supposed bones of Saint Rosalia in Palermo. See Normal Douglas, *Old Calabria*, Penguin Books, 1962.

4. See Herbert Thelen and John Ginther, 'Experiences with programmed materials in the Chicago area', in Wilbur Schramm (ed.), *Four Case Studies of Programmed Instruction*, Fund for the Advancement of Education, New York, 1964, pp. 48

et seq. Of one teacher they write: 'he was aware that the students were bored. ... His inclination was to call the class together and give them instruction, but he felt this would be violating the rules of program self-sufficiency about which he was trying to get evidence.' Similar worries afflicted other teachers. See also Len A. Biran's article in *New University and Education*, April 1969: 'By "building in" the teacher as a partner [the programmer] may end up with a shorter and better programme but how to validate it? Or must he supply a copy of the teacher with every copy of the programme?'

5. It is far from easy to ensure that a test is *valid*. Do the scores derived from it accurately represent the scale of difference in the particular qualities the test claims to reflect? Tests of knowledge or performance are simple enough: but tests of 'ability' or 'understanding' or 'attitude' depend heavily on the test-maker's definition and design (for in such matters there's no objective measure to scale the test against, and imperfect design elicits misleading answers). Often in examining an evaluation one is much more impressed by the subsequent mathematical analysis than by the initial tests and questionnaires providing the raw scores. Sir Josiah Stamp in *Some Economic Factors in Modern Life*, King, 1929, writes: 'The individual source of the statistics may easily be the weakest link. Harold Cox tells the story of his life as a young man in India. He quoted some statistics to Judge, an Englishman, and a very good fellow. His friend said, "Cox, when you are a bit older, you will not quote Indian statistics with that assurance. The government is very keen on amassing statistics ... they collect them, add them up, raise them to the nth power, take the cube root and make wonderful diagrams. But what you must never forget is that every one of those figures comes in the first instance from the *chowkidar* (village watchman) who just puts down what he damn pleases."' Quoted by J. E. Dietrich and F. C. Johnson in *Cost Analysis of Instructional Technology*, Academy for Educational Development, Inc., Washington, 1968.

6. Research in the *Plowden Report* emphasized the importance of parental support (*Children and their Primary Schools*, Report of the Central Advisory Council of Education (England), HMSO,

1967). R. Rosenthal and L. F. Jacobson, *Pygmalion in the Classroom*, Holt, Rinehart & Winston, 1968, illustrate the effects of teachers' expectations. The *Report on Equality of Educational Opportunity* by J. S. Coleman, US Office of Education, 1966, stresses the influence of the social milieu. J. W. B. Douglas's *The Home and the School*, MacGibbon & Kee, 1964, shows how these factors interact to condition a child's academic performance.

7. The National Foundation for Educational Research study by J. C. Barker, *Streaming in the Primary School*, 1970, provides an interesting example of important conclusions perilously drawn by excluding such factors. Two sets of similar and carefully authenticated tests were applied to two samples made up of children from similar socio-economic groups. In sample A the children in unstreamed classes did significantly better than those in streamed classes, but in sample B the reverse was the case. From this the conclusion is drawn that the form of classroom organization has no definite effect on academic performance, hence, in the public announcement of the report, the statement that streaming was shown to be academically irrelevant. But this does not follow at all. Streaming could have been a significant factor, but its effects may have been offset by inequalities between the two samples in some influence not accounted for, for example, in the quality or expectations of the teacher.

8. See especially R. W. Tyler, 'The function of measurement in improving instruction' in E. F. Lindquist (ed.), *Educational Measurement*, American Council on Education, 1957.

9. Robert F. Mager, *Preparing Instructional Objectives*, Fearon Publishers, 1962.

10. See J. C. Flanagan, 'Individualized education', address to the American Psychological Association, 1968: 'However, if we cannot specify any set of judgements by any group of persons which will establish that Exhibit A shows more creative originality in art than Exhibit B, it may be just as well for us to drop this as an objective for our Art Department.'

11. Benjamin S. Bloom (ed.), *Taxonomy of Educational Ojectives*, Longman, 1966.

12. An estimate of how rare is to be derived from the introduction by Stephen Wiseman, Director of the National Foundation for Educational Research, to Clare Burstall's *French from Eight: A National Experiment*, National Foundation for Educational Research, 1968. Wiseman refers to this as an 'interim account' of 'the *first* example in this country of a major evaluation exercise' (my italics).

13. Caroline Wedgwood-Benn, Research Secretary to the Comprehensive Schools Committee, in 'Unstreaming in the comprehensive school', *Where?* Supplement 12, Advisory Centre for Education, Cambridge, 1965.

14. Leslie Greenhill, Introduction to J. C. Reid and D. W. MacLennan, *Research in Instructional TV and Film*, quoted by Helen Coppen, 'The search for evidence: what do we know about the ways in which audio-visual aids helped learners to learn?', *Visual Education*, September 1968.

15. G. O. M. Leith and C. F. Buckle, *Mode of Response and Non-Specific Background Knowledge*, National Centre for Research and Documentation in Programmed Learning, University of Birmingham, p. 19.

16. See Merrill Palmer in *Quarterly Journal of Behaviour and Development*, vol. 13, 1967, p. 70.

17. All of these are chapter or page headings in A. D'Abro, *The Rise of the New Physics*, vol. 2, Dover, 1951.

18. Of an appropriate sort – Bernstein has sharply criticized present practices. See Basil Bernstein, 'Education cannot compensate for society', *New Society*, 26 February 1970.

19. See E. M. Forster, 'Voltaire's Laboratory', *Abinger Harvest*, Penguin Books, 1967.

20. Antony Oettinger writes: 'At least three conditions must be satisfied for the systems approach [earlier defined as the application of scientific method] to be more than an apt metaphor. (a) The system being studied must be independent enough of the other systems which combine with it to form a supra system for interactions among these systems to be satisfactorily accounted for or ignored without dire consequences. (b) The system being

studied must be one for which well-developed and proved research and design tools exist. (c) When designing a system we must know explicitly what it is for ... the education system is far more complex than anything we have hitherto tackled. We should not be misled by the outward appearance of success with the simplicities of our defence systems, moonshots, air, rail or communications network ...' (Anthony G. Oettinger, *Run, Computer, Run*, Harvard University Press, 1969, p. 55).

21. From Julian Huxley, *Memories*, Allen & Unwin, 1970. For an approach of this sort of evaluation at university level see Malcolm Parlett 'Undergraduate teaching observed', *Nature*, vol. 223, 13 September 1969. Such evaluation is described in the article as 'ecological' as distinct from the dominant 'technological' style.

22. The Nuffield Foundation Resources for Learning Project has made a grant to Professor Liam Hudson and Dr Malcolm Parlett of the University of Edinburgh, Department of Educational Sciences, to do a design study in the sort of evaluation that might usefully be applied to something as various as independent, resource-based learning.

23. Quotation from Robert Thouless, *Daily Telegraph*, 8 July 1969.

24. Jacques Barzun, *The House of Intellect*, Secker & Warburg, 1962.

Chapter 12

1. Quoted by E. M. Forster, 'Howard Overing Sturgis', *Abinger Harvest*, Penguin Books, 1967.

2. Paul Brandwein, Report to the Senate Committee on Labor and Public Welfare, Subcommittee on Education, quoted in Anthony G. Oettinger, *Run, Computer, Run*, Harvard University Press, 1969, p. 92.

3. Carl Henrik von Mentzer, 'Summary of an investigation of pupil activities and learning situations in English studies in grade 7', *School Research Newsletter*, no. 34 (1966), National Board of Education, Stockholm.

4. I was informed at a conference called by the Schools Council that expediture on the initial training of teachers as opposed to in-service training was in the proportion 94 : 6.

5. 'Boston – and other cities – like to talk innovation. Innovation has become fashionable and profitable.... Around the urban school system are magnificent necklaces of special programs, head starts, pilot schools, enrichment classes; but the body of education and the results produced remain almost unchanged. In Boston while having enough trial programs and experiments to fill a book, the life of the average child in the average classroom is virutally unaffected. The teachers, the curriculum, the school committee are the same. The books are the same. The attitudes are the same' (P. Shrag, *Village School Downtown, Politics and Education – A Boston Report*, Beacon Press, 1967, p. 117; quoted in Anthony G. Oettinger, op. cit., p. 61).

The need to scale things up carefully stage by stage before making grand claims is emphasized by Oettinger. He is impressed 'on the one hand by the enormous gap between national policy pronouncements and their local effects and on the other by the lack of realism of local experiments laying claim to national implementation without regard to the effects of changing scale ... a design admirable for creatures the size of a housefly or a ladybug will be a miserable failure if similarly built creatures attempted to grow the size of elephants or whales'.

Patterns and Policies in Higher Education

George Brosan, Charles Carter, Richard Layard,
Peter Venables, Gareth Williams

The 1970s will be a decade of exceptional challenge and
opportunity in higher education. As talents that previously lay idle
or wasted knock at the doors of colleges and universities in
unprecedented numbers, the imagination and variety of courses,
and the standards and flexibility of institutes that offer them, will
be tested to the full. Decisions must be made now on how to provide
an education that can be judged, whatever its academic or vocational
flavour, by its contribution to the quality of the civilization we
inherit and live through, at a cost that allows the job to be properly
done.

Many voices will contribute to the debate on choice and decision,
but few with the authority and realism that the authors of this book
offer. From different viewpoints they give alternative appreciations
that both clarify the wide range of issues involved, and face the
reader with the questions that, at a turning-point in the evolution
of a democratic society (for the opening up of education beyond
school is nothing less), every teacher, parent and student must
confront and resolve for himself.

George Brosan is Director of the North-East London Polytechnic,
and was formerly Principal of Enfield College of Technology
Charles Carter is Vice-Chancellor of the University of Lancaster
Richard Layard is Lecturer in Economics and Deputy Director of
the Higher Education Research Unit at the London School of
Economics
Peter Venables was formerly Vice-Chancellor of the University
of Aston
Gareth Williams is Associate Director of the Higher Education
Research Unit at the London School of Economics

Other Penguin Education Specials

Teaching and Learning in Higher Education

Ruth Beard

Provision for higher education is now recognized as a major social
and educational need. In the United Kingdom alone, a million
students by 1980 is no longer a wild statistic, but a realistic basis
for forward planning. At the start of a new decade of expansion,
Ruth Beard has produced a timely and comprehensive analysis of
the nature of teaching and learning in higher education.

Drawing on innovations in teaching methods in universities and
colleges, as well as on findings from educational research, Dr Beard
examines ways in which the current upsurge of new ideas is
affecting curricula, courses and teaching techniques. After a chapter
on different psychological approaches to human learning, which sets
out the theoretical background to the practical problems under
discussion, the middle chapters of the book provide a rigorous
analysis of the educational value of the lecture, the seminar,
laboratory and small-group teaching.

The author, believing that courses cannot be fully effective unless
teachers reconsider their methods in relation to their aims and
objectives, evaluates important preliminary research which has
looked at the interaction between teacher and student in different
learning situations.

Teaching and Learning in Higher Education demonstrates the vital
need to ensure further improvements in the quality of teaching
during the coming years. The book will be of particular value to
teachers in universities and colleges, and also to those who are likely
to benefit most from the raising of standards – the students
themselves.

Ruth Beard is Director, University Teaching Methods Unit,
University of London Institute of Education